SHAPER
HANDBOOK

THE SHAPER
AND ITS EQUIPMENT

Plate 1 Top left: Delta RS-15
5-speed spindle moulder with six
interchangeable spindle arbors.

Plate 2 Lower left: Table rings and
loose arbor of a Wadkin BEM
spindle moulder.

Plate 3 Below: Sectional view of
the spindle assembly of a two-speed
Delta spindle moulder.

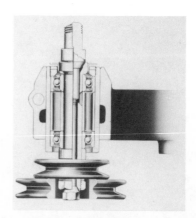

SHAPER HANDBOOK

Eric Stephenson

M.I.M. Wood T.

LINDEN PUBLISHING

FRESNO, CALIFORNIA

SHAPER HANDBOOK

Originally published as "Spindle Moulder Handbook".
by Stobart and Son Ltd. London

© Eric Stephenson
1986

ISBN: 0-941936-09-0

35798642

First United States publication October 1987.

Library of Congress Cataloging-in -Publication Data

Stephenson, Eric.
    Shaper handbook/Eric Stephenson.
        p.   cm.
    British ed. published under title: Spindle moulder handbook.
    Includes index.
    ISBN 0-941936-09-0
    1. Shapers.   2. Woodwork.   I. Title
TT180.S738   1987
684'.083—dc19   87-23713
                                            CIP

Linden Publishing Co.
3845 N. Blackstone
Fresno, CA 93726 USA

To my Wife and Family who afforded me the time and opportunity to devote to writing.

PREFACE

Although technologies for other woodworking machines have changed a great deal over the past few years, in the smaller workshop the role of the spindle moulder (shaper in The United States) has changed very little, but even so, change it has. This book has been prepared as a practical guide to all users and students of these machines, to update well-established practices covered in earlier and quite excellent books on this subject and to cover changes that have affected the spindle moulder. The techniques described apply both to small home-use machines and the larger production types. They are described in a way which hopefully is both informative and easily readable.

ACKNOWLEDGEMENTS
Preparation of this book has only been made possible with the help, encouragement and guidance of my many friends and colleagues, together with numerous manufacturers and establishments who have willingly provided data, technical assistance and photographs. A full list is given in alphabetical order.

I would, in particular, like to thank Mr. Malcolm Crank M.I.M. Wood T. who checked my original script and suggested numerous improvements and additional material. These are based on his own wide experience of machine woodworking, and, in particular, of the spindle moulder. I am also very grateful to Mr. C. Horsefield, H.M. Inspector, Woodworking National Industry Group of the Health and Safety Executive. He advised on those aspects relating to safety and the interpretation of the present U.K. legislation, and also suggested the inclusion of some additional material. Finally I would like to thank Mr. Henry Clayton, President of the Institute of Machine Woodworking Technology, for his introduction.

To each one I express my sincere gratitude for the help given. I would emphasize, though, that the views expressed are those of the writer alone. Great care has been taken to give unbiased viewpoints and to lay great emphasis on the safety aspects of the spindle moulder, in particular those relating to UK regulations.

It should be noted that in some cases photographs from manufacturers show guarding which in the author's opinion is inadequate, often because the manufacturers remove essential guards so that the operation illustrated is more clearly shown. However, the safety aspects are fully amplified within the text.

ERIC STEPHENSON 1986

Acknowledgements

Autool Grinders, Sabden, Blackburn, Lancs.
De Beers Ind. Diamond Division (Pty) Ltd, Johannesburg, S.A.
Delta International Machinery Corp., Pittsburg, PA, U.S.A.
Dominion Machinery Co Ltd, Halifax, W Yorks.
Elsworth Ltd, Sheffield, S Yorks.
Equipment Ltd, Hickory, NC U.S.A.
ETP Hydro-grip, FFV transmission AB, Linkoping, Sweden
W. Fearnehough Ltd, Bakewell, Derbyshire.
FIRA, Stevenage, Hertforshire.
Forest City Tool Company, Hickory, NC, U.S.A.
General Electric Company, Worthington, Ohio, U.S.A.
Graycon Tools, Wabash, Indiana, U.S.A.
Hammer Machinery Co Inc, Santa Rosa, California, U.S.A.
Holz-Her, Nuertingen, W Germany.
Inca Maschinen und Apparate AG, Teufenthal, Switzerland.
Interwood Ltd, Hornchurch, Essex.
JKO Cutters Ltd, High Wycombe, Bucks,
Gebr. Leitz GmbH & Co, Oberkochen, W Germany.
Leuco International, Horb am Neckar, W Germany.
C.D. Monninger Ltd, London.
Newman Whitney, Greensboro, NC U.S.A.
Northfield Foundry & Machine Co, Northfield, MN U.S.A.
August Oppold, Oberkochen, W Germany.
Pacific Grinding Wheel Co Inc, Marysville, Washington, U.S.A.
Powermatic Houndaille, McMinnville, TN U.S.A.
Thomas Robinson & Son Ltd, Rochdale, GM.
Rye Machinery Sales, High Wycombe, Bucks.
SCM International Spa, Rimini, Italy.
Sedgwick Woodworking Machinery, Leeds, N Yorks.
Joseph Scheppach GmbH & Co., Inchenhausen, W Germany
Sicar Spa, Carpi, Italy.
Sigrist & Muller, Rafz, Switzerland (Saturn).
Spear & Jackson (Industrial) Ltd, Sheffield, S Yorks.
Startrite Machine Tool Co Ltd, Gillingham, Kent.
Stehle GmbH & Co Memmingen, W Germany
Deloro Stellite, Belleville, Ontario, Canada
TRADA, High Wycombe, Bucks.
Universal Grinding Wheel Co Ltd, Stafford.
Wadkin PLC, Leicester.
V.R. Wesson, Waukegan, Ill, U.S.A. (Tantung)
Whitehill Spindle Tools, Luton, Beds.
WMSA, Loughton, Essex.

ROCHDALE,
LANCS.

SPINDLE MOULDER HANDBOOK.

I am very pleased to have been invited to introduce this book
written by Eric Stephenson which I am certain readers
acquainted with this type of machine will relish.

Only someone with the confidence born of wide experience
allied to a finely tuned analytical capability, and a flair for
illustration, would dare to tackle such a subject in so
comprehensive a manner. The simple title gives no indication
of the breadth of cover given by the author to the essential
preparation and back-up procedures supporting the actual
cutting process.

The manufacture and use of templates, jigs, fences and guards,
so essential to safe and efficient operation, are profusely
illustrated and described. Not only are the many optional
cutters, cutterblocks and cutter steels comprehensively
covered, along with their maintenance, but the selection, use
and dressing of the various abrasive wheels for this purpose
are similarly treated. Cutter profile development includes the
method of making useful development scales. Full coverage is
also given to optional equipment and its use for dovetailing,
stair housing, routing and even tenoning.

The book is so comprehensive, it must be put on record, not
only for the present but probably more so for future
generations the scope and versatility of this basically simple
machine. In the hands of a craftsman it is probably the most
versatile of woodcutting machines, but we must also remember
- potentially the most dangerous. Eric Stephenson, to his
credit, has treated both properties with equal respect.

H. CLAYTON F.I.M.Wood.T.
PRESIDENT
INSTITUTE OF MACHINE WOODWORKING TECHNOLOGY

CONTENTS

CHAPTER 1
INTRODUCTION 1
Spindle speeds 4
The cutting action 5
Operational safety 12

CHAPTER 2
MACHINE OPERATION 15
Preparation 15
Straight moulding 20
Shaping 21

CHAPTER 3
CUTTERHEAD TYPES 25
French head 25
Slotted collars 28

CHAPTER 4
CUTTERHEAD TYPES 33
Square blocks 33
Circular Cutterblocks 38

CHAPTER 5
CUTTERHEAD TYPES 45
Profiled heads 45
Disposable cutterheads 47
Chip-limiting heads 48
Router cutters 49

CHAPTER 6
CUTTER PREPARATION 53
Checking to a sample 53
Geometric development 55

CHAPTER 7
CUTTER GRINDING 59
Grinding without a rest 59
Grinding techniques 61

CHAPTER 8
PROFILE GRINDING 63
Copy grinder 64
Profile grinder 65

CHAPTER 9
PROFILED CUTTERS 71
Setting the cutting angle 71
Indexing the cutter 72
Grinding techniques 73
Grinding faults 74
The Q3S system 75

CHAPTER 10
CUTTER GRINDING 81
Grinding wheels 81
Superabrasives 87
Tool steels 89
Non-steel tools 89

CHAPTER 11
GENERAL MOULDING 91
Through-fences 93
The bed 100
Guards 102
Safety aids 104
Rebating 105
Grooving 107
Bevelling & chamfering 109
Mould profiles 110
General moulding 112
Types of jigs 118
Stop moulding 120
End grain moulding 127
Trimming operations 132
Corner rounding 134
Trimming circles 136

CHAPTER 12
SHAPING 139
Table rings 140
Ball bearing follower 141
Ring fence 143
Straight fence shaping 144
Template types 145
Cutting against the grain 151
Cut relieving 155
Curve-on-curve work 157

CHAPTER 13
ROUTING 165
Using guides and jigs 165
Stair housing 169

CHAPTER 14
DRAWER AND FRAME JOINTS 177
Dovetailing 177
Finger jointing 185
Tenoning 187

Index 189

CHAPTER 1

INTRODUCTION

The earliest woodworking machines were pole lathes, foot-powered in a very simple way by a band or cord wrapped around the piece being turned and connected one end to a foot pedal and the opposite end to a supple tree branch overhead acting like a leaf spring.

As with many early machines the cutting tool was stationary or moved only under hand control. The workpiece revolved as with a lathe, or moved in a straight line when planing and moulding with what was then the machine equivalent of smoothing and moulding hand planes.

Rotating cutterheads originated around the time mass-produced parts were needed for a rapidly expanding navy, the wooden walls of England, and amongst the first applications was in making ships' blocks at Chatham Dockyard.

The spindle moulder in its present form is a fairly recent innovation dating from an 1853 patent by a Mr. Andrew Gear of Jamesville, Ohio, U.S.A. The machine had a vertical spindle through the centre of a horizontal wooden table very much in the present style. From this machine evolved the present spindle moulders, also power-feed shapers in their various forms with sprocket-fed jig, rotary table, linear table or powered horizontal roller feed.

Fig. 1 Typical spindle moulder shown using a straight fence (Wadkin Bursgreen).

Another version had an overhead spindle for recessing and panel raising on the surface of large pieces which were manually moved around whilst flat on the table. This variant evolved into the high-speed router, originally with hand feed and later with mechanical feed and now with a powered table and fully automatic computor numerical control.

1

The type of work the spindle moulder was originally intended for was then called irregular moulding, that is the shaping and square-edging or edge-profiling of table tops, chair arms and legs, etc. Straight mouldings were invariably produced on early versions of the four-sided planer and moulder (roller-fed machines which plane and mould on four sides at a single pass through, rather than a single face at a time as on the spindle moulder).

The spindle moulder was also made in two-spindle form. The spindles carried identical but opposite-hand heads and the two heads rotated in opposite directions, the work being interchanged between them so that the cut was always with the grain.

Most spindle moulders now have only a single spindle as modern high-speed tools allow slow-speed cutting with or against the grain with little tear-out.

There are some variations: for example, a tilting spindle type to reduce cutter overhang on deep moulding, multiple quick-change spindle machines for repeated, short-run work, and traversing table machines.

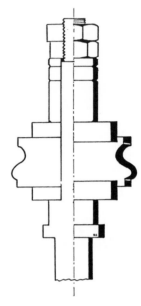

Fig. 2 Sectional elevation through a typical spindle arbor fitted with slotted collars.

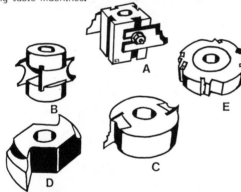

Fig. 3 Various cutterheads used on a spindle moulder
A - square cutterblock:
B - slotted collars:
C - Whitehill type (circular moulding) cutterblock:
D - solid profiled cutterhead:
E - disposable-cutter type cutterhead.

The basic machine

The main spindle is usually a plain, parallel arbor and the cutterheads have a matching plain bore. They are held between a shoulder on the spindle arbor and a top locknut (or locknuts) with spacing collars between. Cutterblocks commonly used on this plain spindle include slotted collars, square and circular heads, profiled heads and disposable-cutter heads.

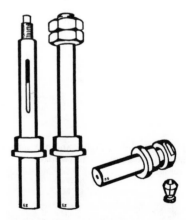

Fig. 4 Alternative spindle arbors:
Left: French head:
Centre: plain arbor:
Right: collet arbor for router and similar cutters.

Fig. 5 Ring fence for shaping with a French head. The workpiece is sandwiched between the template and a base. Although not shown a cage or bonnet guard is essential.

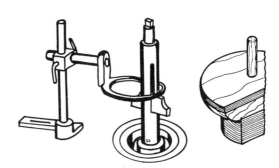

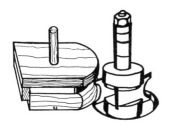

Fig. 6 Ball-bearing follower shown with slotted collars and the template directly on the workpiece. Again, a cage guard is needed.

On the more sophisticated machines the spindle arbor removes and can be replaced by other types, allowing a wider variety of tools to be fitted. These include a slotted or French spindle and a collet head for router, dovetail and similar shanked tools.

Regular equipment with the spindle moulder usually includes a one or two-piece fence for straight moulding, a ring fence or ball-bearing collar for internal or external shaping, together with the necessary guards, dust hoods and pressures. Additional equipment available for some machines includes attachments for stair stringing, dovetailing and corner-locking, etc.

Fig. 7 Chart showing maximum spindle speeds for different cutterhead diameters and types.

The sloping lines represent different cutterhead types:
S - solid profiled and disposable-cutter types.
P - planing heads.
K - keyed moulding heads with loose cutters.
F - friction-held, loose-cutter moulding heads.

Where vertical lines from the cutterhead diameter scale cross the sloping cutterhead-type lines, follow horizontally to the left to find the highest recommended speed.

The example shows in dotted outline a 150mm diameter planing head with a top recommended speed of 7 000 revs/min.

TOOL SPEED CHART

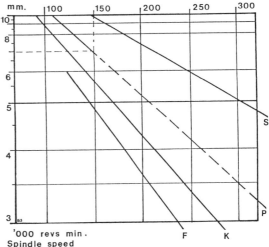

SPINDLE SPEEDS

Spindle speed variation is essential where tooling of different cutting diameters is used. A speed range of between 3,000 and 9,000 revs/min is fairly normal. If provided with a single speed only this must not excede the top speed for the largest diameter cutterhead used, otherwise there will be a problem with balance, and heads are unsafe when run at higher speeds than those stated. In the same way heads should not be run at too low a speed or they tend to snatch.

A speed/tool diameter chart shows the recommended combinations. Note that different types of heads have different maximum spindle speeds. Some European cutterheads have the maximum stated speed stamped on them, check against this or with the maker, taking the speeds given in the Chart as a guide only.

Plate 4 5-step vee-belt drive on a Delta RS-15, showing ease of speed change

Spindle drive types

For the bigger machines run off industrial power supplies the normal drive arrangement is via a flat or vee-belt from the drive motor. Multi-speed drive is often provided via stepped pulleys on the motor and a single flat, parallel pulley on the spindle arbor, with speed changed by moving the belt onto another step on the motor pulley and re-tensioning.

The golden rule with belt drives is that the belt should run with the least tension needed to transmit the power required. Too little tension and the belts wear out fast, too much and long-term damage is done to the bearings, belt life is shortened and excessive power is wastefully absorbed. There are two pointers to correct tension. A belt that squeals is usually under-tensioned and a belt that runs hot or absorbs an undue amount of power is usually over-tensioned.

When changing vee-belts it is essential to completely release tension so that the belts can be positioned whilst slack. Do not force vee belts into position under tension as this will damage the load-bearing cords.

The ideal solution is infinately-variable speed drive as this allows the speed to be matched precisely to the cutterhead type and diameter and nature of the work, but this is rarely provided. With it the belt tension is automatic via an internal spring so tensioning in the normal way is not necessary.

Some spindle moulders have a direct-drive from a motor mounted on an extension of the spindle arbor. When this is an industrial mains motor powered from a three-phase electrical supply the frequency of the supply governs the speed of the motor. Direct connection from the mains supply gives too low a spindle speed for regular spindle moulder work, so motors of this type are powered via a frequency changer to run faster.

The frequency changer is actually a rotating transformer driven by a normal mains motor either directly-coupled or with a short-centre-belt drive. In the former case it is possible to change the spindle speed by simple electrical switching, but speeds are restricted.

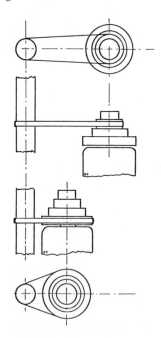

Fig. 8 Flat-belt drive from a stepped pulley on the motor (right) to a single parallel pulley on the spindle arbor.
Showing a four-speed drive from a 50 Hz motor giving 4,500 revs/min. spindle speed (above) and 9,000 revs/min. (below).

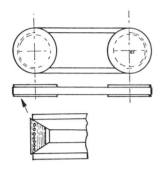

Fig. 9 Above: Vee pulley drive showing the load-bearing chords (inset) in the vee-belt. The drive is 1:1 giving 3,000 revs/min spindle speed.
Below: Infinately-variable drive. As the motor pulley halves (left) are forced together the belt contacts the sides of the vee pulley further out towards the rim to raise the speed.

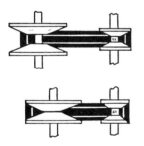

Fig. 10 The quality of the surface finish produced by a rotating cutterhead can be measured as the pitch of the cuttermark 'K'. The cuttermark depth 'L' is more when using a cutterhead with a smaller diameter so the surface appears worse for the same pitch.

On U.K. machines with electrical switching for speed change, control should be such that the machine always starts at the lowest speed before switching to a higher speed. This is an essential safety feature. Control of this sort is possible with newer electrical gear which can also give infinately variable speeds on direct drive.

With a belt-driven frequency changer it is possible to change speeds by electrical switching, or by a stepped pulley drive and manually changing belts.

THE CUTTING ACTION

Certain factors affect the cutting action of all rotary cutterheads and it is important to know what these are and what restrictions they place on the user. They affect the life of the cutters, their efficiency, the choice of cutterhead and the operating speed, but most importantly they affect the surface finish.

Surface finish

A rotary cutterhead does not produce a perfectly flat surface but a series of scallop-like cuttermarks, each mark produced by a single cutter at each rotation. Although the surface is not flat technically it is commercially acceptable provided the cuttermarks are close and evenly-spaced. The spindle speed and the feed speed together determine the cuttermark pitch which is used to measure the quality of the surface finish. (The number of finishing cutters also affects the surface finish, but as only single cutter finish is normal on a spindle moulder this factor is ignored.)

Poorer surface quality is produced when the cuttermark pitch is large, i.e., when the feed speed is fast and/or the spindle speed is slow. In addition to the prominent cuttermark pattern formed the chips are thicker so tear-out and other machining defects increase.

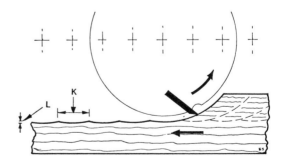

Better quality results when the cuttermark pitch is small, i.e., when the feed speed is slow and/or the spindle speed fast. Too fine a pitch, however, produces more dust, and there is a greater tendency to burn.

5

To a lesser extent the surface quality is affected by the size of the cutterblock. Small cutterblocks give a deeper and more prominent cuttermark for the same pitch, so a smaller pitch is needed to give the same quality of surface finish. This is shown in the feed speed chart, Fig. 11.

As a manual feed is normally used on a spindle moulder, feed speed is difficult to judge accurately except from the appearance of the finished workpiece. This shows the defects described if wrong, but only after the event. A smooth, steady feed without hesitation gives the best results. What should be avoided is a series of fast movements interspaced by a stoppage whilst the operator changes hand grip.

Obviously a mechanical feed gives the best results as the feed is continuous and can be set to a precise speed. Use a mechanical feed instead of hand feed wherever possible on straight mouldings. A guide to maximum feed speeds relative to cutterblock diameter and spindle speed is given below.

FEED SPEED CHART ①

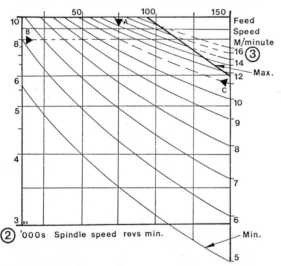

Fig. 11 Chart showing maximum feed speeds for mechanical feeds on straight moulding which give an acceptable finish.

Trace horizontally along the spindle speed line to the cutterhead diameter, then follow the curved line to show the maximum recommended speed.

Example shows: A maximum feed speed of 11 m/min. 'C' is possible for a 75 mm. diameter cutterhead 'A' running at 8,000 revs/min. 'B'. The feed speeds are correct for shallow moulding on good quality timber. For deeper cuts or with more difficult timber much lower speeds are needed. When the finish is not exposed the feed rate could be increased to double the figures given.

Hand-fed machines, such as the spindle moulder, are invariably fed with rotation of the cutter against the direction of feed. This is conventional or resistance cutting.

The timber tends to split and rive ahead of the cut and bunches of slivers often tear-out below the finished surface when cutting against the grain, that is when the grain of the timber slopes towards the cutting head in the feed direction. This can occur when straight moulding, but always when shaping. It also happens around knots and with curly-grained timber, sycamore for example, and with interlocked-grain timber which grows with alternating growth-slope angles in narrow bands.

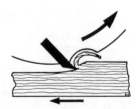

Fig. 12 Conventional or resistance cutting, cutters rotate against the feed.

Fig. 13 With large cutting angles the grain rives to split ahead of the cut. Bunches of fibres often tear out below the finished surface to spoil it when cutting against the grain.

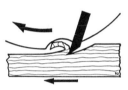

Fig. 14 Climb cutting, cutters rotate with the feed. This is never used except with a mechanical feed and secure clamping of the timber, or with a very light cut and a holding jig.

Fig. 17 Right: cutting angle of collar cutters 'E' - usually 30 degrees.

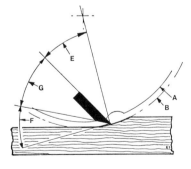

Fig. 15 Various cutting angles, etc:
A - cutterhead.
B - planing circle.
E - cutting angle.
F - clearance angle.
G - bevel angle.

Grain tear-out spoils the finished surface which then needs a lot of extra finishing. Even when correction is carefully carried out the surface never looks uniform and, unfortunately, the process is always time consumming and costly. Tear-out can usually be reduced by reducing the feed speed and/or the cutting angle.

Very occasionally the cutter rotates with the feed, which is known as back or climb cutting. The advantage of climb cutting is that the cutters cut into the timber and there is virtually no tear-out, even when cutting against the grain.

It is used only on machines with a strictly controlled mechanical feed and a clamped workpiece. Whilst climb cutting is possible with a hand-feed machine it should be undertaken only with the greatest of care as the cutters could grab the timber and throw it violently in the direction of cutter rotation. Only the lightest of cuts should be taken and the timber must be securely held and very carefully controlled using some form of holding jig.

CUTTING ANGLE

This is measured between the leading face of the cutter and a line drawn from the cutting point to the centre of the spindle arbor. Measure it with a protractor after sketching the precise shape of the cutterblock used. The way to measure it is shown in the sketches. The cutting angle is very important as it determines the aggressiveness of the cut and the quality of finish it gives.

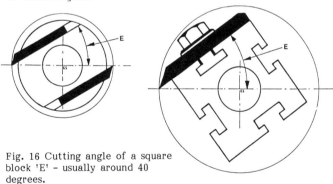

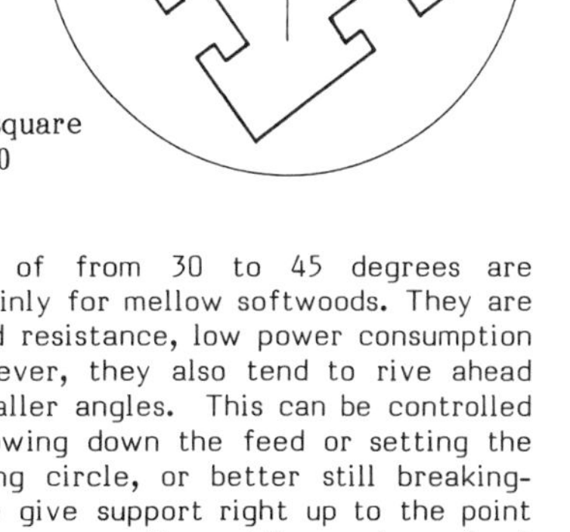

Fig. 16 Cutting angle of a square block 'E' - usually around 40 degrees.

Large cutting angles of from 30 to 45 degrees are aggressive and are used mainly for mellow softwoods. They are free-cutting, have low feed resistance, low power consumption and low noise level. However, they also tend to rive ahead much more readily that smaller angles. This can be controlled to a certain extent by slowing down the feed or setting the fences close to the cutting circle, or better still breaking-through a wooden fence to give support right up to the point of cut. The real cure is to use a smaller cutting angle or front bevel, but both have drawbacks.

Some timbers are prone to chip bruising, that is hooking of severed chips by the cutting edge to be carried round and indent on the finished surface. Chip bruising is common with larger cutting angles, on heavy cuts, with wet timber and when cutters are dull. The affect is worsened where the exhaust system is inefficient - often a spindle moulder dust hood is full of air leaks. If no air connection is fitted check that the chip path is clear at the back. Adding extra non-cutting cutters can sometimes reduce chip bruising by creating extra draft.

Small cutting angles, 5 - 10 degrees, prevent riving ahead and tear-out even on interlocked grain timbers, but take more power, give more feed resistance and are noisier. Smaller angles also reduce chip bruising.

Medium cutting angles, 20 - 35 degrees, are the most commonly used as they allow cutting of most commercial timbers without serious down-grading or having to restrict feed speed.

Cutting angle change

With most cutterheads it is not possible to change the cutting angle. It might seem simple enough to alter a profiled head cutting angle but this is not practicable as it also alters the profile slightly. The normal practice is to choose a cutterhead with the most suitable cutting angle for the work intended.

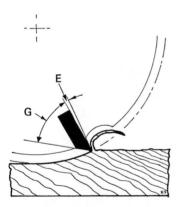

Fig. 21 A small cutting angle 'E' allows cutting against the grain with little tear-out.

With planing heads is it possible to reduce the cutting angle by adding a front bevel to the cutters but this is only necessary with the worst interlocked-grain timbers. It is rarely practiced on a spindle moulder as difficult timbers can be worked satisfactorily using regular cutting angles simply by slowing the feed rate. It is not practical to increase the cutting angle.

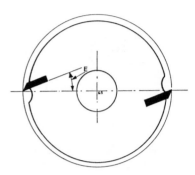

Fig. 18 Cutting angle of a circular moulding block 'E' - usually around 27 degrees,

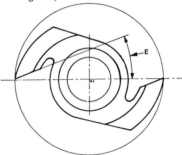

Fig. 19 Cutting angle of a solid profiled head 'E' - usually around 20 degrees.

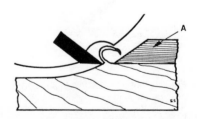

Fig. 20 A close-set fence 'A' helps to prevent riving ahead.

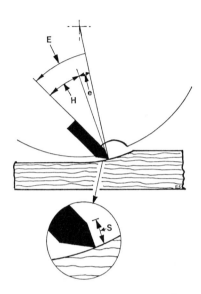

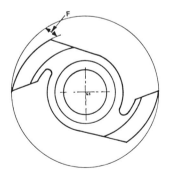

Fig. 22 A front bevel 'H' can reduce the cutting angle 'E' to a smaller one 'e' to give the same effect as a reduction in seating angle of the cutter. The depth of bevel 'S' should be at least 1.5 mm.

Fig. 23 Radial relief 'F' on a solid profiled head.

SPECIES	GREEN	DRIED
Basswood, Cedar, Chestnut, Cypress	25	20 - 25
Soft Elm, Hemlock, White Pine, Redwood, Spruce, Ash, Beech, Plain Birch, Hard Elm	25	15-20
Fir, Gum, Mahogany, Plain Maple, Plain Oak, Yellow Pine, Poplar, Walnut, Curly Birch, Hickory, Quartered Oak	20	10-15
Bird's eye Maple	5	5-10

Source - Graycon Tools.

Clearance angle

This is measured between the trailing face of the cutter and a line tangential to the cutting circle at the cutting point.

Too small a clearance angle allows rubbing and in extreme cases burning. It does not allow subsequent honing to re-sharpen the edge, and natural wear produces a dulled condition much more quickly. Too large a clearance angle leaves a weak cutting edge. The clearance angle is normally between 15 and 30 degrees.

True clearance is a snail-shell curve with the gap between trailing face and cutting circle increasing pro-rata the distance behind the cutting edge. This is called radial relief and is normal on solid profiled heads, router cutters and similar. This face is not touched in re-grinding as this would spoil it. Regrinding takes place only on the leading flat face.

With square and circular heads, slotted collars and French heads the bevel angle formed when profiling and re-sharpening them affects the clearance angle.

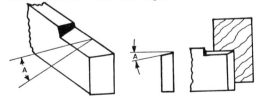

Fig. 24 Side clearance 'A' is needed when, for example, rebating.

Side clearance angle

Most cutters also have side clearance. This avoids burning where the cutting edge is almost square to the cut - the edges of rebate cutters for example. Normally 5 degrees is enough.

Bevel angle

This is the ground angle of the cutter measured between the leading and trailing faces. When using too small a bevel angle the cutting edge is weak, breaks down quickly and is prone to damage. If the bevel angle is too big the cutter dulls more quickly and the clearance angle is less.

The recommended minimum bevel angle is 35 degrees for HSS and similar cutters, and 45 degrees for tungsten carbide types. Maximum bevel angle in both cases is 60 degrees.

BEVEL ANGLE CHART

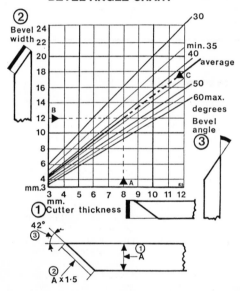

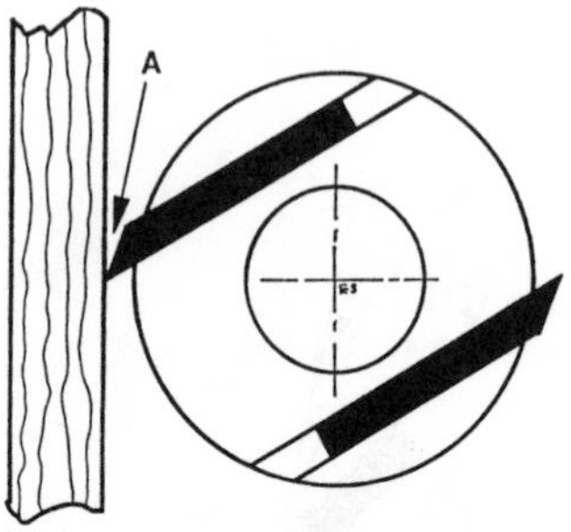

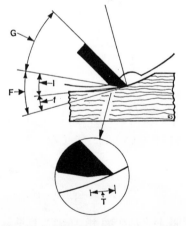

Fig. 25 Rotate the cutterblock with the cutters in contact with a sample piece to check for clearance at 'A'.

Fig. 26 Left: Chart showing relationship of bevel angle to cutter thickness and bevel width.

Example shows:
A – cutter thickness of 8mm.
B – bevel width of 12mm.
C – bevel angle of 42 degrees.

The sketch, lower left, shows the rule of thumb used to measure an average bevel angle of 42 degrees.

Fixed angles cannot be stated either for the bevel angle or the clearance angle as both vary according to the cutting angle and the cutting diameter of the cutterhead. It is possible to relate them to tables, but the simplest and most direct way to check if they are correct is to set the cutters to a sample piece of timber and rotate the cutterhead. There should be visible clearance between the fixed timber and the trailing heel of the ground face. If no gap can be seen, increase the clearance angle by reducing the bevel angle. If the gap is wide the bevel angle can be increased to give a stronger cutting edge. A rule of thumb is to make the bevel width 1.5 times cutter thickness to give a bevel angle of 42 degrees, which is a good average for many cutterheads.

A secondary clearance angle is commonly formed on cutters when honing, to give a stronger tip. This is also used for tungsten carbide cutters. The smallest practical clearance angle in this case is 5 degrees.

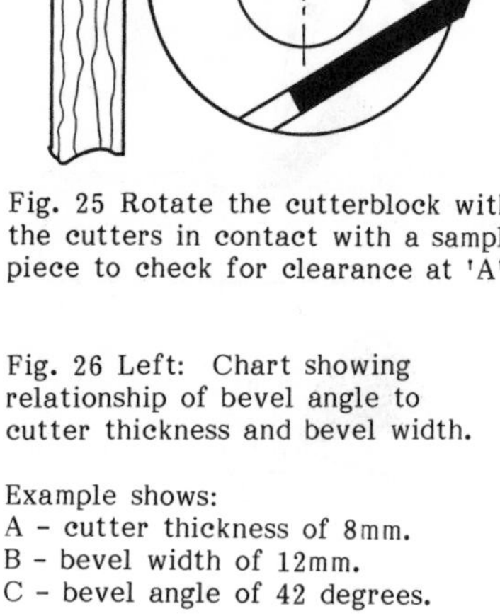

Fig. 27 A secondary clearance angle 'I' reduces a large clearance angle 'F' to a smaller one 'f'. 'T' is the width of the land, usually not more than 1.5 mm.

Plate 5 Top left: This Dominion BCB spindle moulder has infinitely variable spindle speeds between 3 000 and 9 000 revs/min.

Plate 6 Lower left: Showing easy removal of the spindle arbor on a Delta RS-15 spindle moulder. It is secured by a locknut with differential threads.

Plate 7 Lower right: This Powermatic Model 26 spindle moulder has four spindle speeds.

Operational Safety

The spindle moulder is a versatile machine capable of a wide variety of work in joinery and furniture production. The tools it uses operate at higher speeds than on most other industrial machinery and certain basic safety precautions are essential.

Specific safety points are detailed for the different cutter-head types and machine operations. Other safety points are more general in nature and apply to all types. Both should be observed in preparation and operation and a check list run through immediately before start-up.

Machine setting

Isolate the machine electrically before setting-up or making alterations.

Use the cutter equipment recommended for the job. Ensure that arbor mounting, cutterblock and cutters are clean and free from grease, rust-preventative, rust, wood residue and metallic burrs, etc. Check thoroughly for soundness, freedom from cracks and signs of overstrain on cutters and cutter-heads. Replace suspect parts immediately and dispose of them.

Only use cutters in dimensionally-alike pairs formed to the same profile, and balance cutters in matched pairs after grinding. Mount them directly opposite on the cutterblock and both 'to cut' to ensure they balance dynamically. Make sure that cutter projection and retention of the cutter in the cutterblock are as recommended. Cutters wear down in use and are advanced to compensate, make sure they are still safely retained when worn.

Use only the correct spanners when tightening cutters. Never add extra leverage as this strains the bolts, causes excessive strain and leads to undue wear. Some manufacturers recommend the use of a pre-set torque spanner, but not all makers agree on this point.

Discard spanners when they wear. Tighten cutters progressively, rotating the cutterblock in the process, never fully tighten one cutter with the other still loose. When the cutterblock has several bolts or screws cross over to tighten each a little in turn until all have equal tightness. Never exceed the recommended maximum spindle speeds given in the Chart (Fig. 11). Lower speeds can be used but keep the difference as small as practicable.

Make sure that all parts are secure, the loose arbor, cutter-block and cutters. Use table rings to give support right up to the cutterhead or use a wooden false table. Guard the cutter-head as well as practicable and fit a through-fence to give the narrowest practicable fence gap, allowing ample clearance of the steel fence plates before fitting the fence. Cover the top, sides and rear of the cutterhead.

Plate 8 Speed change lever on a Wadkin Bursgreen BEL spindle moulder, showing safety interlock covering the stop push button.

Plate 9 Plug-in voltage-change feature on the electronic brake offered by Delta for their machines. The torque and brake time controls are variable, and the arbor is free to rotate when the braking cycle is completed.

Plate 10 Straight moulding on a Scheppach HF33, using roller hold-downs.

Plate 11 A power feed, such as this Holz-Her, is faster, safer and better for straight moulding.

Use top and side Shaw guard pressures to hold the workpiece down on the table and control it sideways when straight moulding. This steadies it and prevents vibration which could cause a kick-back. Hand-fed pieces can never be properly controlled unless some form of mechanical pressure is used. This also guards the cutterhead when timber is not in position.

Check that fences and pressures are correctly positioned and properly secured. Rotate the cutterhead manually to make sure that no part fouls the machine, with extra clearance allowed for subsequent adjustment should it be necessary.

When handling small parts, when dropping-on and when shaping, use a jig with handles to control the operation.

Remove all loose items from the machine. Fit all guards and connect the dust hood to the exhaust system or make sure that the chip exit is clear before starting the machine even if only making a pre-run trial cut.

Finally check that the direction of rotation and spindle speed are correct before starting up.

Operation

Hand-feed timber past the cutterhead in as smooth and continuous movement as possible. Hold it firmly down on the table and against the fence. The operator's hands should not pass immediately across the cutters whenever practical as slippage or kickback could have serious consequences. If possible alternate the feed between both hands so that one hand maintains momentum whilst grip is changed with the other.

When straight-moulding a series of short sections, push the piece in the cut through with the following piece rather than feeding them individually. Push the last one through with a push-stick. Stand at the side rather than in line with the feed, just in case of kick-back. Spikes and push-sticks should always be used to avoid close contact with the cutters. Before starting make sure that these are close at hand. Use a jig where recommended.

Certain operations are inherently dangerous, for example stop moulding, shaping, etc. Make sure that proper precautions are taken.

Do not wear clothing that could be caught up in the machine or the cutterblock, avoid loose ties and unbuttoned cuffs, etc.

Do not overfeed. If the cutterhead slows down immediately slow down the feed. Use the brake to slow down the spindle, never run timber into the cutter to slow it. Make sure the spindle is stationary before leaving it, then isolate the machine electrically.

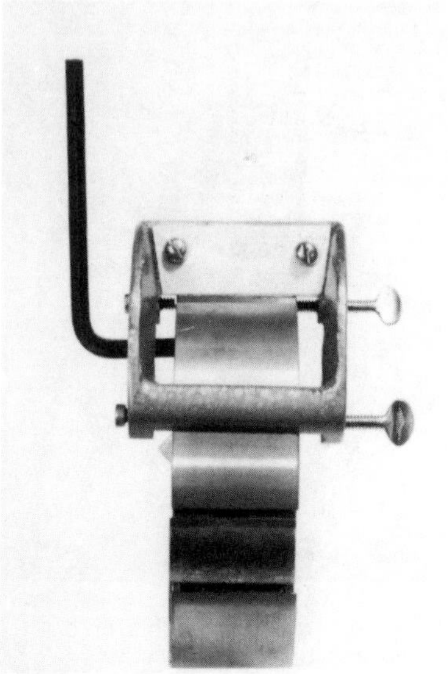

Plate 14 Top right: This Dominion cutterblock has facility to allow a cutter setting template to be fitted.

Plate 12 Top left: The Northfield spindle moulder is a heavily built machine with up to a 10 hp motor drive. It has rear-mounted Shaw-type guards.

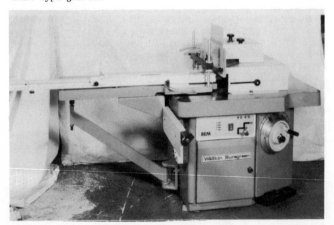

Plate 13 Lower left: Some machines, such as this Wadkin Bursgreen BEM, can have a tenoning table fitted.

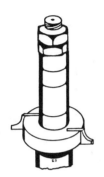

Fig. 28 A cutterhead mounted correctly near the top bearing.

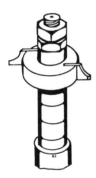

Fig. 29 Avoid this by raising the arbor.

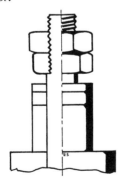

Fig. 30 By having insufficient spacing washers the nuts can lock on the arbor without gripping the cutterhead.

CHAPTER 2

MACHINE OPERATION

This chapter outlines the general principles of setting and operating the spindle moulder on two of its most common operations, straight moulding and shaping. Later chapters fully detail the techniques briefly mentioned here, along with other operations.

Preparation

All spindle moulders have an overhung spindle arbor with bearings below the arbor only; this should be borne in mind when setting-up. Very heavy spindle moulders with a removable top bearing were once used for shaping curved parts of wooden-bodied vehicles but are rarely used now.

As a general guide set the cutterblock directly on the machined collar of the spindle arbor rather than on spacing collars. Use cutterblocks which have a suitable depth for the mould wanted and use the arbor vertical adjustment to position the cutters rather than altering the height of the cutter or the block. This is not always possible, but in all cases the point of cut should preferably be close to the top bearing.

Before fitting the cutterblock make sure that the arbor is secure and that the arbor and the cutterblock are free from grit, grease, wood residue and metallic burrs. On machines with a removable key for the loose arbor make sure the retaining collar is properly fitted to secure the key in position. After fitting the cutterblock add the necessary spacing collars above it so that the top face of the top collar is a few millimetres above the thread shoulder. (Failing this, the nut may lock on the arbor itself without actually securing the cutterblock). The cutterblock must be on the plain part of the arbor - never on the threaded part.

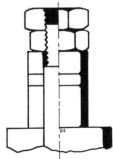

Fig. 31 Do not have the top nut barely gripping as shown here.

Don't have the top collar too far above the thread shoulder as this reduces the grip of the nut. Part of the thread should be above the nut when secured.

15

Add the top nut (or nuts) to fasten the assembly.

Spindle moulder arbors rarely have keys so the cutterhead is held only by friction - make sure it is properly secured. Use the arbor lock when doing this, or use a second spanner on flats on the top or the base of the arbor itself. (The spindle arbor securing nut or ring should not be used). Don't use inertia tightening, e.g.- swinging the spanner against something solid or hitting the end with a mallet.

When no key is provided the nut must tighten with rotation of the spindle, i.e, with normal counterclockwise rotation the nut should tighten in a clockwise direction. When the spindle can run in either direction it is essential to use double locknuts or an intermediate keyed washer. In this way no mistake is made when reversing the spindle direction.

The following sections: cutter selection, grinding and setting, refer mainly to user-profiled type loose cutters, used on French heads, slotted collars, square and circular heads, etc.

CUTTER SELECTION

Spindle moulder cutters normally shape the under corner rather than the top corner when moulding as the operator is less exposed. In such operations the Shaw guard can be used without hinderance and kick-back is much less likely.

A common practice with deep cutterblocks is to share a complex cut between more than one pair of cutters. This simplifies cutter selection and may allow cutters from an earlier obsolete set to be used. The cut is also broken up into smaller, safer bites.

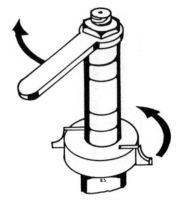

Fig. 32 When only a single locknut is used, rotation of the nut when tightening should be opposite to spindle rotation when running.

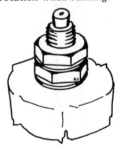

Fig. 33 Double locknuts are essential when the arbor rotates in either direction.

Fig. 34 Sometimes an intermediate, keyed washer can be used, then a single locknut is suitable.

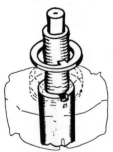

Fig. 35 Cutters normally undercut as shown here. This small section is controlled by two Shaw guards. The gap between the Shaw guard pads is closed-in so that only a spike can pass between. The cutterhead cannot be seen when timber is in place.

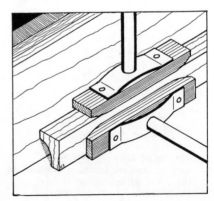

Large cutter projections should be avoided as these put extra strain on the cutters and increase the chance of breakage. It also makes the cutting circle larger and more dangerous and gives more problems in balancing. In all cases the cutting circle should be as small as possible so that the cutterhead gives maximum support to the cutters. If possible 'sink' the cutterhead. A tilting arbor is also useful in reducing cutter overhang.

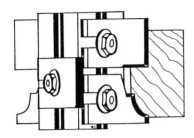

Fig. 36 Dividing the cut between three pairs of cutters on a square block.

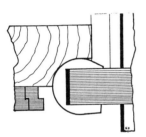

Fig. 37 'Sinking' a Whitehill head into a large ovolo.

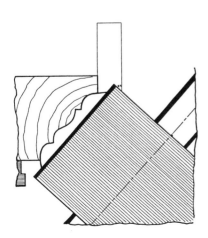

Make cutters deeper than the mould depth by perhaps 5mm. at each side if practicable. If the cutters have a narrow cutting face make them wider and stronger where clear of the through-fence.

CUTTER DEVELOPMENT

The cutter profile normally differs from the mould it produces due to the angle at which it meets the cut, the cutting angle. Only when the cutter meets the cut square-on, as with a French head, is the cutter profile exactly the reverse of the mould it produces. In all other cases the cutter needs to be slightly deeper than the mould, although width-on-cut remains the same.

When the user profile-grinds his own cutters the correct cutter shape must be developed-out. This can be done geometrically, or by using a development rule or a cutter projection template. These give much more accurate results than merely guestimating the cutter shape.

CUTTER GRINDING

With the exception of disposable types, cutters are removed when dull and ground to restore the cutting edge. Many are also hand-honed 'in situ' during a run.

Cutters used on French heads, slotted collars, square and circular heads can be ground off-hand using a twin or multiple-wheel grinder. For better control of cutter profile and ground angles a copy grinder can be used to form the cutter profile to exactly the same shape as a metal template. A profile grinder uses the same basic principle but automatically allows for the difference between the cutter profile and the mould it produces. Cutters must be hand-honed to remove the grinding burr after grinding, otherwise they quickly dull.

Except for the French head, a pair of cutters is used for each mould or section of mould. Normally both cutters are ground to the same profile and should be dimensionally alike, especially when using heavier cutters as on square blocks. After grinding, cutters must be carefully balanced and any inbalance made good by grinding off the heavier cutter. Use a cutter balance or scales to check this. Set both cutters 'to cut'.

If cutters are not properly balanced, or if they are balanced but not both set to cut, the vibration caused will give a poor finish and may damage the machine.

Fig. 38 A tilting spindle reduces cutter projection on some moulds.

Solid and tipped profile heads are ground straight across their face using a universal tool room grinder. Disposable cutters are not re-ground (normally not, they can be but there are practical difficulties) they are simply replaced so grinding and setting does not apply in their case.

CUTTER SETTING

The normal way of setting cutters is 'in situ' on the machine using a sample mould. Place this against the through fence and down on the table. Make sure it is properly seated, particularly if the mould is large and the sample small. It is an advantage to clamp the sample in position, otherwise you may find you need three hands.

Adjust the spindle vertically to give maximum support to the cut. Make sure the bearing housing does not foul the workpiece or filling-in rings fitted later. Make sure the cutterhead and any cutterbolts or lips clear the sample by fitting cutters and rotating the cutterblock. Adjust the fence as needed.

Set both cutters to 'cut', to just scrape the sample mould, and lock them securely in place. It isn't easy to know when cutters are correctly set because contact is difficult to see. Sometimes contact can be seen when viewing along the fences from the infeed, but it is near impossible then to reach the cutters to make adjustment.

Do not simply move the cutter against the sample whilst holding the cutterblock stationary because setting will be wrong, the cutterblock must be rotated.

After cutter setting check and correct depth and height using a straight-edge with short rules fitted. Finally, add the guards, pressures and exhaust hood, then run through a check list before starting-up.

Template setting

Setting is made easier if using a template of some sort. The template can be a simple rectangular piece of plywood, aluminium, plastic-faced hardboard or similar, anything that can be pencilled on and the pencil lines later erased for re-use.

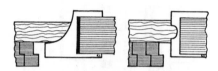

Fig. 39 Cutters should be wider than the mould they produce.

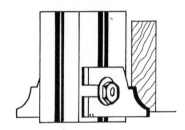

Fig. 40 Cutter setting 'in situ' on the machine.

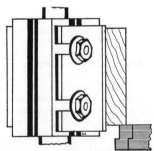

Fig. 41 Left: Set planing cutters to a piece of hardwood clamped across the fences and adjusted to just clear the bolts.
Below: Mark along the cutting edge to show the planing line 'P'.

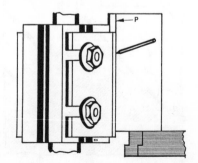

The template should be straight on the underside. It normally rests edge-on the table, up to the cutterblock and with its face against the cutter face. In its simplest form the template merely needs just one basic line permanantly marked on it, the planing line. This can be marked after setting planing cutters to the minimum cutting or planing circle, as follows:-

18

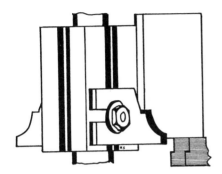

Fig. 42 The template can rest on the table and the underedge taken as the table line.

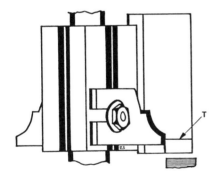

Fig. 43 Alternatively, the template can be notched out to rest on the cutterblock. In this case a table line is added 'T'.

Clamp a piece of straight, flat hardwood across the spindle fences. Mount the cutterblock in the usual way and with the regular thickness of cutters in position. Set the fence so that the inside face of the hardwood clears the cutterblock body, lips, cutterbolts, etc., by 1.5mm.

Set planing cutters so that their cutting edges just scrape the face of the hardwood piece, i.e. to the minimum cutting or planing circle. Place the template in position and carefully mark along the cutting edge of the planing cutter. This is then the line to which planing cutters should be set and beyond which all mould cutters must project to clear the cutterblock.

A second line can be added square to the planing line to show the table line, perhaps 12mm. above the bottom edge to allow cutters to be more easily seen when setting. Using this requires the spindle initially set high, then lowered before use.

It is possible to use the underedge of the template as the table line. As the template rests on the table when setting, the spindle is initially set to the correct height so re-setting is not necessary.

An alternative is to notch-out the template so that a small projection locates on the top of the cutterblock. This type is popular because it is more convenient and can be used off the machine.

The planing and table lines should be permanently marked on the template. The method varies according to the type of template used:

PLYWOOD TEMPLATES - Use birch or some other light-faced plywood about 3mm. thick and mark the lines in HB pencil. Lacquer over the complete template (back and front to prevent warping) using a matt finish lacquer. Finally scrub with wire wool to give a suitable surface to accept pencil marks.

FACED-HARDBOARD TEMPLATES - Scribe the lines with a sharp point then carefully sand level and finally scrub with wire wool.

ALUMINIUM TEMPLATES - Scribe the lines with a sharp point then carefully emery-cloth level, finally use a wet and dry emery cloth, wet, to give a suitable matt surface.

In all cases cutter-profile lines are made in pencil and deleted with a hard eraser. Mark the template for the precise position of the cutters using the planing and table lines as the starting points. The vertical (height) setting is marked-off using a regular rule.

Horizontal setting (depth-on-cut) is marked-off using a projection rule, or by rule-of-thumb adding 2.5-3.0mm. for every 10mm. depth for square cutterblocks and 1.5-2.0mm. for every 10mm. depth for other cutterblocks. This rule-of-thumb is not accurate but good enough in many instances. (See also development templates). The template fits to the cutterblock itself and if there is any damage to the lip accurate setting is not possible.

Pre-setting

Pre-setting in a tool room on a setting stand is easier and simpler that setting on the machine because the cutters and sample or template are clearly visible. A setting stand has a dummy arbor carrying the square or circular cutterhead, setting rollers for planing cutters, clamps for short sample mouldings and usually a template holder for either plain or development templates.

NOTE: Pre-setting is not practicable with conventional slotted collars because cutters slip on transfer to the machine.

Straight moulding

This is used when forming house trim, architraves, door and window sections, etc., when a mould shape, rebate, groove or similar is formed along the full length of timber.

The straight fence should be used with a through-fence for additional support and safe operation. Normally, the fences are in line when face-moulding only part of the depth but can be off-set for edging, to form a bullnose, for example. Timber is usually held down and against the fence with pressures which can be individual spring leaves or finger-like guides. In this case a front guard is essential above the timber, plus other guards to enclose the cutterblock when timber is not in place. Preferably use Shaw guard pressures which also form an enclosing box guarding the cutterblock.

Table rings fill in the table gap so both this and the fence gap are the smallest practicable. Shaw guards are fitted to hold the timber and to enclose the cutterblock when timber is not in position. Guards then complete the enclosure of the cutterblock, one above the timber spanning the gap, and a cover over the back often formed as an exhaust hood.

With deep moulds it is normal to 'sink' the cutterblock to form complex moulds as a series of steps. With deep moulds or small sections the timber may be unstable after leaving the infeed fence, so add a spacer guide at the outfeed fence to support the newly formed mould. Even so, pieces tend to snipe (vibrate to form an unacceptable surface) and it is usual to allow extra length so that these end defects can be cut off.

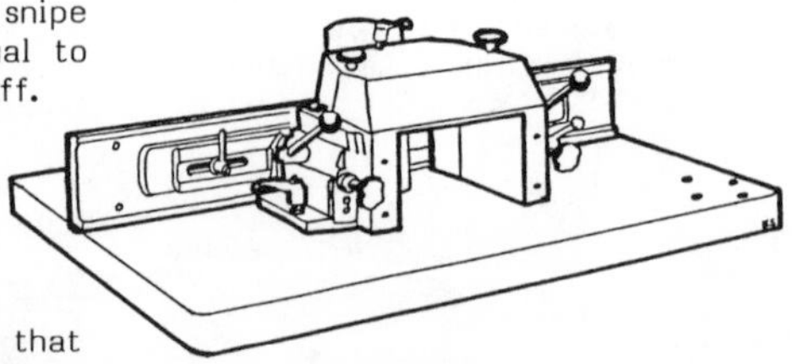

Support long pieces at the infeed and outfeed so that their weight does not lever them off the table. Use a spike in the left hand to avoid close contact with the cutterhead and always use a push-stick or a push-block to follow through. When handling small pieces use some form of jig with secure handholds which afford the operator a firm grip. If stop-moulding, that is forming the mould only part-way along the timber, end-stops must be used. Follow the recommended methods. Never stand directly in line with the timber.

Fig. 44 This shows a straight fence from the rear, complete with a guard fitted but without exhaust hood (Dominion).

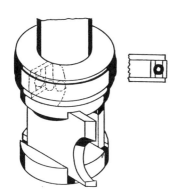

Fig. 45 Slotted collars with a ball-bearing follower.

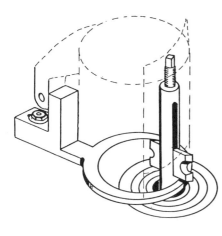

Fig. 46 A ring fence used with a French head. The dotted line shows the cage or bonnet guard.

MECHANICAL FEED

Many users find that a mechanical feed on the spindle moulder not only produces work faster, but also provides a better quality finish, greater safety and makes cutters last longer. The speed can be regulated to give the correct and consistant surface finish on the moulds, whereas hand-feeding gives an irregular finish. It is safer because it guards the cutterhead very effectively and does not need close contact of the user's hands with the cutters.

For feed speeds see Chart 11, Chapter 1.

Shaping

Shaping is forming the outline shape of table tops, chair parts and similar work, either square-edge shaping only, or simultaneously shaping and edge-moulding.

The size and outline of the piece being shaped is controlled by a template made from plywood or similar material. The roughly sized workpiece is fastened to the template so the assembly handles as a single unit. Usually the template is fastened on top of the workpiece, but the template could be underneath. All templates need secure handholds so that the operator can control the work safely, also finger guards where possible. A supporting saddle can be used for compound curves.

SHAPING TEMPLATE

The template edge contacts the pattern follower. This is a ball-bearing mounted on the spindle arbor, a circular 'ring' fence fastened to the table, or a table ring. A cage (bonnet) guard, or similar, protects the spindle above the workpiece, at the rear and around the sides down to table level - leaving the smallest practical gap for the workpiece. Some form of pressure/guard is needed to keep the assembly flat on the table. In shaping, move the assembly around to keep the template in contact with the follower so that the cutterhead simultaneously edge-profiles and shapes the workpiece to the same overall outline.

Ring fence

The ring fence is a static guide having point contact with the template. The ball-bearing type spins with the arbor when running free, but slows down to roll with the template immediately contact is made. This eliminates friction between template and follower and allows that light touch essential to fine detail work. A plain follower can be used, but this rotates with the arbor to create friction and cause wear on the template. It should be used with caution and only when no ball-bearing follower is available.

The template is usually the same size and profile as the finished part to correspond with the planed edge or the highest point of the edge-mould, so template manufacture is relatively straight forward. It is also simple to check the blank against it for size and shape.

Often the blank is first bandsawn to rough shape so that only a light finishing cut is needed. With gentle shapes the spindle moulder can shape and edge-mould simultaneously without pre-cutting. Alternatively, the shape can be formed initially by using planing cutters, and the mould added as a second operation working off the previously formed square-edged shape. In this case the shaped part needs fastening to a jig with secure handholds.

The template can form the edge profile completely around a single piece, for example, a table top. In this case it is essential to ease-in the cut when starting. With a ring fence this is done by starting at any point other than the centre mark on the ring. When using a ball-bearing follower the cut is started against a starting block or by using a lead-in on the template.

Alternatively a template can form only a part of the edge profile, say the inside or outside edge of a chair leg. When handling narrow or small pieces which are only part-profiled use a jigged template which both locates and secures the part in position and has secure handles. The template forms part of that jig.

Often a multi-station jig is used to form part-profiled workpieces, or small and narrow parts in two or more steps. Each part is transfered from one station to another in sequence and several cuts made at a single pass. This is also used to handle full-outline pieces too small to work safely as individual parts.

Plate 15 Above: Setting planing cutters to rollers on an Autool profile grinder.

Plate 16 Below: Setting moulding cutters to a sample on an Autool profile grinder.

CUTTER SETTING

Cutter setting is critical. When a ball-bearing follower is used set the cutters so that the highest point of the mould is directly in line with the contact face of the follower so that the planing diameter is exactly the same as the follower diameter.

When using a ring fence the planed surface or shallowest part of the mould is aligned with the centre mark on the ring. Using a ring fence allows independent adjustment to make small corrections or to suit different diameters of cutterhead.

Cutter pre-setting is as described previously, but the cutting diameter has to be precise when using a ball-bearing follower. This is possible in a number of ways, perhaps using a knife-edge setting roller on fixed centres, or using the Q3S system.

Setting on the machine to a sample part is not easy as cutter contact is difficult to see. Setting, in fact, has to be made both by sight and feel.

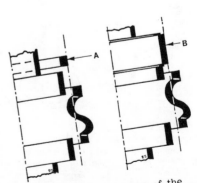

Fig. 47 The highest point of the mould (deepest point on the cutter) should align with the centre mark of the ring fence 'A' or the ball-bearing follower 'B'.

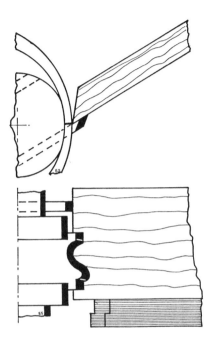

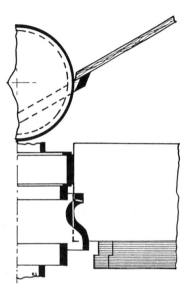

Fig. 48 Cutters can be set with a bevelled-off straight-edge, shown with a ring fence.

Fig. 49 Alternatively a template can be used, shown with a ball bearing follower.

Plate 17 Setting moulding cutters to a template on an Autool profile grinder.

It is possible to use a wooden straight-edge, moving the cutter forward until its deepest point is in line with the bevelled edge set against the follower. Then adjust the spindle vertically until the point corresponding with the underface is in line with the underside of the straight-edge, or at the same height as a jig base if used.

The template is used generally as described previously, but is cut along the planing line and bevelled clear on the reverse side. The planing line then abuts either the ball-bearing follower or the central point on the ring fence to set cutters as with the straight-edge.

In the case of collars the straight-edge or template is used to actually set the cutters. With a ring fence it is used to set the fence to the cutters which are initially set to project in the normal way.

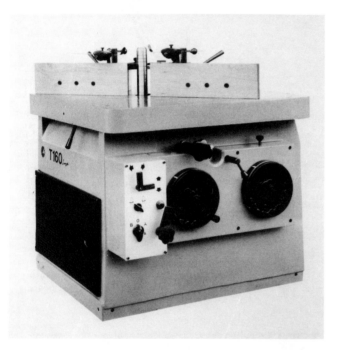

Plate 18. One of several SCM spindle moulders, the T160 features five speeds and a tilting spindle.

CHAPTER 3

CUTTERHEAD TYPES

All cutterheads used on the spindle moulder have one or several cutting edges and rotate at high speed whilst the timber feeds past. Heads vary in size, type and design according to the work for which they are intended.

French head

The single, simply-prepared cutter is inserted through a slot in the arbor (different arbor diameters are available) and is locked by a single vertical screw. The cutter has a slightly negative cutting angle and a poor scraping cut even when properly burred-over.

The steel from which these cutters are made is often unhardened gauge steel, unhardened because it needs to be relatively soft and malleable for burnishing - to bend under pressure rather than fracture. The hardness is much lower than with other cutting tools used in woodworking and as wear resistance is almost directly related to hardness French head cutters dull much more quickly than other types.

Some makers supply a high speed steel type of cutter, tempered-back to be more malleable. This has better wearing characteristics but poorer burring-over capability.

APPLICATION

The French head is small in diameter and for this reason safer than many other common heads, and the slightly negative cutting action gives less tear-out when cutting against the grain. Even after burnishing, the cut is only a little better than a scraping action and nothing like as free as, for example, slotted collar cutters. This can be an advantage when working interlocked grain or when cutting against the grain inside tight corners, but is a disadvantage for other work.

The cutting rate is slow, only light cuts are possible and cutters quickly dull. The tool is best suited for short, non-repeating runs where the low-cost and easy preparation of cutters is an advantage and their short machine life is of little consequence.

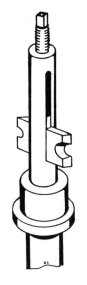

Fig. 50 A slotted arbor or French head.

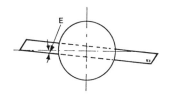

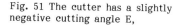

Fig. 51 The cutter has a slightly negative cutting angle E,

The French head was popular for shaping in furniture making for many years as it is suitable for both inside and outside curves down to very small radii. When this type of work grew less the tool was already in decline and with the return of more complex work the router will almost certainly take over.

French head cutters are amongst the simplest to grind as the cutter shape is exactly the reverse of the mould wanted (on most other cutters it is not). It can be checked for shape by holding it square onto a sample mould or flat on a drawing.

Grind the cutter to a bevel angle of 35 - 40 degrees, to give a clearance angle of 50 - 55 degrees. After honing to remove any grinding burr, forcibly burr over the edge using a burnishing tool at two angles against the ground face. Apply relatively heavy pressure and travere along the cutting edge and slightly towards it. A grinding burr is brittle and breaks-off in use, but this cold-formed burr is stronger and does not. Some users also burnish the front face at about 2-5 degrees prior to the burring-over.

The burnishing tool is held at two angles to the ground face to form what is in effect a hook to increase the cutting angle. Some form of lubricant is necessary when burnishing, perhaps a light oil. Traditionally spit is used and old hands claim better results from this, and seem to be right! When the tool becomes dull re-burnishing will partially restore the cutting edge, otherwise repeat the grind-hone-burnish sequence.

Burnishing tools are not easy to come by, most users make their own from a discarded triangular file with the teeth ground-off and the corners rounded-over. Any similar hardened tool will do as only the corners are actually used.

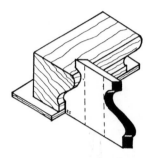

Fig. 53 Cutters should be ground to fit the mould when square-on to it.

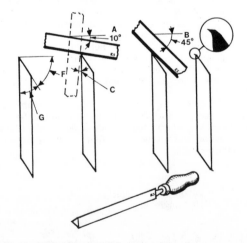

Fig. 53 Bevel angle G should be 35-40 degrees giving a clearance angle F of 50-55 degrees. A shows the first burnish and B the second to give the effect shown. Sometimes the front is also burnished as C. The other sketches show an enlarged view of the burred edge and a typical burnishing tool.

Straight moulding

As with other spindle cutters setting is not critical - the fence can easily be adjusted for cut depth. Cutter projection with a new cutter should include due allowance for subsequent grinding, but must not be excessive.

It is quite common practice for the cutter to cut on one end only with the opposite edge shaped to roughly the same profile and set barely clear of the cut to give reasonable balance. As the cutter is ground down, keep it central on the arbor by reducing diameter to maintain balance.

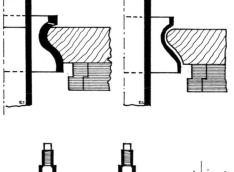

Fig. 54 Left: the cutting end forms the moulding whilst, right: the opposite end is ground to barely clear.

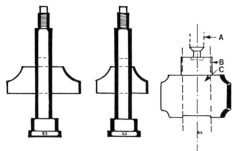

Fig. 55 Left – New cutters.

Centre – The same cutter when worn should still be in balance.

Right – A notched French head cutter C, showing a clamping piece B and the securing screw A.

Shaping

Cutter projection is much more critical if the spindle itself or a plain ring on it is used as a guide. In this case cutter projection beyond the contact face must match the cut depth needed. It is essential to measure this before starting so that the cutter is made to the correct length.

The French head itself can be used as a guide when shaping, but this is not recommended as contact is 'live' against a rotating spindle. At best this gives a 'rough' feel to the feed and at worst could grab and kick-back. Preferably fit a ball-bearing follower to give rolling contact, or use a ring fence.

As wear takes place and has to be advanced to keep the same projection and cutting diameter. The cutter is then no longer central and progressively becomes more and more out-of-balance. Because the tool is physically small in diameter the effect is also small, but the vibration it causes can be transmitted directly to the workpiece via contact of the template with the spindle or follower.

This tool is reasonably safe to use and no special points need making except to ensure that the cutter is safely secured. Some operators notch-out the cutter to engage with a collar underneath to prevent the cutter flying, or notch-out to straddle the arbor seating itself - but this must be accurately milled to give proper seating. Use a top clamp piece so that the cutter top edge is not damaged with the securing screw. Possibly, also, notch the clamp piece to prevent this flying. Never stack French head cutters for multiple cuts; it can be dangerous. For safe cutter projections, see Fig. 56.

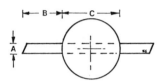

Fig. 56 Maximum cutter projection B should never excede either the retained cutter length C (French-head diameter) or three times cutter thickness A.

Slotted collars

This consists of a pair of slotted collars between which a pair of square or bevelled-edge cutters are clamped. In their original form they were held by friction only between cutter edges and slot seatings and were prone to flying.

Some makers incorporate a safety pin in each slot to engage with a corresponding edge notch in both cutters. These are essential with high spindle speeds and heavy cuts,

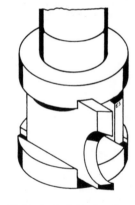

Fig. 57 Typical slotted collar.

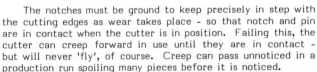

Fig. 58 Right - Slotted collars with a safety pin B and a matching notched cutter A.
Notched cutters, either of this type or the American pattern, are much safer than regular plain-edge cutters.

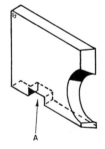

The notches must be ground to keep precisely in step with the cutting edges as wear takes place - so that notch and pin are in contact when the cutter is in position. Failing this, the cutter can creep forward in use until they are in contact - but will never 'fly', of course. Creep can pass unnoticed in a production run spoiling many pieces before it is noticed.

American shaper heads have adjusting screws in the top collar to engage with the notched top edge of the cutters to combine fine adjustment with safe cutter retention. Normally these cutters have a bevelled top edge and collar slots, which allow different thicknesses of cutters to be fitted. A new U.K. cutter system uses the pin as a means of precise cutter setting, the Autool Q3S. See later description.

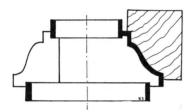

Fig. 59 Unequal collar diameters give more support with this sort of mould.

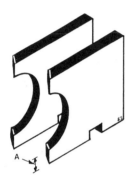

Fig. 60 With collar cutters the edge-to-profile distance A must be identical on both cutters.

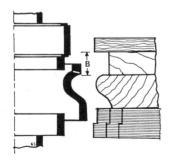

Fig. 61 Distance B should be as small as practicable.

Normally, collars of a matching pair are exactly the same diameter. For the heavier industrial machines they are 75 - 100mm. diameter, and for lighter work 50 - 75mm. diameter. Cutting angle is usually 30 degrees; a good average for most commercial timbers. However, because the cutting angle quickly reduces as the depth of cut increases, the average cutting angle is actually much less.

There have been odd pairs of slotted collar types made in the past; for example, pairs of collars of unequal diameter but equal slot spacing. They are intended for use with large coves and scotias (and other similar assymmetrical, or one-way, moulds) to give more support to the longer cutting edge.

The cutters used can be solid HSS, HCHC, or HSS brazed or welded onto a low carbon steel back. The latter are the most popular, and this type is known as plated bar when sold in the length. Individual pairs of cutters are also available with tungsten carbide, Tantung or Stellite facing.

Collar cutters are normally 6mm. thick and in widths-on-cut from 12 - 75 (or 100)mm. Length is determined by collar diameter and depth of cut. When ordered as pairs, slotted collar cutters are normally supplied 75mm. long - unless otherwise stated, or if supplied by the maker for his own slotted collars. Larger users buy plated bar and cut this off to whatever length is needed. This is more economic and the length can be varied. American shaper cutters can be of different thicknesses to give much more flexibility.

PREPARATION

Slotted collar cutters normally have a bevel angle of 35-40 degrees giving a clearance angle of 20-25 degrees.

Because the cutters are edge-clamped between the collars they cannot be tilted to correct a wrong profile nor can the cutters be adjusted up or down relative to each other. This means that two points must be carefully controlled in cutter grinding.

1 - The distance from the under-edge to the mould must be absolutely the same for both cutters, especially when forming a complex profile using both cutters each to form one part only. When profile-grinding cutters loose, use a side fence to maintain the correct edge-to-profile distance. With hand-ground cutters formed to the same profile the non-finishing cutter is usually deliberately ground to clear the mould. When shaping, the distance of the mould from the upper edge is critical when template dimensions are tight.

2 - The cutter profiles must match the mould precisely when held level with the latter and at the correct cutting angle. The cutter length must be correct to give safe retention when set. The length of a new cutter should be such that the tail end (opposite to the cutter edge) barely clears the cutting circle. The cutters then have the longest possible life and maximum retention in the collars.

29

Always use the largest diameter collars practical as this allows longer cutters to be fitted and these have a proportionately longer life. With larger collars, the longer grip also allows longer, safe cutter projections, and the cutting angle does not change so much in deep moulding. Use small diameter slotted collars only for internal shaping which includes tight curves.

CUTTER SETTING

Straight moulding

Slotted collars are often used for straight moulding. The through fence needs a cut-out for the collars so that the cutters project only enough to give a 1.5mm. working clearance between the collars and the closest part of the piece being moulded. It is also possible to use collars without a fence cut out; but cutter projection beyond the collars then becomes 1.5mm. plus the through-fence thickness. In both cases the top edge of each cutter needs forming with a 5 degree side clearance bevel.

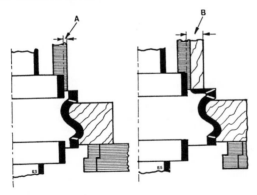

An exception to the general rule is when forming a bullnose or similar moulding when the full edge is being machined. In this case the deepest point of the cutting edge can be inside the collar diameter to give more support to shorter cutters.

Shaping

Slotted collars are ideal for shaping. With a relatively small cutting diameter they are easier to guard, are capable of shaping relatively small internal diameters and are better to work with than other larger cutterheads. Normally they are used with a ball-bearing follower, but can be used with a ring fence. The deepest point on the cutter should line up with the ball-bearing follower or ring fence.

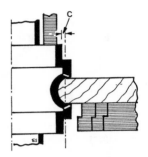

Fig. 62 Normally the cutter should project a minimum of 1.5mm beyond the collars C, but can be inside when bull-nosing or similar. In this case a cut-out in the through fence is essential for the collars. The collars can be edge-bevelled to allow more clearance when inside the planing line. (See Fig. 66.)

Fig. 63 Collar-to-fence-line gap should be 1.5mm. A, left, or 1.5mm. plus through-fence thickness B, right. Alternatively, hollow-out the rear of the through fence so that the top collar needs less cutter projection. It is possible to cut through or into the fence for collar clearance by breaking-through initially at a higher setting and to a smaller cut-depth.

Plate 19 Startrite ring fence and guard, with fine screw adjustments for setting height and position.

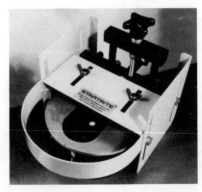

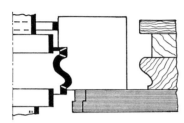

Fig. 64 A setting template can rest edge-on the table or on the jigged template base when setting cutters. (Shown with a ring fence.)

Fig. 65 Alternatively, the template can be marked with the jig base line. (Shown with a ball-bearing follower.)

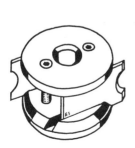

Fig. 66 These Rye collars can be pre-set in a tool room.

Template setting

The template normally rests on the machine table when straight moulding and on either the table or the jig when shaping. Bevel it away to contact the collar when straight moulding or to contact the follower when shaping.

Pre-setting in a tool room is not practical with conventional slotted collars because the cutters shift once the locknut is released. The spindle arbor could be removed completely for setting in the tool room, but this is not practical.

The only types of slotted collar which can be pre-set have separate screws to lock collars and cutters together after setting. This allows pre-setting and transfer back to the machine as a single unit.

Special, simple setting stands using setting fingers or setting wheels can be used in pre-setting and are ideal for shaping applications. Q3S cutters allow precise cutter setting by re-grinding the location notch after profile grinding. See later notes.

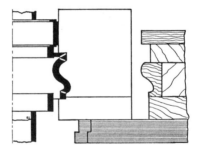

OPERATIONAL SAFETY

Pairs of cutters have to be precisely the same width, parallel and with perfectly square (or bevelled) edges. Makers supply cutters in matched pairs and it is essential to keep them this way; never use odd pairs of cutters, even if of the same nominal width, because different makers, and even the same maker in different cutter batches, cannot guarantee absolutely equal width.

With long bars always make cutter pairs out of the same bar; never one out of one bar and another out of a second. It is also important to make sure that the cutter edges and slots are free from burrs and lumps, etc. and that both are free from dirt, grease, chips, etc., before fitting cutters. Any of the above, singly or in combination, could give incorrect seating and unequal grip, with the loose cutter possibly flying out or slipping on start-up.

There are no specific regulations concerning safe cutter projection. The only guide that remotely applies gives a 20mm. projection as the maximum for a cutter thickness of 6mm. Likewise their are no international regulations concerning the shortest retained cutter length. There is, however, a universally-accepted guide that cutters should be discarded when their retained length is equal too or less than half the slot length plus their projection beyond the collars. As cutters wear their safe limits of projection also reduce; take care to watch this point. Small diameter collars obviously allow less cutter projection.

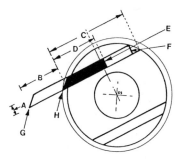

Fig. 67 Cutter retained length D must be greater than half the slot length C plus the distance from the collars to the maximum point of the cutters B.
Cutter projection B must not excede three times cutter thickness A.
Other points are:
G - maximum projection.
H - minimum projection (planing circle).
F - new cutter-tail position.
E - maximum forward position of the cutter tail for planing only - for moulding the tail must be further to the right.

Plate 20 These Forest City slotted collars feature bevelled seatings so that different cutter thicknesses can be fitted, lockscrews to allow pre-setting, and fine screw adjustment via a notched edge to provide precise setting and secure holding of the cutters.

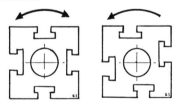

CHAPTER 4

Square blocks

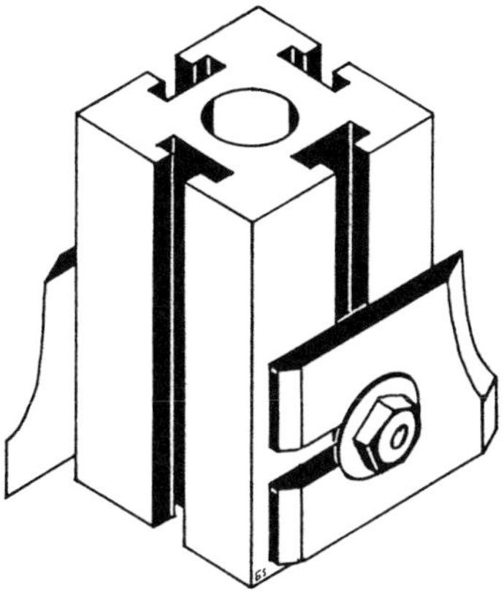

These are square in section and cutters can be bolted to all four slotted faces using nuts and bolts. Cutters of a wide variety of width, length and slot configuration can be fitted. The blocks can be provided with or without lips - but usually for spindle moulder work the unlipped type is used.

The cutterbolt slot can be central in the cutterblock face or off-set. Unlipped cutterblocks with central slots can rotate in either direction. Cutterblocks with off-centre slots must have the slot always closest to the cutting edge of the cutter it secures.

Bolts should be high tensile steel type; use no other type than those supplied by the makers. The correct washers are fully machined, bevelled-off to avoid damage (to be fitted bevel outwards), and are large in outer diameter to give full support to the cutter.

Fig. 68 A typical square, unlipped cutterblock as used on a spindle moulder.

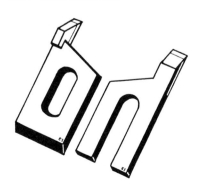

Fig. 69 Left: a centre slot cutterblock can rotate in either direction. Right: an off-centre slot cutterblock must rotate as shown.

Cutters

Cutters are flat, with open or closed slots and usually 9 to 13mm. thick. Thicker cutters are used for heavier cuts, but where a narrow cutter is used for deep grooving it is common to reinforce the back. (There are larger moulding cutters having reinforcement ribs welded to the back, but these are for heavy guttering or cill work on four-sided moulders, not spindle moulders.)

Most cutters are faced, usually with HSS or HCHC for regular work and sometimes with Tantung, Stellite or tungsten carbide for abrasive timbers. The backing material is stiff enough to withstand normal cutting pressures but is intended to bend back rather than break in a smash.

Cutters can have closed slots which are retained by the bolts if slippage takes place, or open-slots which fly completely off the cutterblock if they loosen whilst in use.

Fig. 70 Left: A closed slot type with a reinforced grooving cutter.
Right: An open slot rebating cutter.

APPLICATION

The cutting angle is around 40 degrees and tends to be vicious and with a big 'bite'. It is fine for heavy work on free-cutting softwoods and straight moulding such as large window sections, doors and frames. It is not really suited to light spindle moulder work, is of little use with furniture parts and unsuitable for shaping unless of very heavy section. 'Bite' is the theoretical amount a single cutter can remove with an uncontrolled feed. It can be anything from 12 to 40mm.

Cutters can be set anywhere in the depth of the cutter-block, varied in projection and mounted either square-on or slewed at an angle. (Slewing cutters is poor but common practice which allows a cutter to form a slightly different bevel or profile than that for which it was originally made.) Cutters must be used in pairs; this is absolutely vital, but more than one cutter can be secured to a single face of the cutterblock provided there is room.

All this adds up to a cutterblock which is versatile and low in cost. These are the two main attractions of square blocks which have kept them popular for over a hundred years. However, their very versatility makes re-setting difficult and with their safety now being questioned it seems that other types will replace them.

PREPARATION

Cutter selection

Narrow cutters up to about 80mm. wide have a single centre slot and are fixed with a single bolt. Wider cutters have two slots and need two bolts. Cutters are available in a wide range of sizes and it is important to choose the correct one when initially setting.

Most larger square blocks are fitted with 15mm. bolts, and a few smaller ones with 12mm. bolts or their imperial equivalents, and cutters are slotted accordingly. It is important to use the correct bolt for the slot-width and cutter thickness, so check with the makers.

The slot length is correct if the slot end barely clears the cutterbolt when the legs or cutter tail just clear the planing circle. This is also the correct new cutter position. Cutters for some small square cutterblocks are chamfered at the tail to give extra clearance and the greatest possible contact with the cutterblock. (The planing circle is described by planing cutters set to clear the cutterbolts and cutter lips by 1.5mm.)

Cutter width-on-cut is dictated by the work required. For small moulds a single pair of cutters is used. For intricate moulds it is usual to divide the mould into individual parts and use separate pairs of cutters for each part. This allows cutters to be used for more than one application. For example, different sizes of rebate cutter can be combined with different mould cutters to give a wide range of window-section profiles from relatively few cutters.

Cutter length (cutting edge-to-tail) is dictated by the size of the cutterblock and the mould depth. Planing cutters should be such that when their tail just clears the planing circle the cutting edge just reaches it. Longer cutters can be used, but this increases the planing circle which should be kept as small as possible. Shorter cutters can be set forward to reach the planing circle but this reduces cutter life.

Moulding cutters should reach the full mould depth when their tail just clears the planing circle. Longer cutters can be ground down, or the cutting circle increased. Shorter cutters can be moved forward, but cutter life is lost and shorter cutters are less safe.

It will be appreciated that cost savings are possible when a range of cutters are stocked. A useful aid is to make a full-size drawing of the cutterblock complete with cutting circle. Add extra circles at pre-set distances, say every 10mm. from the planing line, to represent depths-on-cut. It is possible then to actually measure lengths of cutters needed for both planing and moulding.

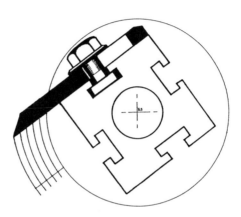

Fig. 71 Draw out a cutterblock full size and add depth-on-cut lines at 10mm. spacings. Use a pair of compasses to draw cutting circles to shown cutter lengths needed for different depths-on-cut.

Whilst cutters are rarely the precise cutter length needed, because of standard sizing, the nearest standard length is readily identified. If a choice of wrong cutter length has to be made, a rule of thumb is that a cutter can be longer by up to 7mm. and shorter by 3mm. As wear takes place with longer cutters the cutting circle will gradually reduce until the cutters are the correct length, after which they are gradually advanced on re-setting.

Grinding

Normally square-block cutters have a bevel angle of about 35 degrees which usually gives enough clearance, but check this at the minimum cutting circle.

A larger bevel angle is essential with tungsten carbide tipped types, but as there is barely enough clearance on square blocks for a larger main bevel angle, a secondary clearance angle is necessary.

Make sure that cutter pairs are dimensionally alike and balance them before using. Square block cutters are larger and heavier than other types and correct balancing is very important.

Setting

Cutters must be used in balanced pairs and mounted diametrically opposite on the cutterblock with both set to cut. Whilst this is also true of other types, square-block cutters must be given special attention because of their weight.

Cutters can be set to a sample or to a template. The template for square blocks is usually notched-out to rest on the top edge of the cutterblock and contacts the cutterblock lip or body. The normal unlipped type of cutterblock gives reasonably accurate registration for the template, but the cutterblock must be cleaned first and be damage-free.

OPERATIONAL SAFETY

Square block cutters sometimes fly out on starting or during use. The weight of these cutters and the speed at which they travel can cause considerable damage and injury.

A simple human error which can cause accidents is to start the machine with the cutters only partially tightened, but other factors which can cause accidents are; The use of dangerous cutters; cutterblocks or cutterbolts; insufficient friction between cutter and block; and chip wedging.

Each cutter must be in full and proper contact with the cutterblock when tightened. Both need absolutely flat faces (some blocks are purposely hollowed to ensure better contact at heel and toe) and both surfaces must be burr and dirt-free. Regularly inspect the cutterblock for damage and deformation. Badly deformed blocks should be returned to the makers.

Old and incorrect cutterbolts can be dangerous, cutterbolts for the square block are of a special high-tensile type. Cutterbolt threads which are stretched or deformed are dangerous. They appear different when compared to new threads.

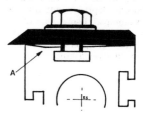

Fig. 72 Some cutterblocks are hollowed, as at A, to ensure better cutter seating.

Thread deformation often causes stiffness when tightening, but this is difficult to distinguish from normal tightening resistance. Check resistance with the cutterbolt and nut removed. Both faults result from persistant over-straining and/or over-long usage.

For safe operation use cutterbolts in rotation and examine each before fitting. Immediately discard any showing wear or deformation of the thread, cracks, rounding of the corners of the nut, etc. Never use a non-matching cutterbolt and nut.

Sometimes a cutter can bend or twist and then shift on tightening. This is not merely a nuisance when setting, it shows incorrect seating and the chance that cutters could shift again in use. Check cutters for bend and twist on a flat plate. Do not just use a thin straightedge as this only shows bend, not twist.

Some users flatten bent and twisted cutters by controlled bending in the opposite direction, but this could well lead to fatigue failure, or to invisible and dangerous cracks forming. Bent cutters should really be discarded.

The use of packing between cutter and cutterblock is widespread as a means of increasing frictional resistance to prevent cutter creep. The thickest packing recommended is thin brown wrapping paper. Cutter slippage on tightening when using only this is a sure sign of something else wrong which wants making right, not thicker packing adding.

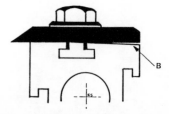

Fig. 73 If used, thin paper packing is inserted at B.

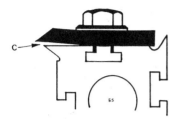

Fig. 74 Chip packing starts at C - particularly on a lipped block as shown here.

Fig. 76 Maximum cutter projection C should not be more than 3 times cutter thickness A, dimension F should never be less than 8mm. and washer G should cover the cutter tail at H.
Other points are:
J - New cutter tail position
H - Worn cutter tail position
E - Minimum projection (planing circle)
D - Maximum projection.

Chip packing or wedging results from dust being forced between cutterblock and cutter, forming a thickening wedge of hard, resinous material. Packing starts when the cutter seats badly, or because of damage to the lip or corner. Check all these points regularly.

The spanner used to tighten the nuts should be the one supplied by the makers. Never add pipes or other extensions and use only normal hand pressure. Some makers quote a specific torque and can supply a pre-set torque spanner, but not all makers agree with this practice.

The maximum cutter projection is about 3 times their thickness beyond the cutterblock. (There are no specific guidelines, but the figure given is widely accepted.)

Cutters wear down through re-grinding and have to be advanced to compensate. Cutters have a limited life, and this is reached when the washer no longer covers the legs or when there is less than 8mm. purchase behind the slot, whichever occurs first.

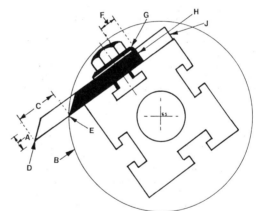

The closed-slot type of cutter can only be moved forward until the slot-end contacts the bolt. The slot on cutters from reputable makers is dimensioned so that enough grip remains when in this position. Other closed-slot cutters have a shorter distance slot-end to tail, so with these the 8mm. minimum purchase behind the slot applies.

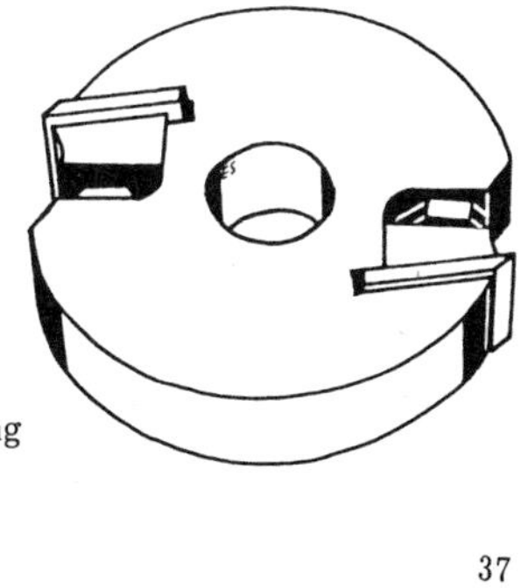

Fig. 75 A typical circular moulding head.

Circular cutterblocks

These are basically circular in section and usually have two cutters when made for the spindle moulder. Three-cutter heads are sometimes used, also four-cutter heads which are suitable for complex moulds.

Cutters are usually solid HCHC, HSS, or with a low-carbon steel back and facing of HSS, Tantung, Stellite or tungsten carbide. Thickness varies from 3mm. for planing only, to about 8mm. for deep moulding. Cutter width is normally the same as the cutterblock itself, or the wedge length if two or three wedges are used, but wider than the cutterhead when narrow moulding heads are used.

Circular moulding heads are infinitely safer than square heads. The cutting action is much less vicious and the cutters are smaller, lighter and cause less damage if 'thrown', something which is less likely to happen anyway. The 'bite' is also much less and the cutting diameter smaller.

The first circular moulding cutterhead was the Whitehill type and this has been copied around the world. Whitehill cutters are thin and are normally profiled all-round for use on any one of their four cutting edges. A regular range of shapes made by Whitehill (and others) make up into a surprisingly large variety of compound shapes. Whitehill cutterblocks are used widely for moulding, planing and rebating. They are extremely versatile as the cutter can be turned to any angle. The cutterhead can be readily sunk to give maximum support to the cutter on deep and stepped cuts. They are very popular with spindle hands.

Whitehill heads normally have two cutter seatings for 4mm. thick cutters. Other versions may accept a different cutter thickness, or a range of cutter thicknesses. It is important to find out from the makers just what can be fitted as fitting a wrong cutter could be dangerous. Don't use cut-up planer cutters, for example, they are too thin for moulding.

The normal cutting angle is around 25 degrees, a good average for most commercial timbers. One cutterhead, the Monninger Diangle, gives a choice of two angles, one for softwood and general use and the other for interlocked-grain timber.

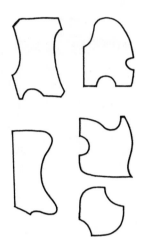

Fig. 77 Some of the Whitehill range of cutters.

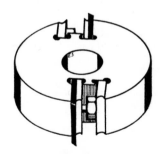

Fig. 78 A Monninger Diangle cutterhead having two cutting angles.

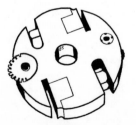

Fig. 80 Whitehill cutterhead with spur cutters for rebating.

Some cutterheads are formed to angles other than 25 degrees, and some makers will produce them to any required angle, but on a spindle moulder this really isn't justified.

Fig. 79 Whitehill cutterhead with backing support.

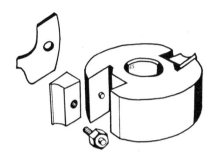

Fig. 81 A pin-type safety head.

Fig. 82 A serrated-back cutterhead

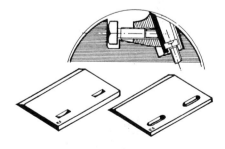

Fig. 83 A Rye screw-adjusted plan-
ing head.
Below: two types of cutter slots.
Left: recessed slots.
Right: through slots.

Circular moulding cutterheads range in diameter from 100mm. to 250mm., and in width on cut from 25 to 100mm. or more. Some types have an edge-chamfer to give more support on deep scotias and similar. Special versions are available with spur cutters for rebating and with back supports for excessive cutter projections.

Most circular cutterblocks use a form of internal wedge in front of the cutter to force this back against its seating on tightening. There are various forms but they all work on the same basic principle with either a nut tightened by a spanner or a socket screw tightened by an allen key.

Cutters were originally held only by friction between their faces and the wedge and slot seating. They are still produced and used in this way and remain the most popular type for spindle moulders with an excellent safety record. The remote possibility of cutters flying during use has recently led to a profusion of keyed-cutter type circular moulding heads for spindle moulder work. Examples are: cutters with a large through-hole or face counterbore to engage with a pin or screw, serrated-back cutters which engage in matching serrations milled in the cutter seating, or with one or more notches and some form of fixed key or keys.

Pin type

This usually has a central pin fitted either to the wedge (always key-locked with this type) or through the cutterblock body. Retained cutter types always need more assembly than friction-only types as in fitting the pin must engage in the hole or recess. The pin positively retains the cutter if normal grip is lost and restricts cutter adjustment to within safe working limits. It does not, however, prevent cutter creep nor twist until pin and cutter are in positive contact, by which time spoilage and damage may have taken place. Some newer types have an adjustable key, or two or more pins for better stability.

Serrated-back type

The cutters have serrations at 1/16 in. spacings to engage with matching serrations in the cutterblock. When the cutters are secured the serrations positively prevent outward cutter movement. Various wedging actions are used similar to the friction-held types. These heads are extremely safe in use.

Blanks are available for profiling by the user - but this sets a problem. The serrations which hold the cutter so securely also prevent adjustment outwards except in 1/16in. increments, and they cannot be tilted. For this reason cutters need grinding with precision, to be absolutely correct when fitted in mould depth, slew and alignment. Hand-grinding is impracticable, they are intended for grinding with the cutters mounted in the head using a profile grinder. A drawback is that the planing circle varies as wear takes place, so they are not ideal for shaping using a ball-bearing follower.

Slotted types

Some cutterheads incorporate an adjusting screw with a cap head that engages in a slot in the cutter. These offer fine adjustment of the cutter and safe retention. Another type, the Q3S, has two pins formed on the wedge engage in precision edge notches in the cutter which pre-determine cutter projection.

APPLICATION

Circular moulding heads are used for virtually every spindle moulding application. The Whitehill types are extremely versatile as the cutter can be seated at virtually any angle to produce a wide variety of shapes from only a few basic cutters. For example, a single, straight cutter will form any angle of bevel or chamfer simply by altering its setting.

Unlike most other cutterheads, Whitehill cutters are intended to project both above and below the cutterhead for 'sinking' the head into the cut. In this way the head gives maximum support to the cutter on deep cuts, so both cutting circle and bite are appreciably reduced when compared to other heads. The heads with top and bottom chamfer give better support on certain profiles and are, perhaps, the most universal type.

It is possible to run Whitehill heads in tandem and span a long cutter between the two, but it is important to use only a matched pair for this work. Never attempt to use two non-matched heads as the cutter slots may not align. Tandem heads are manufactured as a pair for perfect slot matching.

Continental versions of the Whitehill head are much less versatile as the cutters supplied are profiled or intended to be profiled only on one edge and the degree of tilt is more limited. Deep circular heads are also intended for single-edge cutters but not for 'sinking' - except for rebate cutterheads with spur cutters fitted. Conventional serrated-back heads are excellent from a safety standpoint but need profile-grinding and are primarily intended for heavier work on a four-sider.

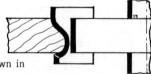

Fig. 87 The moulding cutter shown in position.

PREPARATION

The bevel angle on all circular cutters is normally between 35 and 45 degrees, but this depends on the cutting angle. Check for clearance as previously described and record the bevel angle for future use. Cutters are ground on an open, copy or profile grinder and are then balanced before fitting.

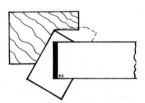

Fig. 84 A Whitehill planing cutter tilted to form a bevelled rebate. Normally the top edge is formed at a slight angle to give a clean underface (as shown in dotted outline).

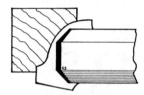

Fig. 85 A Whitehill chamfered cutterhead gives more support for moulds of this type.

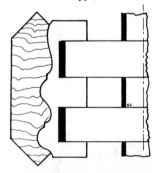

Fig. 86 Whitehill cutterheads used in tandem. They must be bought as a matching pair.

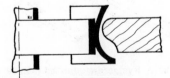

Fig. 88 The same head as Fig. 87 showing a balancing cutter set close to the profile. Both cutters must weigh the same.

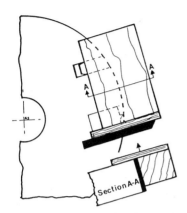

Fig. 89 Above: A Whitehill template can be fixed to a shaped block to register better.
Below: Mark on it:
D – Planing line.
E – Maximum depth of cut (12mm.).
B – Block clearance line (allow 2mm.).
C – Maximum projection above and below (12mm.).
A – Minimum cutter retention line (18mm. into the slot).

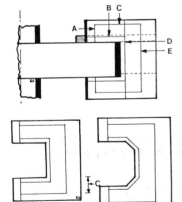

Fig. 90 Setting out a template for any circular moulding head
A – Cutter retention,
B – Maximum cutter projection in depth-on-cut,
C – Maximum cutter projection above and below.

Cutter setting

Cutters are easy to set with all circular heads. The cutters are usually tightened enough to snug only whilst checking them against the pattern, and they can then can be gently tapped into correct position. Use a soft mallet for this - but remember to fully tighten when set.

The Wadkin type with a spring-loaded ball-bearing in the wedge for steadying the cutter is ideal when setting in this way.

Cutters are normally used in matching pairs, but for the smaller heads it is permissible for one cutter to form the mould, balanced by a second cutter of equal weight but with a non-matching profile. The balancing cutter should be set as close as possible to the cut, but without actually touching, to keep the running balance true. Template setting makes this easier.

Wide circular heads have cutters of the same width as the head and often have no means of drawing-out a cutter if wrongly set. Take care with this type not to set the cutters in too far, otherwise they have to be released and re-set, which is something of a nuisance.

The cutterhead types with screw adjustment are more convenient. There are two versions: One has recessed or slotted cutters into which the screw heads lock to move the cutter 'in' or 'out'.

The other has plain cutters to seat on the screws which can only move them 'out'. With these the normal practice is initially to set each cutter slightly too far 'in', then screw out to the correct setting. If initially set too far out, the cutters could be tapped back a precise amount after setting-back the screw, but they are easier to adjust as described.

Standard serrated-back cutters are set in the head prior to profile grinding, not after, usually on a setting stand using a sample. Insert spacing pieces under the cutters so that they engage into corresponding serrations. It is practical to re-set previously-ground serrated cutters and use them without a further re-grind, but only one cutter will finish.

Template setting

The most convenient way to set circular-head cutters (other than standard serrated-back and Q3S types) is to use some form of template.

For the continental and wider heads both the table-mounted and notched types of template are suitable and are used generally as described for square heads.

Templates for Whitehill types should be notched for about 20mm. inside the planing line to project both above and below the heads.

The template can register against the cutter clamp, but is more accurate when fastened to a hardwood block shaped to fit the outer curve of the cutterblock, and with a ledge to rest on the top face.

Mark the planing line, top and bottom block clearance lines (including bevels if any), and minimum cutter retention line. Set-out the cutter shape within these outlines so that the cutter profile just clips the planing and clearance lines for maximum support by the head.

Dominion supply a setting template which fixes to their circular moulding head for cutter setting. Tool-room setting is more convenient than setting on the machine.

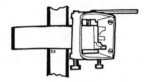

Fig. 93 Dominion provide a template which clamps to their cutterhead.

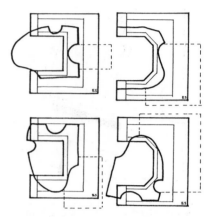

Fig. 92 Set cutter profiles just to clip the minimum projection lines and be within the retention line.

Fig. 94 Cutter projection B should not excede either cutter retention D or three times cutter thickness A. C should not normally be less than 10mm. (Manufacturers recommendations vary, check this point). Other points,
E - Tail position for a new cutter.
F - Tail position of a worn cutter.
H - Minimum projection (planing circle).
G - maximum cutting circle.

NOTE: Cutter projection is not normally more than three times thickness, but can be more at lower spindle speeds and should be less at high spindle speeds.

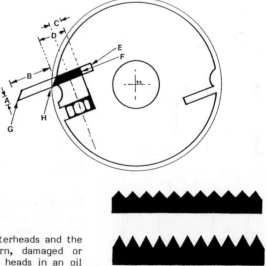

OPERATIONAL SAFETY

Regularly strip, clean, oil and inspect the cutterheads and the clamp assembly in particular. Replace worn, damaged or suspect parts before returning to use. Store heads in an oil bath if used infrequently. Take care to wipe oil from the cutter slots before use.

If using serrated-back cutterheads note that two different types of serrations are commonly used, both with the same pitch. Make sure the cutters used have matching serrations as otherwise the hardened cutter could damage the cutter seating when clamped. The Fearnehough universal serrated cutter is the only type, to date, which fits either type of serration.

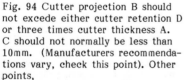

Fig. 91 Two profiles are used on serrated-back cutters;
Above: 45/45/90 degree angles.
Below: 60/60/60 degree angles.
Check that you have the correct one, or use Fearnehough cutters with universal serrations which fit either.

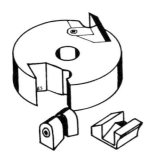

Fig. 95 A Dominion twin wedge-lock cutterhead taken apart for cleaning and to show the double-wedge clamp.

Safe cutter projections beyond the cutterblock directly relate to cutter thickness and cutter retention within the cutter slots. Ensure that cutters do not exceed the safety guides. With the original Whitehill heads the only cutter thickness used is 4mm., so maximum cutter projections can be shown quite specifically setting the template out as Fig. 89.

In all cases an overriding factor is the need of safe retention by the clamp or wedge in front of the cutter. In no circumstances should the inside edge of the cutter be closer than 10mm. to the securing screw centreline, but some manufacturers use the inside edge of the clamp as a guide beyond which the inside edges of cutters must not be set. With serrated-back types the makers usually state the maximum distance between the bottom of the cutter seating and the inside edge of the cutter.

The cutter should not normally be narrower than the cutterblock, except when two or more wedges are used in one cutter seating. In all cases the cutter must be as wide as, or wider than, the wedge. When using cutters narrower that the cutterblock, fill up to the full seating width by adding extra wedges and cutter blanks.

Plate 21 Startrite two-cutter circular moulding cutterblock with alternative moulding cutters and grooving segments.

Plate 22 Left: Forest City serrated-back circular moulding head with hydraulic fitting.

Right: Forest City shear-cut and segmented planing cutterhead.

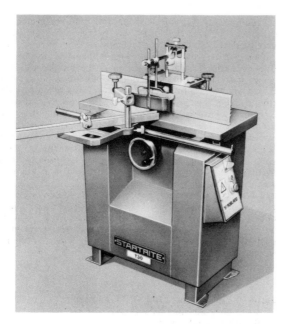

Plate 23 Left: The Startrite T30 has a built-on sliding table and a spindle speed of 6 000 revs/min.

Plate 24 Centre: This two-part tipped profiled cutter is mounted on an ETP Hydro-Grip sleeve CXE. This provides fine screw adjustment of the two halves, plus secure hydraulic locking on the arbor.

Plate 25 Lower right: Forest City tipped profiled cutters; left, for straight-bore mounting; right, with hydraulic sleeve mounting.

Fig. 96 Solid profile cutter.

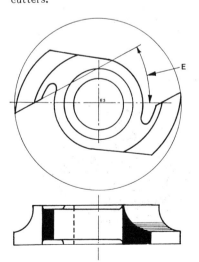

Fig. 97 Tipped combination profiled cutters.

CHAPTER 5

Profiled cutters

With these heads the profile is formed by the maker during manufacture and the user merely grinds the flat leading face when sharpening. The two basic types are: solid heads completely made from tool steel, or a non tool-steel body with HSS or tungsten carbide facings brazed-on. The second type has a common body with interchangable bits or cutters which are profile-ground by the maker. These are used commonly on four-sided moulders, but rarely on spindle moulders, mainly because their cutting diameters are too large.

The type normally used on a spindle moulder is a two-point solid or faced profiled-head, though three and four point types are also used as a one-piece or as part of an interlocking combination.

Profiled-heads can be made with a cutting angle to match the timber to be moulded. This or the class of timber being worked should be stated when ordering, or the head will be made to the manufacturer's standard angle to suit most commercial timbers. If the cutting angle is important, for example, to work interlocked-grain timber, it is essential to emphasize this when ordering because the angle cannot be altered later.

Fig. 98 Left: Cutting angle E measured at the planing circle. The cutter has no side clearance.

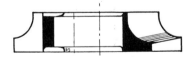

Fig. 99 Above: A one-way solid profiled cutters with side relief.

The cutting angle can be measured at the planing circle or at the deepest point of the cut. As the difference between the two can be large, clearly state both cutting angle and where measured. Previous tables state the cutting angle at the planing circle.

The outer surfaces are precision ground to profile and radial relief and are never ground or honed in use. It is usual for the makers to grind side clearance on heads where clearance is only in one direction, i.e. for quadrants and coves, etc.

This is not normal on shapes where both left- and right-hand clearance is needed, unless including cutting edges square or almost square to the arbor which otherwise burn. When left- and right-hand side clearance is formed on a one-piece head the profile alters as wear takes place. Alteration is small enough with faced types to be disregarded, but not with a solid head.

If pattern change is not acceptable when needing two-way clearance, the head can be made in two or more interlocking and overlapping parts each with clearance in one direction only. The change in profile on grinding is corrected by bringing the parts closer together or further apart using thin removable shims or screws. Take care when using shims that dirt is not trapped to tilt the head. The best adjustment is by using an ETP Hydro-grip sleeve CXE. This is a double sleeve with hydraulic grease to centre the tool, and which also incorporates fine screw adjustment.

Combination heads are now sold by some makers consisting of several cutters which combine in various ways to make up into different and often complex profiles.

Profile heads are straight-bore for mounting on a plain arbor. Cutting diameters for use on a spindle moulder are normally about 100-130mm depending on the depth of profile. These heads usually have a common outer diameter so that the planing circle varies with mould depth.

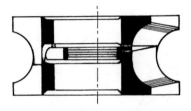

Fig. 100 Showing alteration of profile width A to B through wear on a one-piece solid profile cutter having two-way side clearance.

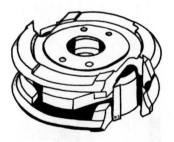

Fig. 101 Change in profile width can be avoided by making the cutter in two interlocking halves and adjusting their spacing by use of shims or screws. Alternatively, use an hydraulic sleeve with fine-screw adjustment, such as the ETP Hydro-Grip CXE. See Plate 24.

Fig. 102 A combination head with section shown

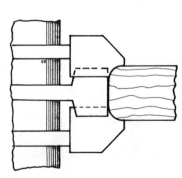

APPLICATION

The biggest advantage of profiled heads is that the maker forms the profile which then remains true for its full life. No setting is needed except for mounting the head, correcting width if two-part and setting height and depth.

It is very quickly put into production and is ideal for repeated runs of identical mouldings. The heads are used for all types of moulding including shaping, but with a ring fence rather than a ball-bearing follower because of diameter variation.

46

Plate 26 Leuco disposable-cutter type cutterhead fitted both with straight and moulding cutters for planing and corner rounding.

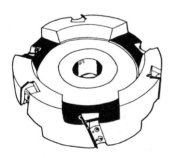

Fig. 103 A disposable-type edging head with opposite-hand shear cutters.

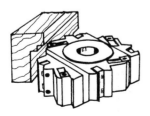

Fig. 104 A disposable-type, double-rebate head.

PREPARATION

Grind flat on the leading face only, making sure that the original cutting angle is maintained. The outer face must not be touched except to remove any slight grinding burr. The only setting required is to correct the width on multi-part heads.

OPERATIONAL SAFETY

Profile heads are exceptionally safe due to the one-piece construction. The normal safety guides apply but no special measures are needed. One point to watch when grinding worn solid-type heads is to avoid forming a sharp corner in the gullet which concentrates stress and could start a crack. Avoid this by well-rounding the grinding wheel, and discard heads when worn to the minimum tooth width.

Disposable-cutter heads

This type is a recent innovation. It uses special heads with small, solid tungsten carbide cutters which are used once only on each cutting edge and are then discarded. Most cutters of this type have two usable cutting edges, but some square ones are made with four usable edges.

The cutter seating is milled precisely in manufacture so cutters always seat in exactly the same position and are pin-retained for safety. The cutters themselves are precisely made to a uniform width and with a highly-honed cutting edge. Conventional cutter grinding and setting is not needed and the cutting circle remains exactly the same regardless of the number of replacement cutters used.

The heads are straight-bore and are available in different diameters, numbers of cutters and width-on-cut using cutters of standard size. Cutting angle is normally about 15 degrees.

Two-cutter heads are used for edge-planing solid timber. When edge-planing faced particle (chip) boards with a straight cutting action the outward pressure can edge-splinter and lift the facings. Avoid this by using a special shear-action head to enter the cut at the outer face and shear in towards the centre. On these the plastic is severed ahead of the point where splintering occurs and pressure is turned harmlessly inward. With double-faced boards opposite-hand shear cutters are used. These are fitted to cut inwards from both facings to meet and overlap in the centre.

This type of head can have tungsten carbide scribing cutters for rebating, and combinations are manufactured to use regular tungsten carbide cutters to produce any mouldings which can be formed by intersecting straight faces and a few regular curves. Cutterheads are also made for special profiles to customer's drawings with a guarantee of exactly-shaped replacement cutters to the same profile. Users are, however, begining to regrind these mould cutters themselves on a profile grinder or send them to a service centre.

APPLICATION

These heads are simple and safe. Cutters can be replaced quickly, accurately and without need of normal setting. Regrinding is not recommended as the cost of replacement cutters is less than re-grinding costs - according to the makers. If ground, most cutters can only be used in a fractionally smaller cutterhead in any event, so cutterhead costs double or treble if doing this.

The primary application is in edge-planing or edge-moulding particle boards, but increasingly this type of head is being used to form profiles in solid timber. The main attraction is simplicity of use, ease of cutter replacement and maintenance of profile and cutting diameter. A fixed cutting diameter is essential when shaping using a ball-bearing follower.

Cutter setting

Cutters locate on their inside cutting edge against the milled seating and are locked and keyed usually by a taper-locking action which pulls them firmly into the seating.

OPERATIONAL SAFETY

These heads are very safe in use with a mild cutting action and a small bite. As the cutters are retained by one or two pins they never fly out in normal use. The normal safety points apply. Any special points are given by individual makers.

Chip-limiting heads

Many cutterheads have an aggressive cutting action when the cutting angle is large and if the timber is insecurely held, knotty or badly-grained. This can cause vibration and spoilage, and in extreme cases the timber can be grabbed and thrown back at the user.

A chip-limiting head restricts the bite of individual cutters to within safe limits to steady the cut and prevent kick-back. Purpose-made shoulders or a formed chip-limiter project close to the cutting circle to actually contact timber under excessive feed conditions and prevent a dangerous bite being taken.

Special circular moulding heads are produced with profiled chip-limiters fitted at a negative angle immediately in front of the cutters. Setting of both cutter and chip-limiter has to be exacting, but control is absolute through the full mould depth.

There are other versions: for example, solid or tipped profiled cutterheads which serve the same purpose. Profiled cutters may have a negative-rake profiled chip-limiter similar to the loose-cutter type, or chip-limiting shoulders to align with flat or angled sections of the profile. The latter are more easily maintained at the proper height than the fully-profiled type.

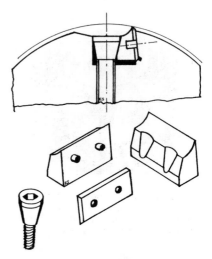

Fig. 105 One method of fitting disposable cutters, showing the wedge viewed front and rear together with one cutter and screw.

Fig. 106 A chip-limiting head with loose-type cutters and chip-limiters.

Fig. 107 A solid-profiled chip-limiting head.

48

Plate 27 Oppold circular moulding head with keyed cutters and chip-limiters.

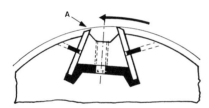

Fig. 108 The chip-limiter A is immediately in front of the cutter, facing the opposite direction and fractionally below the cutting circle.

Fig. 109 A typical collet arbor fitting for a loose-cutter head.

APPLICATION

Chip-limiting heads can replace most other comparable cutter-heads for virtually any straight moulding or shaping operation on the spindle moulder. Their main advantage is that they are the safest head available with virtually no danger of kick-back.

PREPARATION

Loose-cutter type heads need both cutters and chip-limiters profile-grinding accurately in profile and overal length tip to tail because they rely on precise seating for accurate projection. The cutter must project no more than 0.75 mm. beyond the chip-limiter as otherwise it will not act as intended. If the cutters are set too high a bigger and unsafe bite will be possible. If the cutters are set too low the cutterhead will simply not cut at all.

Profiled head types are reground as regular profiled heads, but as the cutting tip is worn down the chip-limiter must also be ground down in step to maintain the original height difference.

With the negative-angle profiled type, the chip-limiter face is ground-off by the same amount as the cutter face to do this. With the simple, flat-shoulder type the shoulders are ground down as needed, but when new tips are fitted their projection must correspond with the height of the worn chip-limiting shoulders. Cutting tip to chipbreaker height should be as the loose-cutter type.

OPERATIONAL SAFETY

These heads are extremely safe to use provided normal safety guides are followed, the cutters correctly secured when of the loose-cutter head type, and the chip-limiter height maintained.

Chip-limiting heads are for hand-feed only. Never use them with a mechanical feed unless the feed is very slow. A mechanical feed usually makes chip-limiting unnecessary in any event, and over-feeding could actually cause a jam or run-off.

Router cutters

These are usually shanked tools for mounting in a collet-type arbor. The common type has a parallel shank, the diameter of which may vary according to tool diameter. A few router cutters have a form of morse taper and/or screw fitting.

There are two basic router cutter types: the single flute (or spoon bit) and the twin flute.

One type of single flute cutter is ground concentrically on the outer surface and is fitted in an eccentric chuck to give the necessary clearance; it is then mounted in the collet and carefully balanced by adding, removing or switching small screws.

It has a clean and free cutting action and allows a small amount of adjustment either to maintain a constant cutting diameter or to give slight cutting diameter variation. Several eccentric chucks are needed when a range of single-flute cutters are in use. The advantages of these cutters are more important on a router, they are not commonly-used on a spindle moulder. Other single-flute router cutters are ground eccentrically for mounting concentrically in the collet.

Twin-flute cutters have two cutting edges and, as their outer surfaces are radial-relief ground, they lose diameter as wear takes place. Straight router cutters can be solid HSS, tipped with tungsten carbide, solid tungsten carbide, or have disposable tungsten carbide tips. Profiled router cutters are usually solid HSS or tipped with tungsten carbide and often have a shear-cutting action when the profile is deep.

Fig. 110 Loose-cutter shank-type tool.

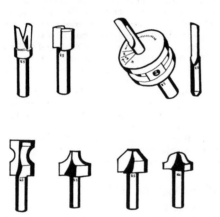

Fig. 111 Typical straight router cutters:
Left, twin-flute.
Right, single-flute router cutters loose and mounted in an eccentric chuck.

Fig. 112 Profiled router cutters.

The normal heavy-duty profiled type is radially-relieved, but a lighter-duty type (known also as a wing cutter) can be formed on a profile grinder from blanks either by the maker or the user. Some router cutters can have a ball-bearing follower mounted on them for shaping work. Small diameter cutter-blocks integral with an arbor are also used. These have loose, bolt-on cutters or are of the Whitehill type.

APPLICATION

Router cutters are used for relatively shallow profiles and light cuts only where regular heads are too large in diameter or are unsuitable. Examples are in shaping twisted handrails, spade-handle grips and tracery. They are also used for cutting grooves along or across the grain and with attachments for stair trenching or drawer dovetailing. The cutting angle is small but the finish produced is good whether cutting with or against the grain provided a high spindle speed and a slow and steady feed are used.

Fig. 113 Whitehill shank-type cutter-head with a taper/screwed shank.

PREPARATION

Solid and tipped cutters are ground in the flutes only using a tool and cutter grinder with some form of dividing head. The wing type can either be flute or profile-ground. Loose-cutter types are prepared in the same way as small flat cutters.

No setting is needed except to secure the shank in a self-centring collet (except the loose-cutter type which needs cutters setting first). Make sure that the shank corresponds in size to the collet used and is of the same measure (either imperial or metric). Collets can squeeze onto a smaller shank than that for which they were made, but will not grip the cutter correctly or safely.

Problems may arise with routing on a spindle moulder because the cut is underneath the workpiece and cannot be seen until complete. For this reason the spindle moulder is not a substitute for the router.

OPERATIONAL SAFETY

Router cutters, being one-piece, are a reasonably safe tool to use and no special precautions are necessary. Make sure proper tools are used for routing, though; the wrong type can be dangerous. Never use twist drills or other non-routing tools when routing, they have insufficient strength and could snap in use.

Plate 29 Above: Flute grinding a router cutter on a Sigrist and Muller (Saturn) universal tool grinder.

Plate 28 Lower left: Various Forest City tools tipped with PCD for machining the most difficult materials.

Plate 30 Below: Oppold carbide inserts for disposable-cutter tools.

51

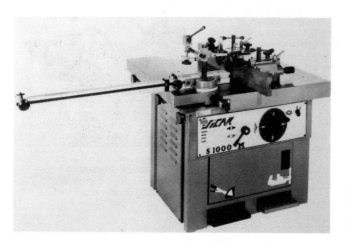

Plate 31 The Sicar S1000M features
a sliding table and extended rear
fence for tenoning and similar
work.

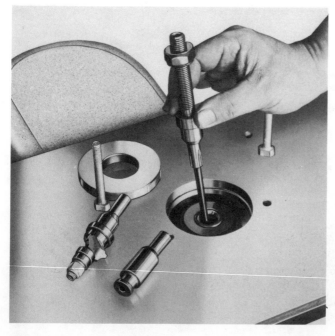

Plate 32 Interchangeable arbors on
a Delta two-speed spindle moulder.
Note the router cutter with a
ball-bearing follower on the left.

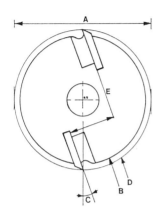

Fig. 114 Typical circular cutterhead showing:
A - planing diameter.
B - cutterhead outline.
C - cutting angle.
D - planing circle.
E - cutter spacing.

Fig. 115 Check the cutter profile against a sample mould at the correct cutting angle C. For accuracy support the cutter with a plywood triangular-shape piece. E is the reciprical of the cutting angle (90 degrees - cutting angle).

CHAPTER 6

CUTTER PREPARATION

The cutter profile normally differs slightly from the mould it produces due to the angle at which it meets the timber - the cutting angle. If it cuts square-on, i.e, with zero cutting angle as a French head, the cutter and mould profile fit one another precisely when the cutter is held square to the mould. With all other cutterheads the cutter profile must be deeper than the mould profile to compensate for the cutting angle.

The amount of 'throw' - the difference between the cutter profile and the mould it produces - is greater with large cutting angles and less with small cutting angles. When checking the cutter profile allow for 'throw' by holding it against the mould at the proper 'cutting angle'. Alternatively, develop-out the profile using geometry, a development rule, a development template, or a profile grinder.

CHECKING TO A SAMPLE

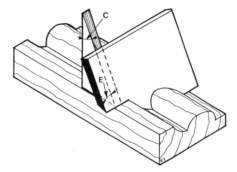

The most ready and practical way of checking the ground cutter profile is to hold the cutter at the same angle to the mould as when cutting - the cutting angle of the cutterhead. Obviously the angle has to be accurate, but most experienced grinders simply estimate this, relying on the skills developed over the years.

For the less experienced some form of guide is needed. Draw out the cutterhead full size and measure the cutting angle with a protractor. Make a triangular piece of plywood to the cutting and reciprical angles, and use this to support the cutter when checking it's profile. The reciprical or support angle is 90 degrees minus the cutting angle, e.g.; cutting angle 30 degrees, support angle 60 degrees, third angle 90 degrees.

Another way is to saw-off the moulding at the 'support' angle and check the cutter against this. Alternatively, place the moulding angled-face down on a piece of paper, plywood or a template and scribe or draw around the profile.

There is an error in all these methods because they are based on a single cutting angle but, in cutting, this continuously changes. For greater accuracy the 'cutting angle' used should be that measured at mid depth-on-cut - so a different support is theoretically needed for each mould. Unless the mould profile is exceptionally deep, the cutting angle large or the cutter small there is little angle change, so only two or three supports are needed for each cutterblock catering for cut depths of, perhaps, 10, 20 and 30mm.

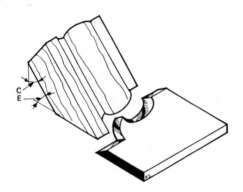

Fig. 116 Another way to check cutter profile. Cut-off the sample mould at the reciprical angle E. C is the cutting angle.

The error can best be seen in checking the cutter shape needed for a 45 degree bevel, which has to be be slightly rounded to produce a perfectly flat surface. By using these methods the cutter profile has the correct slope but a perfectly straight cutting edge and produces a slightly rounded surface on the timber. A similar distortion applies to all moulds, so slightly deformed profiles are always produced. This is usually acceptable for most applications, but not where a precise matching profile is needed.

When a mould profile is critical a better method is needed. Either geometrically develop the cutter profile, or use a development rule or template.

Two basic cutterblock dimensions are needed, the cutter spacing and the planing (or minimum cutting) circle. The shape, type and size of cutterblock does not affect cutter development, two different types with the same basic dimensions need exactly the same cutter profile.

The cutter spacing is the shortest distance between the leading face lines of cutters fixed on opposite sides of the head. With a three-cutterblock the cutter spacing is double the distance between one face line and the cutterblock centreline. The planing circle is the diameter as measured from the cutting point of one cutter to the cutting point of the opposing cutter when both are set to the minimum cutting circle. See Fig. 114.

GEOMETRIC DEVELOPMENT

With this a section is taken geometrically through the mould and projected against a radial line drawn from the centre of the cutterblock, around the centre of the cutterblock then square-off the cutter face line.

Draw out the cutterhead full size complete with cutters, bolts, etc. Draw a radial line from its centre parallel to any cutter-face line (the leading face of the cutter). Add the planing circle (the smallest circle which clears the cutterblock body, bolts, etc.) and draw a line square to the radial line from where it crosses the planing circle. This is the planing line. Draw out the mould full size with the fence face on this line and with the mould on the opposite side to the cutterblock.

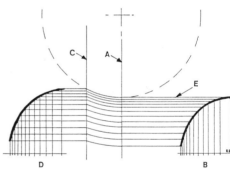

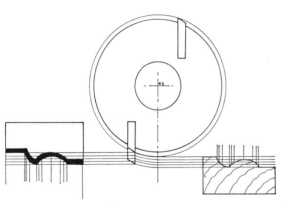

Fig. 117 This shows the general layout for development with the sample mould shape on the right and the developed cutter profile on the left.

Fig. 118 As Fig. 117, but showing:
A – radial line.
B – mould profile.
C – cutter-face line.
D – cutter profile.
E – planing or fence line.

Draw several lines square to the planing line to divide up the mould profile. Draw parallel lines at the same spacings at the far side of the cutter-face line and clear of the cutterblock. The number of lines and their spacing is not critical, but for the best results divide along the profile itself at even spacings. The more lines and the greater the accuracy - but development then becomes complex. To make development easier number or letter each corresponding line.

From the intersection of each dividing line and the mould profile draw a line parallel to the planing line and up to the radial line. Using a pair of compasses continue the lines concentric to the cutterblock centre to meet the cutter-face line. Finally draw lines parallel to the face line from all these points to intersect with corresponding dividing lines already drawn. Join the intersections to outline the true cutter profile. This is the profile to which the cutters must be made.

Cutter profile developer

The Robinson cutter profile developer is a device which duplicates the movements of any cutter to mechanically develop out the correct cutter profile from a true section of the required mould. It adjusts to any cutterblock size.

Cutter projection rule

This is a simple rule divided on one edge into regular spacings and on the opposite edge into the equivalent projected dimensions. Make one as follows:

Draw out the cutterblock full size, and add the radial and cutter-face lines. Divide up the radial line into regular divisions from the planing circle outwards. Draw concentric lines from each point up to and square from the cutter face line to form the projected scale. Also mark on this the cutterblock lip or body line. Mark the projection rule on opposing edges with these two scales. Label the radial scale-edge as the 'measure mould' scale, and the cutter-face scale-edge as the 'mark cutter profile' scale. Cut the rule off along the 'lip' line.

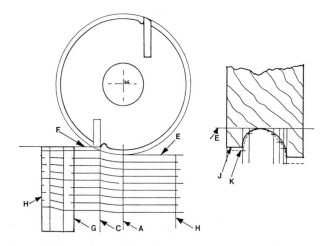

Fig. 119 The basis of a cutter projection rule showing:
A – radial line.
C – cutter face line.
E – fence line.
F – 'lip' line.
G – mark cutter profile scale.
H – measure mould scale.

A typical use is shown with the mould profile in solid outline J and the cutter profile in dotted outline K. Fence line E is added together with several lines at right angles to this. The mould is measured from the fence line using rule H and the same measurements set out with rule G and seen as short lines. The profile is finally developed out by joining these points.

In use draw out the mould profile full size and add lines square to the face (fence) line at any suitable spacings. Measure along each dividing line from the face line to the mould profile using the 'measure mould' scale. Mark corresponding points on the same lines also measured from the face line, but this time using the 'mark cutter profile' scale. Join the developed points to outline the true cutter profile. Draw the cutterblock 'lip' line square across to show cutter projection needed beyond the cutterblock.) If using with a template the cutterblock 'lip' line should also be the template cut-out.

Cutter projection template

This is a board of plywood, faced hardboard or aluminium marked out as previously described (Chapter 2), but with additional permanent lines marked as a graph in depth and width-on-cut.

The width-on-cut lines are marked out with the 'measure mould' scale of the development rule and are square to the planing line. When the template is marked with the table line or cutterblock clearance lines, as in the case of a Whitehill block, start the scale at these lines.

The depth-on-cut lines are marked out with the 'mark cutter profile' scale of the development rule and are parallel to the planing line. When making a projection rule for a Whitehill block the template is divided up for depth-on-cut both inside and outside the planing line and all are projected as lines onto the template.

The required mould is measured at several points in width from the table line and in depth from the fence line. Corresponding points are marked on the template using the graph as the measure. The cutter profile is developed out by joining these points.

Each different size of cutterblock needs its own projection template, and each template is suitable only for the cutterblock for which it was made.

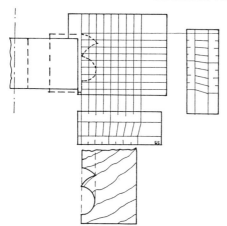

Fig. 120 Use a projection rule to make a projection template as shown here. Measure the mould with a regular scale but set it out on the template using these lines as the measures.

Robinson Estephagraph

This is a commercially-produced template system designed by the writer for use with most common types of moulding head. It comprises a gauge for measuring the mould profile and a series of templates for different cutterheads. The gauge has a graph with an inverse-development scale in mould depth and a regular scale in mould width. Each template has a graph to regular scales in both width and depth, with the planing and table lines also marked.

The mould required is traced onto a plastic sheet and placed on the gauge, face uppermost. Development of the cutter profile is by draft projection, i.e., marking corresponding points on the template to those on the gauge where the mould profile intersects them.

The difference between mould and cutter profile, the 'throw', is determined by the spacing of the depth-on-cut gauge lines and is varied by placing the mould profile at different positions on the gauge. The position for any size of cutterblock is found simply by moving a sliding scale until the cutter spacing and planing circle measurements align with one another. The section needed is shown by an arrow and by numbered lines which correspond to those on the template.

The templates themselves are individually fitted to the cutterblock by cutting them away until the planing (adze) line corresponds with the edge of a planing cutter set to the planing circle.

The gauge and graph lines are permanently sealed-in under plastic so that guide lines can be pencilled-in and erased. A single gauge can be used with any number of templates used 'in situ' or on a setting stand.

Plate 33 Sedgwick medium-duty spindle moulder GW.

Plate 34 The Northfield double spindle moulder cuts with the grain regardless of outline shape by passing the assembly between the two spindles. These rotate in opposite directions. Note the rear-mounted Shaw-guard pressures.

CHAPTER 7

CUTTER GRINDING

Free-hand grinding is the conventional and accepted method for spindle moulder cutters. The old-fashioned multiple wheel grinder, probably the best type for this operation, allows several grinding wheels of different thickness and profile to be mounted at the same time on the same arbor - but used independently. The conventional practice is to form one wide and one narrow wheel to a square section, and the remainder to half-round sections of different radii.

Flat sections of cutters and external curved profiles of large radius are formed on the widest of the square wheels. Small external curves are formed on the largest diameter half-round wheel. Internal curves are formed on the half-round wheel nearest too, but smaller than, the curve needed. The narrow square wheel is used only to form grooves and similar. By using these different combinations reasonably smooth control is possible for all profiles.

A smoother internal curve is formed if the shape of the wheel closely fits that wanted on the cutter. The profiles of many cutters combine curves of different radii, and cutters are freely transferred from one wheel to another in grinding. This is the great advantage of the multiple wheel grinder, rapid interchange between wheels without having to change them.

Many popular grinders, though, are now either the single wheel section of a plane and mould cutter grinder, or a double-wheel grinder. Multiple-wheel techniques are impracticable on these machines as constant wheel changing would be needed to match the wheel profile to that of the cutter. This slows down the process and is also bad practice. Grinding wheels should be changed as little as possible to avoid damaging them and to reduce the wasteful re-shaping always necessary after fitting.

The usual compromise is to use one flat wide wheel and one narrow half-round wheel. However, smooth movement is difficult on the larger internal curves - more skill is needed in grinding and the result is never as good. The alternative is to re-shape a commonly-used wheel each time a different curvature is to be ground. This gives better grinding conditions but plays absolute havoc with grinding wheel usage.

GRINDING WITHOUT A REST

Mould-cutter grinding wheels all grind peripherally (on their rim) and usually grind into the cutter, from cutting point to heel.

Grinding on an open grinding wheel without a rest is difficult but not impossible - as experienced grinders prove every day. The skill is to hold the cutter securely, at the correct swivel and tilt angle to the wheel, whilst moving it around to form the correct profile.

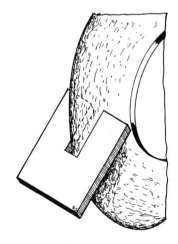

Fig. 121 The best cutter grinding support, or rest, extends on both sides of the grinding wheel. Keep the wheel-to-support gap small.

With an open wheel there is always the chance of the wheel snatching and damaging the cutter. The danger time is on first contact with the grinding wheel. Preferably lightly contact first with the cutter heel, then carefully tilt downwards until the full grinding face makes contact. If contact is made first with the cutting edge the chance of damage is greater.

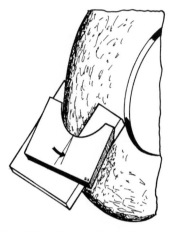

Fig. 122 Swivel to the right to form side clearance on the left-hand side.

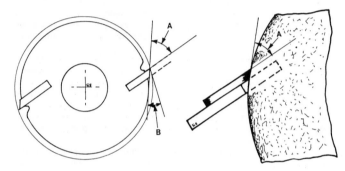

Fig. 123 Above: Set the support to form the correct bevel angle A to give a clearance angle B of between 15 and 30 degrees.

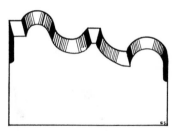

Fig. 124 Right: A typical completed cutter with main and both side clearance angles ground-in.

Fig. 125 Below right: Swivel to the left to form side clearance on the right-hand side.

GRINDING WITH A REST

The cutter rest should be slotted to support deep-profiled cutters at both sides of the grinding wheel. The wheel-to-rest gap at sides and front should be the absolute minimum, and give support right up to the wheel to reduce the levering effect of the down-cutting wheel. This makes the cutters easier to control and the operation a great deal safer. Maintain a gap of not more than 3mm. by adjusting the rest as the wheel wears - and after changing grinding wheels.

Set the rest to the correct bevel angle - to suit the worst conditions at the planing circle. Check the setting using a cutter ground to the correct angle. When forming side clearance angles keep the cutter flat on the rest but swivel it between 5 and 15 degrees to form a 5 degree side clearance angle. It is not possible to precisely control side clearance, but with practice a reasonable degree of repetition is possible.

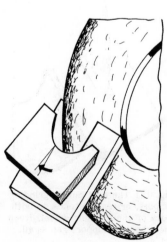

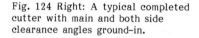

GRINDING TECHNIQUES

When forming the profile, move the cutter around flat on the rest whilst maintaining it at the correct swivel angle. Grind slowly, removing weight in two or more light grinds rather than in a single heavy grind, and keep the cutter well quenched by frequent dipping in water. (Some early machines had a drip feed which proved so messy that the type was abandoned; most grinders are now dry.) Keep the cutter moving continuously and smoothly, and use wheel profiles which closely fit the internal curves needed. Check the final shape against the sample or a template. Finished cutters should be dimensionally alike to aid balancing. When heavy cutters are used always grind both cutters of a pair to the same profile, don't use one finishing and one balancing cutter.

Blanking cutters

It is normal when blanking-out cutters (forming a profile from a square blank) to initially grind with the cutter rest set to form a square edge instead of a cutting edge. By doing this the profile is easier to see and the cutter is less likely to burn. When the profile is fully formed re-set the rest to the correct grinding angle and finish-grind to a cutting edge.

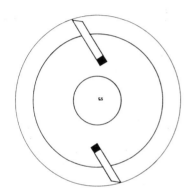

Fig. 127 Use cutters in pairs and of the same profile and weight.

Above: When both project alike the cutterhead balances.

Below: With unequal projection the cutterhead will be dynamically out of balance.

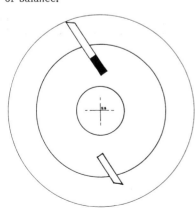

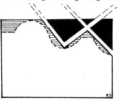

Fig. 126 Relieve the cut by cutting-out vee-sections, shown in black, leaving only the shaded portions to profile-grind.

Where excessive grinding is needed it is quicker and easier to first cut-out sections. Mark the cutter face with the developed profile, then add vee cut-outs from the edge to skirt the profile and show where cuts can be made. Fit a special, reinforced, cut-off grinding wheel. Set the cutter rest square to the wheel and feed the cutter slowly into the grinding wheel following the marked lines. Use it like a circular saw by feeding straight onto the periphery, take care to avoid side movement. Keep the cutter well quenched.

BALANCING CUTTERS

It is essential that the cutterhead is in perfect balance; if not it will vibrate to deflect the arbor and produce an erratic cuttermark pitch and a poor finish on the surface of the timber. Excessive vibration eventually ruins the arbor bearings and could cause an accident.

All cutterheads must have a true running balance, large ones especially because, as cutting diameter increases, so does the affect of imbalance. Even a small imbalance creates problems at high spindle speeds.

Because the effect of centrifugal force increases by the square of the increase in speed, the greatest care has to be taken when balancing heads for high arbor speeds. The correct method is to use cutters in perfectly matching pairs, balance them, then finally set both 'to cut'.

Cutters need balancing after grinding to correct any imbalance that grinding may have produced. Use a pair of sensitive scales or a cutter balance. Some check the balance of a complete head using a balancing stand. This is necessary with heavy cutterblocks, but rarely necessary with small spindle moulder heads unless very complex set-ups or high spindle speeds are used. (It is also essential that all cutterheads and other fast-running parts are accurately balanced on a dynamic balancer. Usually the makers see to this.)

Balancing stand

The simplest has two level knife-edged bars fitted knife-edge up. Mount the head on an arbor and gently place it so that the arbor rests on the knife edges with the head between them.

To check balance roll the arbor along the knife edges and mark the head at the top when it comes to rest. This is the lightest point. If it comes to rest very quickly and quite positively the head is badly out of balance. If this happens slowly and indecisively then it is almost in perfect balance. Final balance is correct when the assembly does not stop at any particular position. To balance, remove and grind the heavier cutter on the tail, then re-set and re-check.

Most modern balancing stands now have two pairs of knife-edge rollers in place of the knife-edge bars and are much easier to use.

Balance can only be checked statically, i.e. when stationary, not dynamically as when running. There is an important difference which must be appreciated. Take an example of a cutterblock with cutters which have the same weight and projection and are also diametrically opposite. The cutterhead would show as being in balance on balancing rollers - and would also be in true dynamic balance.

If the cutters are shifted sideways, one to one end of the cutterblock and the other to the opposite end, the cutterblock would still be in static balance, and seem correct when on the balancing stand. It would, however, be dynamically unbalanced because the pull from the cutters is not directly opposite - so the head would vibrate badly when run.

Put in a nutshell, each pair of cutters should be dimensionally alike, balanced as a pair, set diametrically opposite and to exactly the same projection, and both set 'to cut'. If this is carefully carried out the cutterhead will be in true dynamic balance.

Fig. 128 Above: This head is dynamically out of balance because cutters are not set directly opposite - even though it might be in perfect balance and appear correct when checked on a balancing stand.

Below: This head is in perfect dynamic balance with pairs of identical cutters mounted directly opposite one another.

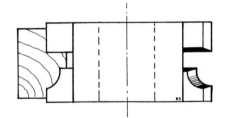

CHAPTER 8

PROFILE GRINDING

When moulds are regularly repeated it is quicker and better to grind cutters using some form of copy or profile grinder. Both machines use a metal template to control the cutter profile in grinding. The cutter and template are normally fixed to a horizontally-floating carriage. The cutter is opposite to the fixed grinding wheel and the template moves with it to contact a fixed copy pin or stylus.

The grinding wheel grinds down, and the cutter is commonly held face-down to grind from the heel to the cutting edge. This seems wrong but isn't. The excessive wire edge initially formed when rough grinding almost disappears when finish-grinding.

The metal template is formed to the reverse of the mould profile required. It can be cut-out on a fine bandsaw or jig-saw, then the edge ground, filed, and finally highly polished using fine emery cloth - wet. For the best finish finally burnish the edge (follow the profile with a hardened tool whilst applying relatively heavy pressure).

Most users make templates from sheet iron. Normally this wears well enough, but some makers recommend that templates are hardened after manufacture. It is also possible to make templates from plastic sheeting which is much easier to work - but these wear badly.

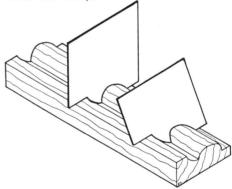

Fig. 129 A template for a copy grinder must be developed out to compensate for cutting angle, so tilt it when checking against a sample, right, or develop the shape geometrically. With a profile grinder the template fits square-on, left.

In grinding, the carriage is moved around so that the profile on the template follows against the stylus, whilst the the cutter profile is formed simultaneously by the grinding wheel. This type of machine normally has a coolant system using an oil and water mix to allow rapid cutter grinding without burning.

Copy and profile grinders vary in design and operation but are basically similar. The following describes specific machines but which are fairly representative of their types.

Copy grinder

On copy grinders the cutter is ground to precisely the same shape as the template, so the template profile first needs developing-out using any of the methods previously described. If the same shape has to be formed by two different cutter-heads, then two similar but slightly different templates are needed. This is necessary, for example in window work, when using a square cutterblock for moulding straight stiles and slotted collars to form the curved rail above the top light, both of which must have matching mould profiles.

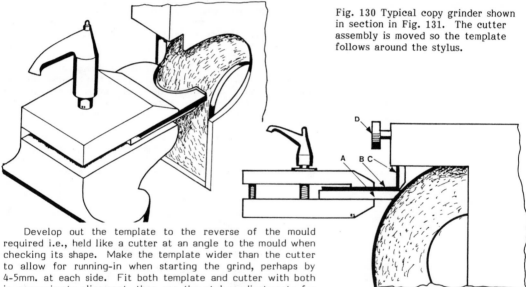

Fig. 130 Typical copy grinder shown in section in Fig. 131. The cutter assembly is moved so the template follows around the stylus.

Develop out the template to the reverse of the mould required i.e., held like a cutter at an angle to the mould when checking its shape. Make the template wider than the cutter to allow for running-in when starting the grind, perhaps by 4-5mm. at each side. Fit both template and cutter with both in approximate alignment, then use the stylus adjustments for fine setting. Setting is correct when, as the stylus is traced around the template profile, the grinding wheel precisely follows around the cutter profile. Cutters should be roughly ground to shape before copy grinding.

The grinding wheel normally forms a grinding angle of around 40 degrees regardless of wear. Dress the grinding wheel, whilst running, by adjusting it outwards towards a diamond dresser operating through a slot in the clamp-on guide. Finally adjust the stylus to contact the template all the way along whilst the cutter barely clears the grinding wheel.

Start the grinding wheel and the coolant, and trace around the stylus keeping the template in light contact. Adjust the stylus so grinding takes place, and continue grinding and adjusting until the full cutting width is ground.

As with all grinding operations allow the grinding wheel to grind freely, don't crowd it, and regularly dress it. Add side clearance by swivelling the cutter holder.

Fig. 131 Section through a copy grinder showing:
A – Cutter.
B – Template.
C – Stylus.
D – Adjustment for the stylus.

Plate 35 Profile grinding on an Autool PR230H. The template and stylus can be seen at the front left-hand side.

Fig. 132 Section through a profile grinder showing:
A - Cutter ground in the head.
B - Cutter support.
C - Stylus.
D - Template.

The template mounting moves with the carriage as F.
The stylus can be adjusted for grinding cut as E.
The grinding wheel adjusts to compensate for wear G, and for clearance angle H.

Profile grinder

With a profile grinder the cutters are usually fastened to a block on a rotating arbor and are supported on a rest directly in front of the grinding wheel. Cutters can be ground in the head or on a dummy block (which must match the parent cutterblock in cutter spacing and diameter).

When grinding, the template remains level and the cutter rocks on the rest to repeat the same cutting angles as when moulding, so the true cutter profile is developed-out automatically by the grinder. As development is therefore not needed, the templates for profile grinders are simpler to make as the exact reverse of the mould required. Make each to match the full-size drawing of the mould, or to fit a sample mould square-on. Allow overlaps of both cutter beyond the mould and template beyond the cutter.

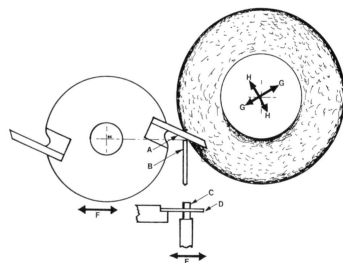

Fit the template, then set the closest point of the cutterblock to clear the cutter rest by 3mm. Holding the carriage in this position, adjust the stylus to contact the deepest point of the template profile (usually the planing line). Set cutter blanks far enough forward for the edge to contact the grinding wheel when the carriage is reset so that the stylus touches the shallowest point of the template profile. Cutters can project slightly more if necessary. It is also possible to draw cutters out to touch the grinding wheel if short, but grinding life is then lost and cutters are less safely held. With previous-formed cutters fit them and set the machine as described under 'Re-grinding'.

There are three main movements in addition to the two-way free movement of the table or carriage. One is a screw-adjusted forward movement of the grinding wheel during or after dressing. This adjustment is normally on an angle so that clearance-angle setting remains the same regardless of grinding wheel wear.

The second grinding wheel movement alters its vertical position to vary the clearance angle between about 15 and 40 degrees. As the profile grinder maintains a fixed clearance angle, the grinding angle on the cutter varies in step with changes in cutting angle. This ensures that clearance is never less than the minimum set, and that the cutter is given the maximum possible cutting-edge strength.

(In grinding tungsten carbide tipped cutters it is normal to alter the clearance angle setting between facing and backing to grind them independently and with different types of grinding wheels. With HSS and similar cutters a single clearance angle setting is used and is commonly the same for all heads).

The third movement on some machines allows the grinding wheel to be tilted to 5 or 10 degrees either side of vertical to add side clearance. On other machines the grinding wheel remains vertical and the carriage is slewed to add side clearance.

GRINDING WHEEL DRESSING

A built-in diamond dresser keeps the grinding wheel true. Regular dressing is essential to maintain grinding wheel profile and cutting ability. Always dress the grinding wheel prior to finish grinding.

In dressing, the grinding wheel and dresser are brought into contact, whilst rotating or traversing the diamond, until the grinding wheel is fully formed. When the dresser is fixed at the point of grind the grinding wheel adjusts and aligns automatically with the stylus on dressing - making operation simple and error-free. When the dresser adjusts in dressing, it is necessary afterwards to manually re-align the dressed grinding wheel with the stylus. This takes longer and is prone to error.

The grinding wheel is dressed to a half-round section by rotating the diamond dresser on its axis. For square and angular dressing, the dresser is moved across the wheel usually in a swivelling action. The dresser is only used for conventional grit grinding wheels. Diamond and CBN grinding wheels are already formed to profile and should not be dressed.

Grinding wheel profiles

The regular grinding wheel shape for rough grinding, and for finish-grinding all profiles other than internal squares and angles, is half-round. The grinding wheel thickness is usually between 4 and 6mm. This allows fairly small radii to be formed, yet is of reasonable width so that the grinding wheel does not wear excessively.

Plate 36 Above: The grinding head tilts to give side clearance on this Autool PR grinder.

Plate 37 Below: The Autool PR grinders feature point-of-grind dressing, in this case dual-radius.

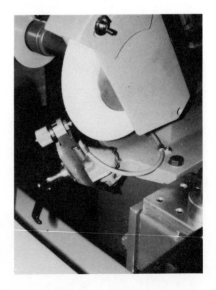

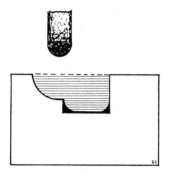

Fig. 133 Above: Finish-grind as much as possible using the half-round grinding wheel.

Below: Grind-out remaining corners only using a square wheel.

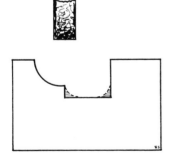

Thinner grinding wheels are used, but normally only for the small internal corners that the regular half-round grinding wheels cannot form. It is possible to use thin, regular-grit grinding wheels, but they are fragile and damage too easily; preferably use a thick, tapered grinding wheel.

Regular grit grinding wheels with small radii and sharp corners should be fine-grit types, but these are not suitable for fast grinding. It is possible to form small internal radii grinding slowly using the corners of a square grinding wheel, but the finish is poor and corner-wear rapid. Keeping regular-grit grinding wheels to a sharp profile is a problem on profile grinders - a better solution is to use a formed CBN grinding wheel instead, or a dual template.

GRINDING TECHNIQUES

The best technique is to finish the cutter profile as completely as practical with a half-round grinding wheel, then merely clean out the internal square or angular corners and small radii using a grinding wheel of different profile. When changing the grinding wheel it is essential also to change the stylus as the two must always match. The stylus must also accurately align with the grinding wheel. After replacing both grinding wheel and stylus, check both for alignment by traversing along the fully finished section of the profile, then correct any mis-alignment by adjusting the stylus.

In grinding, the carriage is moved to make the stylus follow the template so that the grinding wheel forms the cutter to the correct profile. The cutter must maintain contact with cutter-rest immediately in front of the grinding wheel, so exert pressure via a handwheel on the cutterblock arbor. With a profile grinder the cutting edge cannot easily be seen because of the angle and the coolant, so watch the template and stylus to anticipate the movements needed. This is contrary to hand-grinding practice and, perhaps, the most difficult thing to become accustomed to.

Grinding should be light enough to not crowd the grinding wheel. Allow it to cut freely, if necessary riding on the grinding wheel to leave a gap between template and stylus until the cutter is ground away. Keep the cutter moving and in the smoothest possible way. Grinding is complete when the full cutter width can be traversed with the stylus in full contact with the template.

Direct the coolant to the point of grind to allow fast, burn-free grinding. If anything, coolant should flood from above and below, and at the cutter rather than the grinding wheel, to avoid splashing.

Grinding from a blank

When first using a profile grinder it is an advantage to set the stylus to give a shallow grind of only 2-3mm. at the deepest point. When this has been fully formed step-back the stylus by stages of 2-3mm. to allow further grinding until the cutter is fully profiled.

Mark the stylus position before grinding the second cutter so that this exact setting can repeated. With this method much less can be ground-off the cutter and a new operator feels he has more control - so confidence is built up quickly.

Invariably, though, most operators eventually grind the full depth at a single setting, allowing the cutter to initially ride lightly on the grinding wheel, progressively grinding down to the full depth.

When profiling cutters from a blank the recommended method is to make a series of parallel plunging cuts directly into the grinding wheel to form a series of close slots, finally traversing across to remove the scallops remaining. However, I prefer to traverse across in small, deepening arcs applying pressure only from the furthest point to the deepest point until the full profile has been formed.

Always have the grinding wheel vertical or the carriage square-on when grinding from a blank, adding side clearance later. If the grinding wheel is tilted or the carriage slewed when plunged in, it could apply side pressure to possibly shatter the grinding wheel. Pressure must only be applied to the periphery of these grinding wheels.

Profile grinding is exceptionally fast when compared to other methods as coolant makes continuous grinding possible and template control prevents errors. A Whitehill cutter, for example, can be formed along one edge from blank to finished cutter in just three or four minutes.

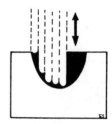

Fig. 134 Above: Plunge-grinding to remove weight.

Below: Part-circular roughing is a better alternative.

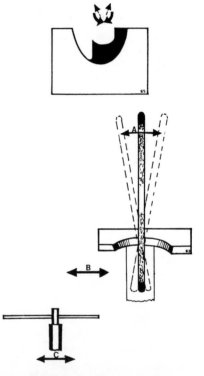

Grinding side clearance

As a last operation, side clearance is added. On some machines the grinding wheel is tilted to one side and the cutter reground, then tilted to the opposite side and ground a second time. Side clearance angles are controlled mechanically and repeat precisely.

On some machines additional adjustment is necessary during this operation to grind to a feather edge where side clearance is added, and to avoid spoiling the cutting edge elsewhere. Autool profile grinders and a few others require no additional adjustment when adding side clearance, so machine setting is simple and error-free - and the two grinds blend perfectly.

With swivelling-table machines the table is swivelled in the appropriate direction individually for each section, but grinding is a continuous sequence. On some machines the swivel angle has to be estimated. This needs greater skill and is complicated because different swivel angle settings are needed when the machine setting is changed. In swivelling the table, because the grinding wheel presents a slightly different profile to the cutter, only half-round and knife-edge grinding wheels can actually be used in the way described. With other wheel shapes a different grinding wheel and stylus profile are needed for grinding square-on, also for left- and right-hand side clearance.

Fig. 135 Adding side clearance on a tilting-head profile grinder as viewed from the rear. The movements are:
A – side clearance tilt.
B – carriage sideways movement.
C – stylus sideways adjustment.

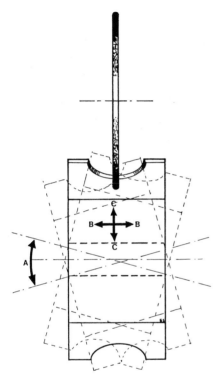

Fig. 136 Adding side clearance on a swivelling-carriage profile grinder as viewed from above.
The swivel movement A varies with changes in cutting and clearance angles.
The two arrows B and C are the operating movements of the carriage.

Finish grinding

Because the cutter profile is mechanically controlled it is practical to 'spark-out' the grind by making repeated passes without adjustment to the stylus. For absolute accuracy the process should be repeated two or three times, dressing the wheel between operations. This is normally necessary only when blanking cutters or when grinding-out excessive cutting-edge damage.

The surface finish is greatly improved by sparking-out even when using a relatively coarse grinding wheel, so that the cutter then produces a better surface and lasts longer. The more the process is repeated, the better the finish. Sparking-out should always be part of normal grinding practice.

When the first cutter is completed grind the second. If grinding in the head simply rotate for the next cutter. If grinding on a dummy block replace the first cutter with the second making sure both seat against the side guide and back fence so they finish exactly the same size.

Because they are dimensionally alike, of the same profile and with the same grinding and clearance angles, the cutters remain in balance, so balancing after grinding is not needed.

Re-grinding

Re-grinding is similar to grinding from a blank, except that roughing-out is usually unnecessary. First, accurately align cutters with the grinding wheel using the side and front-to-back adjustments of the stylus. Once alignment is correct the only adjustment needed is depth-on-cut to progressively increase the grind until the cutting edge is fully restored.

Slotted collar cutters are best ground individually on a dummy block. Whitehill and other circular and square-head cutters can be ground in the cutterblock or on a dummy block as preferred.

Grinding in the head

The correct technique is to first balance the blank cutters in pairs, then pre-set both equally so they project enough to be fully profiled without resetting. Check that the cutterblock does not foul either the grinding wheel or the cutter support when at the deepest point of the grind.

Use a setting stand in pre-setting. Notch-out the end of a sample mould square to the face and to a parallel depth just beyond the deepest point of the mould. Position it so that the top surface of the notch is in line with the centre-line of the arbor. Set to give normal clearance between mould and cutter-head, plus allowance for regrinding. Set cutters so that the blank cutting edge sits in the corner of the notch to project the correct amount.

By grinding in the head cutters are ground to the same profile, the same radial height and in perfect side-ways alignment. Balancing is simpler, and cutterheads have a better running balance than when prepared in the conventional manner. When cutters remain in the head, regrinding is faster and simpler as there is no need to remove and re-set the cutters each time.

Profiled cutterheads can be re-profiled on a profile grinder after re-tipping in exactly the same way as a conventional cutter. Use a regular grit or CBN wheel for H.S.S tips, and a diamond wheel for tungsten carbide tips.

Tipped router cutters can be ground in the same way, but with a router chuck fitted in place of the regular arbor. In this case the arbor is locked by a dividing mechanism as cutting-edge projections are too small for the cutter support to be used.

Plate 38 Grinding a profiled cutter on an Autool profile grinder.

CHAPTER 9

PROFILED CUTTERS

Profiled-heads and bits are are formed to pattern on their outer surface. They are face-ground only, using some form of dividing head or finger register, on a machine with either a traversing table or a traversing grinding wheel.

Fix the cutter directly onto the grinder arbor, or on a self-centring bush and finger tighten. Cutters can face either direction - unless clearance is restricted. Fit the saucer grinding wheel with its concave face against the ground face of the cutter.

SETTING THE CUTTING ANGLE

Most operators set by trial and error. To do this cross-adjust the grinding wheel whilst turning the cutter loose on the arbor until the two fit snugly, then lock the cutter to the arbor.

Plate 39 A JKO four-wing solid profiled cutter.

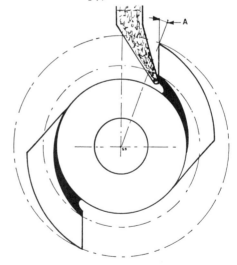

Fig. 137 Grinding a solid profiled cutter using a saucer grinding wheel. Although only touching on the rim, the grinding wheel grinds the full vertical face. The cutting angle is shown at A.

It is difficult to tell when setting is correct as contact is between a flat face on the cutter and the relatively narrow grinding surface of the saucer grinding wheel. Some makers provide a flat dummy metal wheel to fit in place of the grinding wheel for setting purposes. After using this, and replacing it with the grinding wheel, simply cross-adjust as needed to bring the ground face of the cutter and the grinding wheel into contact.

Setting the grinding wheel and cutter face in true contact is technically wrong; it should actually bear harder against the tip to maintain a constant cutting angle (see later note).

INDEXING THE CUTTER

All grinders have some form of indexing to accurately position each face in turn. If indexing is not accurate cutting-edge heights will vary, so take great care in this. Three types are used; dividing head, face registration and peripheral registration.

A dividing head positively locates the arbor at pre-set angular positions by means of plunger to engage in holes or slots. The dividing head is the most convenient type and the most positive.

Having set for cutting angle, set the dividing head for the correct number of points on the cutter and engage the plunger at any position. Index to check that the cutter locates at the required angles. Finally, release the cutter and turn on the arbor to set any face against the grinding wheel, then re-secure. Some dividing heads have fine rotary adjustment to correct a wrong angle setting. Use the cross adjustment of the grinding wheel in setting the cut-depth.

With face registration a fixed finger locates each ground face in turn before locking the arbor. The line of the grinding wheel is off-set from this finger by the depth of grind needed (this setting is also used as cut control). Usually each face is ground once only, regrinding the complete cutter a second or third time if much wants grinding off. Because register is against a previously-ground face, grinding errors can and do build up.

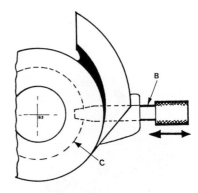

Fig. 138 The cutter can be indexed for position by plunger B and dividing disc C.

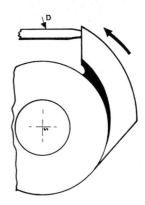

Fig. 139 Indexing the ground face against a fixed finger D.

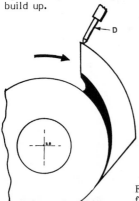

Fig. 140 Peripheral indexing using a fixed finger D or a dial indicator.

With peripheral registration the cutter is turned against normal rotation to bring the outer face of the cutter just short of the cutting face into contact with a fixed finger-stop. The modern version uses a dial indicator instead of a stop, and has fine screw-adjusted rotary movement and a positive arbor lock. Adjustment is made until the dial indicator shows the same reading each time before locking the arbor. This takes more skill as each face needs individual setting, but gives excellent results.

Plate 40 Accurate centering on the grinding machine arbor is guaranteed by using an hydraulic sleeve such as this ETP Hydro-Grip.

Plate 41 Grinding a tipped profile cutter on a Stehle universal grinder. This machine features automatic positioning using a sensor.

Machine setting

Tool-room types with a table-mounted cutter arbor and a horizontal grinding wheel arbor:

Set the grinding wheel height so that its lower edge just clears the inside edge of the ground face. Set the table traverse limits so that the cutter clears the grinding wheel at the operator's end for safe indexing without danger of fouling the wheel, and at the opposite end for working clearance between wheel and cutter.

Radial feed types:

Position the wheel at the deepest point of the cut to project beyond both extreme points by an equal amount. With symmetrical profiles the grinding wheel should be central to the cutter.

With assymmetrical profiles the grinding wheel and cutter need off-setting. This adjustment is possible either by adjusting the wheel or the cutter - which depends on the machine type. Such adjustment may not be necessary with a large diameter grinding wheel, but may be with a small diameter grinding wheel, a wide cutter, or a shallow gullet. Set the forward movement so that the wheel stops just short of the bottom of the gullet.

GRINDING TECHNIQUES

When the cutting edge is badly worn or chipped so that an excessive amount wants grinding off, two different techniques can be used: continuous adjustment, or grinding to a zero.

With continuous adjustment each face is ground in sequence, adjusting the feed after each complete rotation of the cutter until all cutting points are restored.

When grinding to a zero several passes are made on the worst cutting edge, progressively adjusting the grinding wheel feed until the edge is fully restored. All subsequent faces are then ground to exactly the same grinding wheel feed-setting.

Where the grinding wheel feed-adjustment has a scale and pointer, note or temporarily mark the position after grinding the most worn or chipped cutting face. Index the next face, shift the wheel clear, then progressively feed in until the original scale setting is again reached. Repeat with the remaining faces.

On machines with a loose graduated collar and a click-stop, set this to zero after grinding the worst face, then simply grind the remaining faces to zero.

Zero-grinding gives much the same result as continuous-adjustment but does not take grinding wheel wear into account. To do this finally regrind each face at the same machine setting. (If CBN grinding wheels are used the wear factor can be ignored). Whatever method is used grind until no more sparks are produced to give a good ground surface and accurate cutting point height.

Grinding faults

By setting to the previously-ground face this is progressively ground-back in a series of parallel steps. This seems correct because the original setting is apparently repeated, but it is not, the cutting angle and mould depth both slightly increase.

The correct way is to measure the cutting angle on a new cutter and always set to this, ignoring the actual fit of the grinding wheel to the cutter. The simplest way is to shape a metal plate with a vee cut-out to fit the extreme cutting points when new, then check before and after grinding.

Because the grinding wheel normally adjusts in parallel steps, the angle also changes but to a lesser degree when grinding an excessively dull or chipped cutter. In practical terms angle change is very slight and can be ignored - provided setting is made each time to the correct angle and not to the previously-ground face.

Users often think that accuracy is inherent in profiled cutters, it is not; it depends on the accuracy of the cutter mounting and the care taken in the grinding operation. The grinding machine bearings and dividing head mechanism must also be absolutely true - otherwise good results are never possible.

The accuracy of the dividing head is easily checked. Fit and carefully grind any suitable cutter, allowing the grinding wheel to fully spark-out. Re-set the cutter loose on the arbor by one spacing and lightly re-grind the complete cutter. If the grinding wheel contacts the faces unevenly the dividing head is suspect.

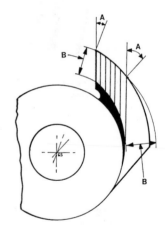

Fig. 141 Above: Wrong method of grinding in parallel steps - this practice increases both cutting angle A and mould depth B.

Below: Correct method of grinding keeps a constant cutting angle A and mould depth B.

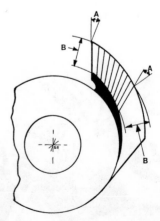

Correcting inaccuracies

If the dividing head is not correct, grind the cutter using a dial indicator mounted on the grinder or, less conveniently, one mounted on the spindle moulder itself. First mark the cutter and the spindle arbor so that the two can be replaced in exactly the same position. Check each cutting point in turn by rotating the cutter past the dial indicator finger - to first contact the heel. Mark the measured height on each point, then grind the faces until the higher points are reduced by the difference between the these and the lowest point.

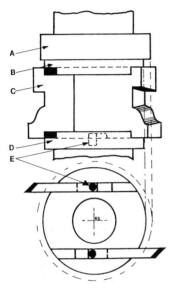

Q3S SYSTEM

This is a keyed, quick-set tooling system designed by the writer for slotted collars and circular heads. The cutterheads have pins fitted to engage in slots in the sides of the cutters. Slotted collars have pins in the bottom slot and circular heads have pins each side of the cutter clamps. Cutters are set so that the slots engage with their pins. This locks them in place to set the cutters quickly, accurately and automatically. Cutter creep is impossible and cutters cannot fly out of the cutterblock.

The same basic attachment and technique are used for both heads. It fits on Autool profile grinders and incorporates an independent dummy block, notch template and separate notch stylus.

SLOTTED COLLARS

Profile-grind both cutters generally as described earlier but using the dummy block section of the attachment. This is fixed at the same diameter and cutter spacing as slotted collars and has a fixed side guide and adjustable rear fence. Cutters are ground individually whilst clamped in place against these so that they finish dimensionally alike.

When a new profile is formed for the first time the opposite end of the template is made as a gauge to set the machine for notch grinding. First make a master gauge for each size of slotted collars to the precise pin-to-planing-circle distance. The planing circle is a maximum of 3mm. beyond the collars when shaping using a ring fence, and corresponds with the follower diameter when shaping using a ball-bearing collar. When straight moulding the planing circle is the collar diameter plus clearance of 3mm., plus double the through-fence thickness. This allows the cutters to cut through the fence without the collars fouling. (It is possible to cut-out the fence for the collars to give less cutter projection. This is more trouble, but gives a smaller and safer cutting circle).

Fig. 142 Q3S slotted collar assembly:
A - ball-bearing follower.
B - top collar.
C - cutter.
D - bottom collar.
E - pins.

To set the cutter, simply move it forward until against the pin - then secure.

Fig. 143 Make a master template for each collar diameter:
H is the distance from the back of the pin to the cutting circle A. Measurements are:
B - 20mm.
C - 5mm.
D - 15mm.

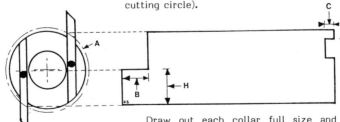

The slot aligns with the cutter edge, allowing the template profile to project beyond.

Draw out each collar full size and measure along the cutter face from the planing circle to the back of the pin (H). Notch out the master template by 20mm. deep to leave this width out from the back edge. For new templates use the master template to mark distance H, then add the mould depth of the profiled cutter, and cut out to form the notch setting gauge.

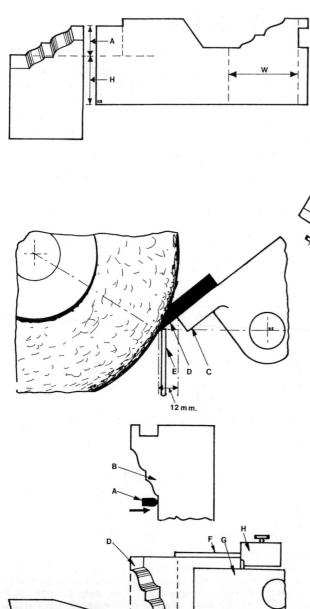

Fig. 144 The cutter width is shown
as W.
Add the mould cutter depth A to H
to give the correct gauge width.

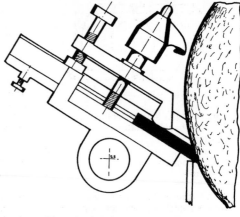

Fig. 145 Section through the Q3S
dummy block showing the cutter
clamped in position and resting on
the cutter support. The dummy block
caters for all collars between 65 and
300mm diameter.

Fig. 146 When setting shaped
cutters, adjust stylus A when against
the planing section of the template
B to give a 12mm gap between
dummy block C and cutter support E.
Cutter D should rest on the cutter
support.
The grinding wheel contacts the
planing section of the cutter when
ground.
The cutter is set against side guide
F, back against rear fence H and is
held by clamp G.

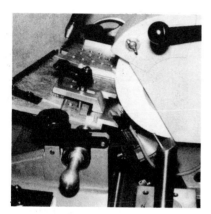

Plate 42 Grinding Q3S cutters loose on an Autool PR230.

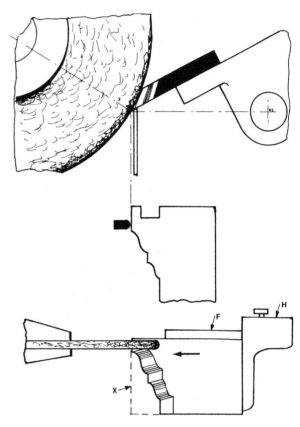

Fig. 147 When grinding from a blank move the carriage so the stylus contacts the furthest point of the template profile, then move the blank cutter forward to contact the dressed grinding wheel. Clamp the cutter in this position against side guide F, and fit rear fence H against its tail. X shows the outline of a blank cutter.

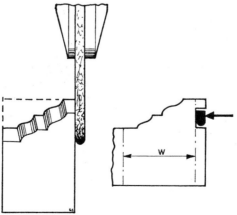

Fig. 148 For sideways alignment butt the cutter against the vertical grinding wheel, and adjust the stylus until against the slot end (this corresponds to the cutter edge). W is the cutter width.

To use the gauge, fit the setting pin in the attachment and place the template end-against the angled guide with the gauge cut-out against the pin. Move the fence tight against the back edge of the template and lock in position, then remove template and pin. Clamp each cutter in turn side-against the angled guide and cutting-edge against the fence. To grind the notch, rotate the attachment on it's arbor so that the cutter rides on the regular cutter support.

To grind, move the carriage so that the notch stylus engages in and follows the slot in the notch template. The notch is then formed automatically in the edge of the cutter at the correct pre-set distance from the cutting edge.

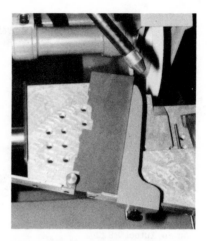

Plate 43 Above, and Fig. 149, left: Fit setting pin A and trap the gauge section of template B between this and fence C. Side guides are at D.

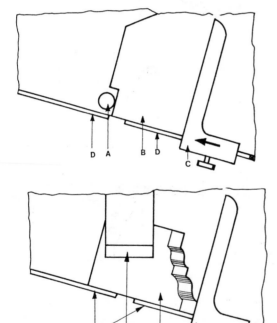

Plate 44 Below, and Fig. 150, left: Remove the pin and template, then butt the cutting edge of profile cutter A against fence C and secure by clamp B.

Cutters are then ready for use. Set them in their slot so the notch contacts the pin, and secure. This precisely aligns the planing line of both cutters with the follower, or sets for normal cutting projection beyond the collar.

When cutters are re-ground they are also re-notched, each time locating the newly-ground cutting edge against the fence pre-set by the gauge. In this way the distance between cutting edge and notch remains fixed throughout the life of the cutter, giving automatic compensation for grinding loss. When setting cutters they repeat precisely their original projection, so cutter alignment remains absolute regardless of cutter wear.

Plate 45 Above, and Fig. 151,
Flip-over the table so notch
template D contacts fixed notch
stylus E. Notch cutter A whilst
resting on the regular cutter
support. The notch template adjusts
for depth after releasing screw F.

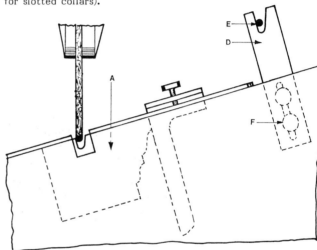

The cutters used are regular collar cutters with plain, squared-edge or bevelled sides. Slots are ground-in on the grinder. The slot grows longer as cutters are worn down. When only 3mm. remains behind the slot the cutters are discarded, so it is impossible to use them when dangerously short. (In some cases a bigger distance should remain; see safety notes for slotted collars).

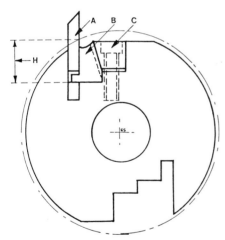

Fig. 152 Above: Section through a
Q3S circular moulding head showing:
A - one cutter.
B - clamp with locating pins.
C - wedge lock.
H - is the minimum pin-to-planing
circle distance.

CIRCULAR CUTTERHEAD

These have the same basic concept as Q3S slotted collars but each cutter has two opposing notches and each clamp has two pins formed on it. The regular cutterhead has four cutter slots and normally has a constant planing circle when used as described for slotted collars.

Q3S circular heads have a different cutting angle to slotted collar cutters, so pre-set the back fence to the setting pin and fit the cutters tail-against this. Set and use the grinder as for slotted collar cutters. To fit cutters remove the clamps and the wedges, locate clamp pins in the cutter notches and insert in the cutter slot. Add wedges and secure. Springs push the cutters out so the notches always contact the clamp pins.

The basic technique is to grind cutters to a constant planing circle, but this is not absolutely necessary. The regular cutter length allows for a 17mm. deep profile. With shallower profiles, cutters can be left their original length to initially have greater projection and a longer overall life. The notches are re-ground only when the cutters wear down to normal projection - and then retain the regular planing circle. The template is not used to initially notch the cutter. Instead, fit the setting pin to locate the tail fence. Place cutters tail-against this to slot for maximum seating conditions.

Plate 46 This SCM spindle
moulder/tenoner combination
features stacked cutterheads to
give rapid programme change-over
from one section to another.

CHAPTER 10

CUTTER GRINDING

Cutters perform best when newly sharpened but, during use, a point is reached when they no longer cut cleanly and the surface produced is not acceptable. Dull cutters take more power, sound noisier, resist the feed more and have a greater tendency to kick back.

Steel-based cutters tend to wear more or less evenly to a rounded point, but sintered cutters begin to break-down rapidly when initial sharpness is lost, so sharpen them before this point is reached.

Grinding to restore sharpness leaves a scratch pattern on the surface. When the ground surface is rough a jagged cutting edge is formed which can break down quickly. To give the best edge and the longest cutter life use a fine grinding wheel with coolant and a relatively slow grinding movement. Finally hone to make the surface as smooth as practicable and to completely remove the burr which grinding forms.

It is important to know when the cutting edge is restored to sharpness because further grinding wastes time and money without improving cutter performance. With HSS and similar cutters a fine grinding burr is formed, so stop when this point is reached. With sintered materials no burr is formed so frequently examine the edge under a good light using a magnifying glass and grind only until the wear pattern is completely removed.

Plate 47 Grinding planing cutters in the head on a Saturn universal grinder.

GRINDING WHEELS

Grinding wheels consist of fine abrasive grains bonded together in a matrix. The grains have naturally sharp edges which cut fine, thin slivers from the tool in grinding. The matrix holds the grains in position whilst they remain sharp, but releases them to expose fresh grains when they loose sharpness. Grain loss or 'shed' results from the extra pressure and heat generated when the grains no longer cut effectively.

Few types of abrasives are used in grinding wheels for woodworking tools. The main type is bauxite (aluminium oxide) which can be natural or manufactured. Natural abrasives vary considerably in performance and have largely been replaced by manufactured abrasives which can be closely controlled for quality and crystal size. Most abrasives are now made by refining and fusing either bauxite ore (clay), or residue from smelting aluminium. Electric furnaces are used for this, and afterwards the end product is crushed, seived and graded to the various grain sizes.

The least pure form, commercially used, is made from the clay and varies in colour from a light or dark grey to brown or blue, according to the origin of the clay and the processing temperature. This type is used for manufacturing general-purpose grinding wheels.

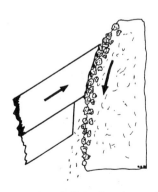

Fig. 153 In grinding, the sharp edges of the abrasive protrudes from the surface of the wheel to pare or abrade-away the metal as thin slivers rather like very fine wire wool.

81

The purest form, made from the residue of aluminium smelting, is almost white and is known as white bauxilite. This generally is the best type for HSS cutters as it grinds exceptionally fast with minimal heat generation. Chromium oxide is added to white bauxilite by some makers, which makes the grinding wheel pink and the grains slightly tougher and less likely to crumble under pressure. This type also has some application in woodworking, but it is used mainly for tool steels of higher alloy.

The other abrasive in regular use is silicon carbide. It is harder and more brittle than bauxite and varies in colour from black to dark and light green. The different coloured abrasives have similar physical properties, although the light green is the purest form. Light green (or green grit) wheels are used in woodworking for rough grinding tungsten carbide. Silicon carbide is also used in a mixture with bauxite to produce grinding wheels for special applications.

The way a grinding wheel performs is due to the grain material, grain size of the abrasive particles, the type and amount of bond used and the closeness of the abrasives. With many combinations used, widely differing performances are possible.

Specifications

The specification of each grinding wheel is printed on its compressive washer (or blotter) usually in six groups of letter and number combinations, but not all makers conform.

ONE: This is the abrasive size. Identification letters vary, but 'A' usually indicates aluminium oxide, and 'C' silicon carbide. Numbers indicate either a specifix mix of abrasive, or a mixture of more than one type.

Fig. 154 Fine (small) grains give a good finish but grind slowly.

TWO: Abrasive grain size, ranging from 8 (large) to 1200 (very small). Grinding is basically an abrading operation with small particles close together each cutting a narrow track across the part being ground. When grains are large (low numbers) heavy cuts are possible so grinding is fast but the surface finish is poor. When grains are small (high numbers) the surface finish is good but grinding is a slow process.

THREE: Grade or bond strength, ranging usually from E - soft to Z - hard. This is governed by the proportion of bond to abrasive and determines the grip the bond has on the grains. When the bond has a strong grip the grains are retained longer and the wheel is termed as hard. Hard grinding wheels wear slowly but tend to glaze and fill-in readily so needing frequent dressing. A soft wheel has a weaker bond and loses grains more quickly to expose fresh grains beneath. These grinding wheels wear relatively quickly but perform well and consistantly. The bond is stated as a letter, or as soft, medium or hard. Hard cutters need a soft wheel, and soft cutters need a hard wheel.

Fig. 155 Coarse (large) grains grind fast but give a poor finish.

Fig. 156 Close-structured vitrified wheels give more support when grinding thin edges.

Fig. 157 Open-structured vitrified wheels have numerous voids and grind cool on large areas.

Fig. 158 Grinding wheel types:
A - plain.
B - cup.
C & D - saucer or dish.

Arrows show the grinding surfaces.

FOUR: Structure, ranging from 1 - close to 15 - open. This indicates how closely the grains are packed. A close-grade wheel gives a steadier and more controlled grind. An open-structured wheel is freer-cutting and less easy to control.

FIVE: Bond type. Four bond types are used in woodworking - vitrified, resinoid, shellac and rubber.

Vitrified wheels are by far the most predominant type in woodworking. They have a porous structure with the grains held together by bridges of glass or similar vitreous material giving a rigid grinding wheel suitable for most operations, and they are used either wet or dry.

Resinoid wheels have a bond usually of phenol formaldehyde, sometimes with fillers to form a more flexible grinding wheel which gives a better finish on flat grinding. Often this type of grinding wheel is used dry as the heat of grinding is the means of breaking-down the bond.

Resinoid, shellac and rubber-bond, sometimes with reinforcements, are used for cut-off applications when parting cutters or relief-cutting.

Types

Plain or peripheral grinding wheels are flat and from 3-36mm wide by up to 300mm in diameter. They mount on an arbor between flanges and are intended for grinding only on their periphery. Often the periphery is formed to a half-round or square section when used for grinding flat cutters to a profile. Never grind on the side of a plain wheel as this thins and weakens it, also the grinding wheel lacks the necessary support for side grinding and could shatter under side pressure.

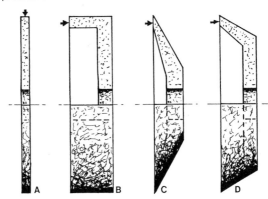

Cup and dish wheels are shaped, as their names suggest, with parallel sides in cup form and with angled, tapering sides in dish form. They mount to overhang the arbor with the securing nut or ring below the abrasive level. They are for flat grinding only on their radial faces.

Cup wheels are used when grinding planing cutters either flat or with a slightly hollow grind. Dish wheels are used for face-grinding profiled-cutters, router cutter flutes, etc., and are tapered back for the necessary clearance.

SAFE USE OF GRINDING WHEELS

There are many safety regulations for grinding wheels. Make sure that these are understood and observed, and that only qualified operators are allowed change the grinding wheels.

Storage

All grinding wheels are brittle and can easily be damaged through mis-use. Take care to handle and store them carefully. Grinding wheels should be stored in medium temperatures away from strong sunlight and high humidity, and where they are unlikely to be damaged.

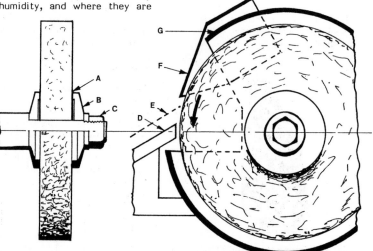

Some grinding wheels deteriorate with age, so do not store them for long periods. Keep only a small stock and replenish this regularly. Handle grinding wheels from storage with care. When moving them around support and protect them from damage. Never use a wheel that has been dropped and never roll wheels along the floor.

Fitting

Before fitting a grinding wheel carefully check it to make sure there are no visible cracks. With vitrified wheel types tap the wheel sharply with a piece of wood (never metal). A crack-free grinding wheel will 'ring' quite clearly.

Fig. 159 A plain grinding wheel for rim grinding showing:
A - compression washers fitted both sides of the wheel.
B - relieved flange.
C - securing nut.
D - cutter rest.
E - cutter shown in dotted outline.
F - nosing which should be set close to the wheel to reduce sparking and to complete the enclosure of the wheel.
G - grinding wheel guard.

Wear eye protectors when grinding, also others in the vicinity.

Plate 48 Grinding the flute of a router cutter on a Saturn universal grinder, using a dividing head for location.

A cracked wheel does not ring and actually sounds cracked. Never fit a cracked or suspect grinding wheel. Resinoid and rubber wheels do not 'ring', so only visual inspection is possible.

Each grinding wheel should have the maximum running speed printed on the blotter. Check that this exceeds the speed of the arbor on which it is to be used, and never use a grinding wheel which is marked with a lower maximum speed.

Before mounting the grinding wheel clean all parts. Check that the mounting flanges are true, also damage and warp-free. They should be equal in diameter and bearing surfaces, and their diameter should be at least one third that of the grinding wheel. Flanges should be recessed to contact only with their rim and the inner flange should be fixed to the arbor.

Ensure that the grinding wheel is a good push-on fit to the arbor. Never force a grinding wheel onto its arbor and do not use a grinding wheel that is a sloppy fit.

Always fit compressive carboard rings (blotters) on both sides of the grinding wheel to cover the entire contact area These cushion the clamping action, give a better grip and lessen the chance of the wheel cracking on tightening. Tighten up the securing nut evenly and progressively, but not excessively.

Before switching-on the grinding wheel replace the guards. Check that all parts are secure and that the grinding wheel is free to rotate. Make sure that anyone around is wearing goggles or a suitable visor, and that no one is standing in line with the grinding wheel - just in case. Allow a newly-fitted grinding wheel to run free for one minute before attempting to use it.

It is possible that the grinding wheel is out-of-balance when initially started up. This is not acceptable and must be corrected before using it. Sometimes dressing will reduce the out-of-balance effect or, failing this, improvement can sometimes be made by turning the grinding wheel on its arbor and again dressing. If the imbalance still persists the grinding wheel should be returned to the maker.

Speed

All grinding wheels are intended to run at a stated maximum speed relating to the peripheral speed when new, a factor determined by the makers. It is this speed, which is usually printed on the blotter, that should not be exceeded.

With plain grinding wheels the peripheral speed reduces as they wear down in use and they then grind as a softer wheel. To avoid this raise the running speed when worn, but always keep below the maximum recommended speed. The effective hardness of a grinding wheel can be changed by altering the running speed; running faster makes it harder, running slower makes it softer.

Peripheral speeds of vitrified-bonded grinding wheels are normally between 25 and 30M/sec., but resinoid-bonded grinding wheels can operate at speeds in excess of 33M/sec.

Plate 49 Profile grinders, such as this Autool PR230H, grind on the rim of thin, plain grinding wheels.

Truing and dressing

Truing is the operation of making a grinding wheel run true (concentric with its arbor) or restoring its profile to the shape required by mechanically removing uneven abrasive. Dressing restores the cutting action of the grinding wheel by dressing-out metal deposits filling-in the pores, and by eroding away high bonding to expose the sharp grains. Theoretically, no sharp grains are dislodged in dressing, but a few usually are. The two processes are often combined as part of the same operation. Normally a rotary mechanical dresser is used, or a single diamond.

The rotary dresser is a either series of star-shaped, corrugated or twisted discs alternating with plain discs on a ballbearing spindle at the end of a handle. This dresser is used dry and is manually held to lightly traverse across the grinding wheel whilst resting firmly on the cutter support. Star-shaped cutters leave the wheel open and fast-cutting, other types leave a smoother surface which is slower-cutting but gives a better finish.

The diamond type is usually a single diamond. This can be used in the same way, by hand, but preferably it should be machine traversed. Traverse slowly, with a only small feed and repeat several times to give the finest surface to the grinding wheel and the best finish to the ground face. A single-point diamond is commonly fitted to profile-grinding machines. Preferably use coolant when dressing with a diamond.

Grinding fluid

Grinding wheels intended for wet grinding should be used with suitable grinding fluid, normally an oil and water mix. This cools the cutter and assists the grinding action by lubricating the cutting points of the abrasive. It also flushes away the grinding chips and helps to prevent wheel loading. Preferably the jet of fluid should be directed at the work rather than the grinding wheel. The fluid is more effective by doing this and there is less spray from the grinding wheel. The supply should be ample and continuous, an inconsistant supply is more harmful than none.

Vitrified wheels are porous and absorb a great deal of coolant which gravitates to the lower half of the wheel when stopped. The grinding wheel then is unbalanced and vibrates on starting. To avoid this start the grinding wheel before switching the coolant on, and switch-off coolant well before stopping the grinding wheel.

The grinding fluid improves the surface finish, allows a faster, burn-free grind and makes grinding wheels last longer. Choose the coolant carefully as it can also cause problems - so get expert advice from the coolant manufacturers.

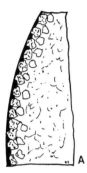

Defects

Glazing occurs with a grinding wheel which is too hard. The grains are retained long after they loose sharpness and take on a glazed appearance. A glazed wheel does not grind effectively because the particles are rounded-over to rub and burn the ground surface.

Loading occurs when material which has been abraded away from the cutter lodges and fills the pores of the grinding wheel instead of being thrown clear. This physically prevents the grains cutting: an effect similar to glazing but with a different cause. Loading can be reduced by using a wax-added grinding wheel when dry grinding, or by using a grinding fluid. (Some grinding fluids are more effective than others, check with your supplier.)

A grinding wheel which is glazed and/or loaded can be made good simply by dressing, but this does not cure the problem if the grinding wheel application or coolant is wrong. One possible solution for both is to is to use a softer-bonded grinding wheel.

SUPERABRASIVES

Two extremely hard abrasives are now being widely used: natural or synthetic diamonds for grinding tungsten carbide, and CBN (cubic boron nitride) for grinding HSS and similar tool steels. The latter is sold as Borazon by The General Electric Company (U.S.A.), and as ABN (Amber Boron Nitride) by De Beers Co., of Johannesburg, S.A.

Superabrasive wheels are available in a wide range of sizes, sections and profiles. The least costly wheels have only a single layer of diamond or CBN crystals electrostatically-plated on a formed wheel. Both abrasives can also be formed in thicker layers with a metal, vitrified or resinoid bond, but mostly the latter for woodworking. They have only a relatively thin layer of diamond or CBN bonded to a metal or phenolic-resin body.

It is possible to vary grit size and bond strength, and both effect the grinding action as with grit wheels. An added factor is the concentration, the ratio of crystals-to-bond. The balanced concentration is 100, but this ranges from 50 to 150.

Diamond and CBN wheels interchange with regular grit wheels on suitable grinders. CBN wears much slower than grit wheels and, whilst costing more, can show an overal saving when grinding HSS and tool steels, and give a higher quality and more consistant finish.

Fig. 160 A - loaded grinding wheel filled-in with grinding debris.
B - glazed wheel with grains rounded-over but not dislodged.
C - dressed wheel with fresh grains exposed after removing dulled grains, debris and high bond.

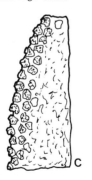

Mounting

Superabrasive wheels for woodworking are pre-shaped and trued by the maker, not on the machine, so it is necessary to mount them with considerably more care than regular grinding wheels.

Take care that all mating surfaces are clean and true before mounting, and do not use blotters. After mounting, check and correct each wheel for roundness and truth using a dial indicator against the register groove (if provided). Preferably these wheels should have individual arbors for morse-taper mounting to maintain accuracy.

If the wheel runs out radially when mounted on a plain arbor, this can sometimes be corrected by turning it independent of the arbor to a different position. When the best position has been determined mark both arbor and wheel at the top as fitted. When re-mounting re-align these marks to give better repetition.

Dress all wheels regularly using an abrasive stick, commonly a fine-grit medium-bond aluminium oxide type, by pressing this lightly onto the running abrasive. With dressing the colour of the wheel surface changes. Rapidly increasing dressing-stick wear shows that dressing is complete. Dressing erodes away high bond left by fragmenting crystals and any grinding debris.

Superabrasives are manufactured for either dry or wet grinding and should be used accordingly - or efficiency suffers. Grinding fluid is usually a soluable oil and water mix, although a neat oil can be used.

Pure diamond is for grinding tungsten carbide only, so separately grind tungsten carbide tips by using different wheels with angles for body and tip which differ by about 5 degrees. Some modern grinding wheels will grind both tip and body of cutters simultaneously. These can be used with a single bevel.

CBN wheels are best for highly-alloyed tool steels, HSS and similar. Do not use them on tungsten carbide and avoid low-alloy steels.

Properly used, superabrasives produce good finishes efficiently and economically. Badly used, they can prove a very expensive mistake. They will not upgrade an old and worn grinding machine to produce better work; the grinding machine should be new, in the best condition and with bearings and arbors which are accurate and true. The machine must also be heavy, rigid and vibration-free, coolant systems ample and dependable and the grinding machine-controlled.

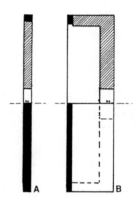

Fig. 161 Typical diamond and CBN grinding wheels.
A - plain.
B - cup.
C & D - saucer or dish.

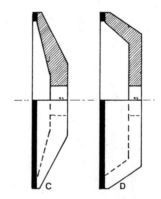

HONING

Natural hones are the Washita which is a coarse and fast-cutting type used for initial sharpening, and the Arkansas, a harder and denser type more suitable for fine finishing. Artificial hones have a grit either of aluminium oxide or silicon carbide. The bond is normally vitrified and hones are available in different grits similar to those in grinding wheels.

Silicon carbide, usually a light green in colour, cuts faster than aluminium oxide and grain sharpness is retained longer. It gives fast results but is less than ideal for finishing. Aluminium oxide is best for finishing as the grit more readily levels-off and evens-out when lightly honing. Colour varies from brown to blue-grey.

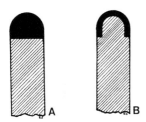

Fig. 162 Shaped superabrasive wheels can have a solid tip on a square body A or a shaped body B. Electrostatically deposited wheels C have only a thin layer of metal-bonded crystals. They cost less but have a short life.

The normal practice is to use coarse or medium-grit for initial work, then finish-off with a fine grit. Flat hones are used for straight cutters and external curves, and shaped hones for internal shapes.

Hones should be used with a light oil or oil and paraffin-oil mix to give a fine finish and save wear on the hone. Use a circular movement where possible as this evens-out flaws and is quicker. When finishing-off, if possible move more along than across the cutting edge to remove any peak and valley effect.

Hones wear hollow and occasionally need dressing level using a grinding wheel. They also may glaze or load. Soaking in paraffin oil or cleaning with petrol and a wire brush helps to clear loaded hones, but glazed hones need dressing.

Completely remove the grinding burr on newly-ground cutters using a hone, or the burr breaks-off in use to leave a jagged edge. Dull cutters can be honed, often without removing them from the machine. In sharpening hold the hone flat on the ground face of the cutter until a honing burr is formed, then alternate between front and ground faces to remove this burr. Honing is quicker on very dull cutters by holding the hone at an angle to the ground face rather than flat, but take care not to round the edge over or the cutter will rub on the heel.

TOOL STEELS

Most tools used in woodworking are made from, or contain, alloys of steel, and are hardened and tempered to give a hard, tough cutting edge. The most commonly-used type is HSS (high-speed steel). One of the most important alloys is tungsten, the content of which varies from 3 to 22 percent. In general, cutters with high tungsten content last slightly longer on harder timbers.

Another steel used is HCHC - high carbon, high chrome, a lower-cost steel which gives reasonable results on softer timbers. Some cutters are now made from a very low-alloy steel which is carburised and heat-treated. This gives a very hard but shallow skin which compares favourable with through-hardened steels on softer timbers. Carburised cutters are particularly susceptable to hardness loss even with modest grinding temperatures and must be ground wet and with care.

NON-STEEL TOOLS

Three non-steel cutting materials are used in woodworking tooling: Tantung, Stellite, tungsten carbide and PCD (poly-crystalline diamond).

Stellite is a cobalt-based metal which is most commonly-used in rod form for weld-depositing, either in making a new tool or in building-up a worn one. The cutting edge outlasts HSS by a factor of about 10 when cutting slightly abrasive materials. Tantung is a similar solid cobalt-based metal brazed onto softer-backed cutters. These metals can be ground with regular grit or CBN grinding wheels.

Tungsten carbide is a sintered metal brazed or mechanically clamped to a cutter or solid head. The cutting edge outlasts HSS by a factor of about 100 on highly abrasive materials and is essential for such as chipboard edging and plastic trimming.

Tungsten carbide cutters need special treatment. Small bevel angles must be avoided, make them not less than 45 degrees and grind slowly and without excessive pressure. Tungsten carbide is susceptible to cracking, so make sure the coolant is ample and dependable if used. Re-sharpen tools before becoming dull, otherwise the edge rapidly breaks-down and needs excessive re-sharpening.

A perfectly sharp edge is needed to clean-cut softwoods and give long life. Sharpening takes much longer than for conventional tools and is often wrongly skimped by some users in the name of expediency.

Tungsten carbide is ideal for factory-produced throw-away cutters for use on planing, edging and certain moulding heads, router cutters and drill bits.

Polycrystalline diamond comprises of a polycrystalline aggregate of artificial diamonds of about 0.5mm thick bonded together and to a tungsten carbide substrate from 1.5 - 3mm thick. This is then clamped to a steel body or brazed on at low temperature. The highly specialised material is made under the name Compax by The General Electric Company (U.S.A.) and under the name Syndite by De Beers Co.(S.A.).

This tooling is as yet in its infancy, but already has proved greatly superior to tungsten carbide. Because of its high cost and limited shapes and sizes, applications so far have only been with difficult materials in mass-production lines.

Small cutters for circular heads and slotted collars are made from solid tool steel or a composite with a thin (2-3mm) brazed-on facing of tool steel on a softer steel back. Router cutters are solid HSS, tungsten carbide or a composite. Profiled cutterheads can be solid steel, usually some form of cobalt-chrome, or with a softer body and HSS, tungsten carbide, Tantung or Stellite facing. The HSS types are much less costly to produce than solid profiled heads, but have a limited life compared with them.

Plate 51 Above: Wadkin PCD router cutter.

Plate 50 Below left: Solid profile cutters normally are of a cobalt-based steel. This shows a Saturn cutter.

Plate 52 Below right: This Leuco panel-raising cutterhead has carbide disposable cutters fitted.

CHAPTER 11

GENERAL MOULDING
Straight moulding

Straight moulding is undertaken by feeding the workpiece on the table and edge or face-against a straight fence. The workpiece is controlled by pressures and guides to keep it running true, and is manually fed by hand or using spikes, push-sticks and follow-up blocks. To make the operation safer a through fence and table rings or bed must be used to close up the cutter gap. A feed unit can be set to press timber down on the table or against the fence.

Plate 53 When edge moulding long, thin pieces use an outrigger support as on this Scheppach spindle moulder.

Fig. 163 Using a feed unit A is safer and better even with short runs.

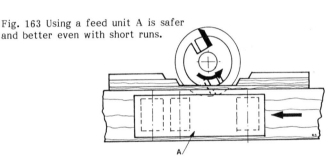

THE FENCE

The fence can be a U type, which can be moved as a unit but with independent adjustment of the two fences, or two separate halves operating in some form of slide or with a keyway to keep them parallel. Most fences allow lever springs or a Shaw guard to be fitted, also a front guard to bridge the fence gap and an exhaust hood.

The fence is first set as a unit to give correct cutter projection for the mould depth wanted, with fence plates adjusted laterally to keep the fence gap small for safety and to give solid support right up to the point of cut. A through-fence should be added, making sure that there is enough clearance between fence plates and cutterhead to allow for the wooden fence to be subsequently broken through safely, also to allow for minor fence adjustments after initial setting.

Fence plates can be steel or wood. The steel type are durable and virtually wear-free but obviously damage the cutterhead if the two come in contact. They usually have counter-sunk holes to screw on wooden through-fences. Hardwood fence plates have some advantages. They need replacing periodically because they wear and are not quite as precise as steel fences, but temporary stops are easily fixed using screws or nails, and because they do not damage the tools it is practicable to cut into them with the cutterhead to close the fence gap.

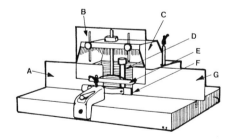

Fig. 164 Typical fence unit:
A - outfeed fence.
B - transparent front guard.
C - rear cover and exhaust hood.
D - spindle arbor.
E - top Shaw guard.
F - side Shaw guard.
G - infeed fence.

Setting aids

Settings for cut depth (beyond the fence face) and height (above table) need to be accurate so that repeated re-settings and test runs are kept to a minimum.

Often a test cut is wrongly (and in the U.K. illegally) made without guards or pressures to save the trouble of later removal for adjustment. Unfortunately, test cuts are often the time when accidents occur which proper guarding would prevent or make less serious. To avoid the problem use precise setting devices.

Plate 54 Micro adjustable controls to a two-part fence on a Wadkin Bursgreen BEL spindle moulder.

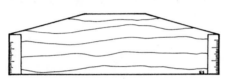

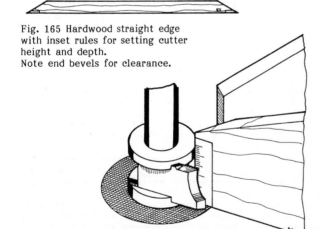

Fig. 165 Hardwood straight edge with inset rules for setting cutter height and depth.
Note end bevels for clearance.

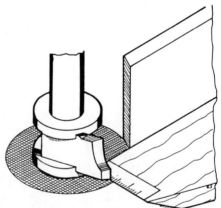

Make a seasoned hardwood straight-edge with vertical short rules inset at both ends on the same face. Sand or plane the ends to leave the rules as pointed edges with a 60 or 45 degree bevel. Use the straight edge vertically edge-on the table to set height, and horizontally against the fence to set depth. Some shapes are difficult to measure like this, for example chamfers, bevels and nosings. Use the method later described under 'breaking through a fence' to aid accurate setting.

Fig. 166 Left: Checking cut height.
Right: Checking cut depth.

THROUGH-FENCES

These are an essential safety feature. They leave a gap-free surface round the projecting cutters to prevent small sections and flexible timber dipping into the fence gap. A softwood through-fence fastens to the normal fence plates or replaces them. (Plywood could be used but it abrades and prematurely dulls cutters. Hardwood fences tend to warp and twist).

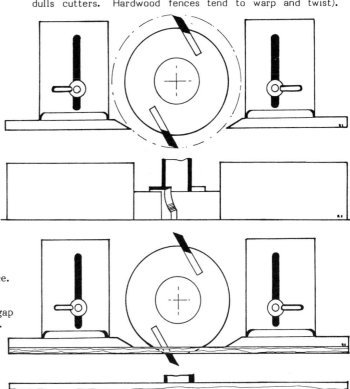

Fig. 167 Above: Fences as the makers supply them, note the wide open gap for cutter clearance.

Below: The same set-up with a through-fence fitted. The cutter gap is closed to the absolute minimum.

Normally the through-fence is the same overall length and depth as the regular fence, but may be longer if using end-stops, or shorter if moulding bent timber. (When feeding large section and rigid parts such as door casings and window frames hollow-side against the fence, long fences prevent face contact at the cutters - so the mould or rebate is formed shallow. With a short fence the cutting depth remains consistant but the part is less stable in feeding).

When replacing regular steel fence plates the through-fence must be thick and stiff enough not too deflect in use. Fasten it either through the fence plate slots by studs screwed into the back, or by countersunk coach bolts, washers and wing-nuts.

When a through-fence is fitted to existing fence plates, these give extra support so a thinner piece can be used and cutter projection beyond the block can be less. Most steel fences have holes to secure wooden fences from the back - using woodscrews. If they haven't, add them. 'G' clamps could be used but may interfere with the feed. When the machine has wooden fence plates the through-fence can be nailed or screwed in position (but don't fix a back-stop to a nailed fence). Perhaps the best combination is to fix 20mm thick wooden fence plates to the steel fence plates, onto which a 10mm false fence can be nailed securely - but quickly and easily removed.

Fig. 168 Different types of false fences.
A - Thick fence fence 'A' replaces the regular fence.
B - Thin false fence 'B' screwed to the fence plates 'C'.
C - Thin false fence 'A' nailed to wooden fence plates 'D'.
D - Front view of sketch C showing nail positions at 'E'.

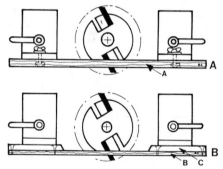

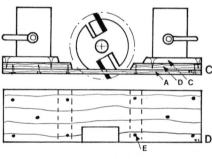

Plate 55 A through fence fitted on a Delta light duty spindle moulder. Guards other than that fitted to the arbor have been removed for clarity.

To use a through-fence properly the cutterhead should break through it when running. An irony is that the through-fence is much safer to use than a two-piece fence, but breaking through can itself be hazardous.

When breaking through follow a strict sequence in addition to taking all normal precautions. First pre-cut the gap using a bandsaw so that less needs cutting out with the head itself. Keep a stock of through-fences with different-size cut-outs already in them. Initially make the fences deeper than really necessary so the under edge can be planed off to remove an oversize cut-out for further use.

Check that the cutter is suitable for cutting through the fence by grinding a clearance bevel on the top edge, and by forming the mould shape close to the top edge of the cutter so that the least amount of fence is cut out. Bevel both edges when intended for over-cutting, as with grooves and similar, keeping the projecting cutter as narrow as practical - but within safe operating limits, of course.

PRE-SETTING

The through-fence should be temporarily attached to, or replace, the original fence plates; a gap should be left below to allow cutters to be rotated. Where practical fit cutters to project above the block to clear-cut through the fence and possibly sink into the mould. Set the head to the proper height and cut depth beyond the outer face of the through-fence using the straight-edge. Check that cutters and cutterblock amply clear all parts both when in the starting position of the fence before break through, and when in the operating position.

Whitehill type cutterheads allow cutters to project above the top face and below the under face to give ample cutterblock clearance on both sides. With heads that are not sunk check that the through-fence misses the cutterhead. If intending to chipbreak with the through-fence check that the subsequent adjustment needed for edge renewal is allowed for by leaving clearance between cutterhead and infeed fence plate, or between the through-fence securing bolts and the slot end.

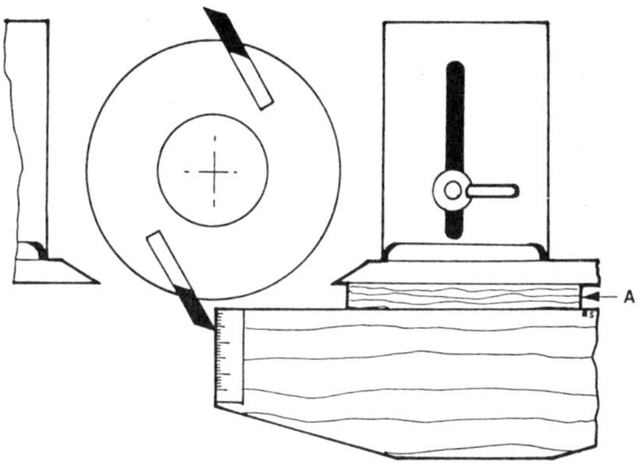

Plate 56 Wooden fence plates fitted to a Delta two-speed heavy-duty spindle moulder.

Fig. 169 Checking cutter depth before the through-fence is fitted. Sandwich the through-fence or a piece of equal thickness between the regular fence and the straight-edge as at A.

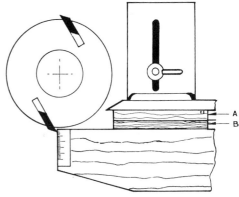

Fig. 170 Sometimes the cutterblock prevents depth measurement as shown, so sandwich a piece of hardwood of specific thickness B in addition to the through-fence A. Add thickness B to the depth measured.

BREAKING THROUGH

Most users break through by moving the fence back into the rotating cutterhead. With an undercut it may be more practical and safer to break through by raising the cutterhead under power whilst the fence remains fixed in place. Mark or note the correct vertical setting of the spindle or set a stop to give absolute repetition, then lower the spindle to clear. Finally fix the through-fence.

With the spindle running and the vertical movement lock slackened, raise the spindle slowly to cut upwards into the fence until the previous setting is reached. As a check, mark the highest point of the mould on the fence with a pencilled line parallel to the table. Note the deepening cut on breaking through and stop when at the proper height.

Raising the spindle is a safe way of breaking through on the right machine. Not all machines are suitable, only those where vertical adjustment is via an easily accessible hand-wheel, and where the machine runs steadily and vibration-free with the rise and fall lock released. The drive must also allow vertical spindle movement when running, not all do.

Moving the fence

Breaking-through a fence live must only be attempted by experienced spindle hands. Vibration is created to give an entirely different feel to normal movement and which can be dangerous. New users should first roughly shape the cut-out, then chip away the wood fence by rotating the cutterhead manually whilst easing back the fence. This is a tedious, but a safer, operation.

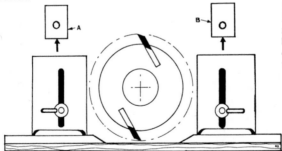

Fig. 171 After setting for cut depth fix back stops A and B against the rear of the fence to limit movement back. The fence is shown drawn clear of the cutters before breaking through.

For the experienced the method of breaking through using a live spindle is as follows:-

After setting the fence in the correct running position clamp secure back-stops to the table against the rear of the fence or the two fence halves to prevent over-run on breaking through. Move the fence clear of the rotating cutters before fixing the through-fence and rear guards in place.

Make the usual safety checks, then start up the cutterhead and slowly move the fence back into the cutters, allowing these to cut their way through until they project the amount required. Then stop the cutterhead and secure the fence. Before starting the run, rotate the cutterhead manually to make sure it still clears. If not, chip it away.

Note that if cutters run in contact with the false fence they run noisily and dull quickly. Preferably break through the fence to a depth marginally beyond that actually required, then draw the fence forward to the proper depth - at which it should also clear the fence. (This does not apply when using the fence as a chipbreaker as close fitting is essential).

Plate 57 Rear view of this Delta RS-15 spindle moulder shows the fine adjustments and ample dust chute giving good protection from the rear.

The way in which a fence adjusts determines how safe or otherwise breaking through actually is. The worst type of fence to adjust is the one-piece fence that simply locks down but has no fine adjustment as a unit. With these, the locks need partial tightening only, to allow manual movement without excessive pressure, but provide enough friction between fence and table for the fence to remain in position when pressure is released.

Some operators lock one side as a swivel point and move back the opposite end, then reverse the movement, and so on, moving back in alternate steps. This is safer than with both locks partially released and gives surer control. In either case a back stop is absolutely essential, of course. (If the machine is fitted with this type of fence it is safer and better to raise the spindle to break through a fence already fixed in place, rather than attempt to shift the fence). With one-piece fences allow more clearance of the steel fence plates as the unit may swivel in being moved and come closer to the cutterhead than had been anticipated.

Whenever locking or releasing the fence always retain grip with one hand, and keep hold until the fence is completely locked down. This also applies when the fence is in position and the spindle is being stopped - keep one hand holding firmly onto the fence. By doing this, both hands are kept out of danger.

Some fences have screw adjustment. With single-screw adjustment the whole fence moves together, so breaking through is simple and safe. When the two halves move independently, both handwheels should be moved equally to keep the two plates precisely in line. This is not quite as easy, but break-through is a controlled operation.

Moving the table

On some machines the table adjusts on slides or swivels on a pivot. Moving the table is the safest means of fence break through and, where provided, should be used in preference to shifting the fence.

First set the fence for correct cutter projection and set the table movement back-stop to repeat this position precisely. Move the cutterblock so that the cutterblock clears, then fasten the through-fence in place. Start-up the head and break through in a controlled manner by moving the table and fence as a unit under mechanical control.

GAUGING HEIGHT AND DEPTH

The correct moulding cut height from the table, and depth from the fence, can both be accurately gauged by noting the expanding fence cut-out as this is moved back into the rotating cutters.

The height is precisely the same as the cut height on the timber and can be shown as a horizontal line on the fence face parallel to the table. When moving the fence back on a mould having a level top section, such as a rebate, start with the cutter marginally low, then raise it to the proper height when a cut is clearly visible. This is not practical with a bevelled top edge because the cut deepens as the fence is moved back, so carefully set height before breaking through.

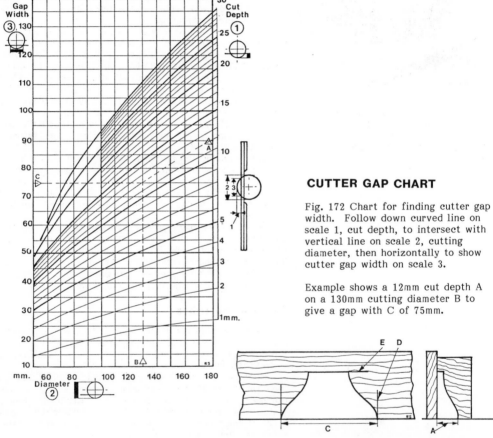

CUTTER GAP CHART

Fig. 172 Chart for finding cutter gap width. Follow down curved line on scale 1, cut depth, to intersect with vertical line on scale 2, cutting diameter, then horizontally to show cutter gap width on scale 3.

Example shows a 12mm cut depth A on a 130mm cutting diameter B to give a gap with C of 75mm.

Fig. 173 Above: Cutting depth A gives a specific width C according to cutting diameter, see chart for details. Mark the fence for cutting height E and width D and constantly check the widening cut-out against these when breaking through.

The width of the fence cut-out gives a very accurate measure of cut depth, being the cord of the cutting circle at this point. Carefully measure the cutting diameter at the furthest points of cut (in the case of a bevel, level with the table when at correct height setting) and note the cord from the chart for the cut depth needed. Using bold vertical lines mark this precise width on the fence face equally each side of the spindle.

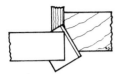

Keep moving the fence back until the cut-out equals the spacing of these lines. This method is particularlly suitable when forming bevels and similar which do not have precise points from which the cut depth or height can be set in the conventional way. With a bevel cutter set the top point just inside the false fence and finally raise it to the setting required to keep the fence gap to the minimum.

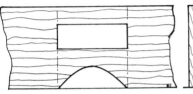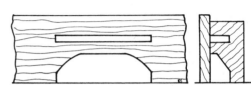

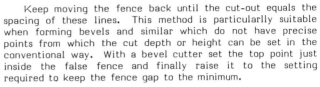

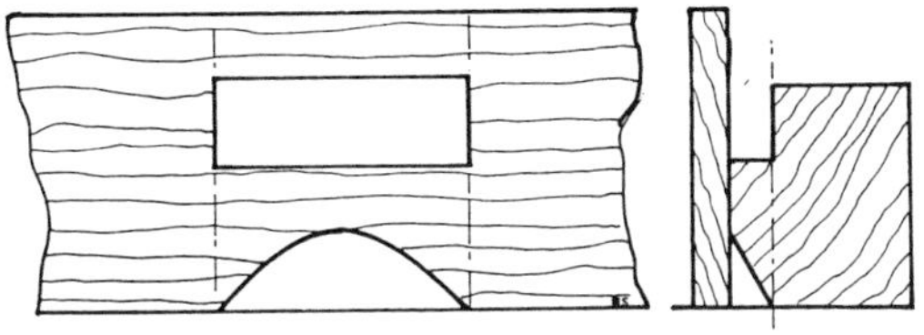

Fig. 174 Above: Cut-out shapes are not always what you expect. A bevel or chamfer produces a shape geometrically called a parabola. It may in fact be a truncated parabola with both halves separated by flat section as shown here.
When bevelling, set the bevel cutter in this way.

Right: Check the cut-out to ensure that sash cutters, for example, project evenly.

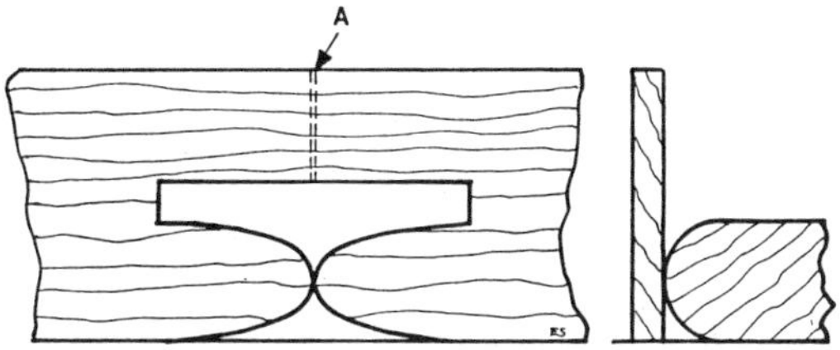

Fig. 175 Centre right: When nosing and edging, barely break through the fence, then split it at A using a fine handsaw.

Fig. 176 Lower right: After splitting the fence, screw back the infeed fence, as B, to give the depth of cut needed.

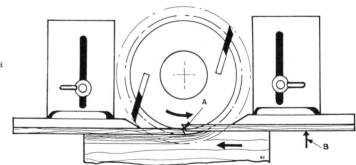

When forming nosings and other similar full-edge moulding where the edge is also to be cleaned-up, move the fence back until the smallest diameter barely breaks through to line-up precisely with the fence face. A gap of only 1 or 2mm is enough. With moulds of this type the infeed fence is normally stepped back to allow for edge clean up (see later details). This isn't possible with a one-piece through fence, so split it from the top to the cut-out using a tenon saw held at a slight angle. By doing this independent movement of the two fence halves can then be made, so finally set back the infeed fence by the cut depth needed.

Checking cutter profile

The fence cut-out clearly shows the cutter profile in deep-ended form where it cuts into the infeed fence. Examine this before moulding to make sure the profile is what you want and, if necessary, correct it before starting the run. Various cut-out profiles are shown in the sketches, check that yours complies. It may be that the balancing cutter interferes with the profile - without this being obvious. If it does interfere, this shows up on the profile cut-out of the fence and can be corrected before running the first piece.

A through-fence gives support across the gap to prevent 'dipping', guards the cutterhead very effectively and fully supports a partially-moulded workpiece so that horizontal pressures can be used across the fence. A wooden through-fence also throws fewer chips at the operator and retains broken pieces of cutter within the guard should an accident happen.

It can also act as a chipbreaker to reduce spelching on the square outer corners of rebates and ovolos, etc. To be effective in chipbreaking, timber has to be tight up against the fence, and the wooden fence must be clean and sharp at the infeed edge. After some use this wears rounded and becomes ineffective, so periodically restore the sharp corner by shifting the fence towards the cutterhead.

First make sure there is enough clearance between steel fence and cutterhead for the movement needed. If not, move the steel fence further out and re-set the through-fence to compensate. Finally, partially loosen the fence plates and, with the spindle running, tap the infeed-fence end to drive the wooden fence 2 or 3mm into the cutters to re-form the sharp corner. Secure the fence and finally check cutter clearance before re-starting.

The same chipbreaking action also reduces tear-out on difficult and interlocked-grain timber to give a better finish. As before, timber and fence must be in tight contact and a sharp corner maintained at the infeed side.

Although normally set for an undercut, the fence can be broken through well above the table line when forming a centre-groove, drip or similar. In this case make sure both top and bottom edges of the cutter have clearance ground-in to cut through the fence to the full depth needed, and use a cutterblock that will not foul in breaking through. A through-fence is useful when stop-moulding as back stops and guides, etc, can be screwed to it quite easily.

THE BED

Table rings

The table normally has removable rings of decreasing size which fit one inside the other. Use them to reduce the gap between table and cutterhead to give maximum support right

Plate 58 Removable table rings as used on a Delta RS-15 spindle moulder.

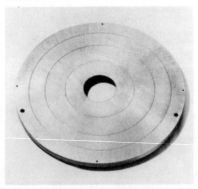

100

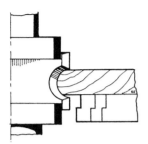

Fig. 177 Above: Fit table rings to fill the gap.

Below: Alternatively shape and fit a wooden bed.

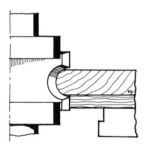

up to the cutters. Where no rings are provided the table may have a ledge to support a hardwood filling-in piece. This should be flush with the table top, have turn-buttons on the underside to hold it in position and a hole to suit the diameter of the cutterhead. Make a range of fill-in pieces with different size holes.

Wooden bed

Another form of support used with a straight fence is a wooden bed or false table.

Slotted tables

This is a piece of seasoned hardwood or laminate, fastened to strips wedged in the fence slots. Shape this to support timber right up to the cutterhead by cutting into the running head. Make the under-strips a good fit and set the bed clear of the cutters. After setting the fence for cut depth, carefully shape the bed by moving it into the running cutterhead until it meets the fence. Use a top Shaw guard to steady the bed when shaping. If an existing bed has a deeper cut-out than needed, saw off or surface this edge so that it can again be used. Make the strips short of the fence edge so that removal is not needed for edging.

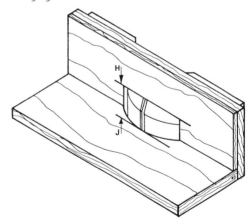

Fig. 179 Mark the fence at H for cut height and the bed at J for cut depth.

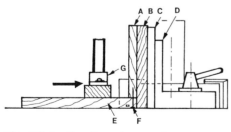

Fig. 178 Section through a wooden bed E nailed to the underside of false fence A which in turn is fixed to the wooden fence plates B. The steel fences are at C and the fence support at D.
Also shown is a Shaw guard G to control movement.

Plain tables

Slots collect chips to score the underside of workpieces and interfere with the feed movement, so modern machine tables usually have a series of tapped holes. With these, first shape the bed, then mark the hole positions from the underside and fit securing screws. The problem is in shaping the bed in the first place.

One way is to fasten the bed-piece using a single screw at one end only close to the fence. Move the bed-piece at the opposite end away from the fence to clear the cutterhead, then start this up and carefully swivel the bed until against the fence. Finally, fasten down with two or more screws. Another way is to slot the bed for the securing screws so that these can be fitted and snugged before shaping, then tap the outer edge of the bed to drive it into the cutters until fully shaped. This is an easier and safer way.

Alternatively, treat the bed as a workpiece and shape by dropping-on using a back-stop. See "Stopped moulds". If the table swivels or traverses use this movement in shaping the bed in preferance to any other way.

The simplest method is to fasten the bed to the underedge of the false fence and break through fence and bed at the same time. Use a Shaw guard on the bed to steady this and control the movement when breaking through. To gauge the height and width of cut, accurately mark both bed and fence with prominent depth and width-on-cut lines.

GUARDS

The Shaw guard - use as a pressure

The best pressure for the spindle moulder is the Shaw guard. This is a wooden pad perhaps 100 to 200mm long fastened to a leaf spring centrally held to a supporting bar. Pad width varies according to use; see later notes. The pad is often cut away for cutter clearance when used as a top pressure for over-cutting, but otherwise use a plain pad with end curves front and rear.

The Shaw guard can be used as a top or side pressure, or two can be used together, either mounted from the same support or individually fitted to the fence and bed. Most types need pre-loading manually for pressure. On some machines the contact pad is held by individual leaf springs at each end, with vertical screw adjustment from a support on the table to control both setting and applied pressure.

The Shaw type is easily the best type, having a large contact area to give even pressure yet allowing a smooth feed. Some wax the underside of the pad and the table to combine effective pressure without making the feed difficult or irregular. This adds safety, as excessive feed-resistance gives a jerky feed movement, a poor finish and more chance of kick-back or accident.

Use as a guard

As its name suggests, the Shaw guard acts both as a very good pressure and as a guard to protect the user by covering the cutters when timber is not in place.

With workpieces which are more or less square in section the top guard pad should extend from the fence to the outer edge, and the side guard pad from the bed to virtually meet

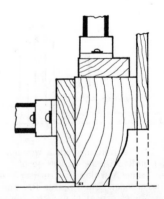

Fig. 180 Use wide Shaw guard pads to enclose the cutter when timber is not in position. Off-set the springs to apply pressure directly opposite the flat vertical or under faces.

the top pad. This boxes in the cutters, so that parts are fed end to end in a continuous stream with the last piece pushed through with a follow-up block. When feeding parts individually leave a small gap for a spike to feed between and past the pressures. Naturally the gap should be too narrow for fingers to reach the cutters.

When a single top guard only is used on wide board edging make the pad much wider than the furthest extent of the cutters. When a side guard is used on wide boards fed face-against the fence, make the pad much wider than the highest point of the cutters. Pad width and distance from pad end to the cutters at both ends relates mathematically to the gap between pad and fence or bed as given on Fig. 181. This gives pad sizes for single pads, also the distance from pad-end to cutters with all pads. Following this guide safely guards the cutterhead when timber is not in place. Pads made to these dimensions give a high degree of safety but may, however, prove unwieldy in use. If this proves impractical, size the Shaw guard to give the best possible protection in the circumstances.

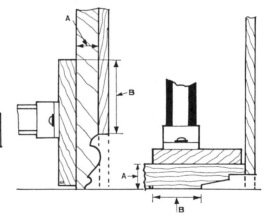

A	6	10	12	15	20	22	30	40	mm.	Max.
B	40	65	90	140	165	190	320	400	mm.	Min.

181

Fig. 181 When using only a single Shaw guard pressure make the pad extra wide. Dimensions A and B should correspond to the table. Distance B should also correspond to the distance of the leading and trailing pad ends from the cutterhead.

Spring pressures

Another type used either as side or top pressure is the leaf-spring. Normally fit one side or top spring before the cutter-head and a second after it. With small sections use two pairs of springs; one pair from the side and the second from the top. Leaf springs are very insensitive and give line contact only. Few operators like or actually use them, though makers persist in fitting them. They tend to resist forward movement on meeting the workpiece and lack the smooth feed possible with a Shaw guard. They do not guard the cutterhead and extra guards are always essential, so throw them away and use only the Shaw guard type.

Custom pressures

Custom pressures can be made from hardwood blocks. The concertina type has band-saw cuts alternately from each end to just short of the opposite end, with cuts close together and parallel to the contact face. With this type light pressure is applied over a large area. Make the part next to the timber thicker to round-off at infeed for easy entry and at the out-feed to avoid flicking. Make them in various lengths and thicknesses to vary spring pressure and to cover the cutters, as with a Shaw guard pad. Slot or drill for hold-down bolts.

The finger type type has several sawcuts close together but at an angle to the contact face. They form a series of close, springy fingers which press individually on the work and give flexible but light pressure. The fingers should be narrow and flexible but not so thin that they snap off. If using hardwood, make sawcuts along the grain by cross-cutting the board at an angle. Alternatively, glue together a number of thin strips and spacing pieces to make up a laminate.

Pressures of this type are fitted with the fingers trailing in the cut to act as an anti-kick-back trap, but give little resistance to forward feed. If a workpiece has to be drawn back first stop the machine, then slacken off the pressure.

Plate 59 The Shaw guard on this Inca spindle moulder is cantilevered from the rear.

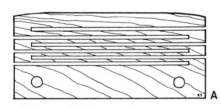

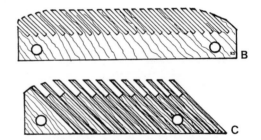

SAFETY AIDS

All these are essential with any hand-fed machine as, unlike fingers, they are easily replaced. A push-stick should be purpose-made; don't use just any old piece of scrap that happens to be lying about. Shape the contact end to a vee cut-out for end contact or fix a spike to dig in at any point. Taper both to a small section which readily passes guards and pressures. Make the opposite end comfortable to grip as an aid to safety, a push-stick is more likely to be used if it looks and feels right.

It should also be handy when needed. Permanently fasten it to the spindle moulder using a piece of cord long enough for normal use but without danger of becoming tangled (which obviously can be dangerous in a kick-back). The cord keeps the push stick where needed and prevents others borrowing and forgetting to return it. It is also practical to provide a box under the machine table to hold the push stick in readiness for use.

Fig. 182 Custom pressures:
A - concertina type.
B - individual finger type.
C - laminate type.

Follow-up blocks are sometimes better than push-sticks for feeding through the last piece of a small section.

Securely fit some form of comfortable handle, as otherwise, being flat on the table or against the fence, there is little to push against. The handle can be a rounded block, a small section of wall handrail, a large drawer handle, or a push-stick cut off at an angle. Most woodworking shops abound with ideal off-cuts. The follow-up piece proper, is best if screwed to a commonly used block so this can adapt to any section. Fix the handle so that both this and knuckles can feed clear past the guards without fouling.

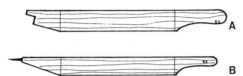

A

B

Fig. 183 Above: Typical push sticks:
Notch type A pushes against the rear of the workpiece.
Spike type B digs-in at any point and is usually held in the left hand in preference to direct hand contact.

Right: Typical push-blocks showing, on the left, as used against the end of wide boards whilst, on the right, with a nailed-on section as a follow-up block. Make sure the handle clears the Shaw guard in feeding past.

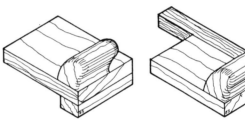

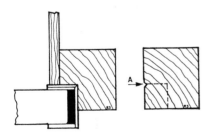

Fig. 184 Left: Rebating cutters should project above the top of the cutterblock, and need relieving along the top edge. Break through the fence to leave a clean rebate edge.

Right: Scribe along the rebate line A, before machining, to prevent spelching beyond.

REBATING

Rebating is possible on any cutterblock using a simple square cutter having a top bevelled edge. When set in the normal way for deep rebates cutters have excessive projection. To reduce projection set the top edge of the cutter slightly above the cutterblock so that rebate depth is limited by the spindle above, not the cutterblock itself. The planing circle in this case is also the rebating circle, and using a cutterblock in this way is termed "sinking" the head. It is commonly used for rebating and deep scotias, etc. A square head is not really suitable for rebating; use a Whitehill or another circular head.

The cutter has a scraping action along a top edge and tends to spelch on the outer corner. Whilst slowing down the feed rate improves this, it doesn't cure spelching on difficult timbers, but there are several techniques that do.

One is to use a through-fence to support timber where spelching occurs. This is effective only if the timber is pressed firmly against the fence and if the fence remains sharp. (See earlier notes).

The second way is to scribe the timber along the rebate line using a joiner's scribe. This severs long fibres so that they break off only up to this line when rebating. The rebate edge and scribe line must correspond absolutely to be successful, but mis-alignment is likely unless that timber is perfectly flat, square and straight. It is possible to fix a scriber to the machine infeed fence in line with the top edge of the cutter to scribe the timber immediately prior to rebating and keep perfect alignment. This needs extra pressure to keep timber and scribe in contact and may, in fact, drag in the cut to give an erratic feed movement.

The third way is to form a scribe on the top edge of the rebate cutter to scribe ahead of the main cut and prevent it spelching beyond. The vee formed in the corner slightly weakens the section remaining, but this is only a problem when double-rebating narrow glazing bars. Cutter projection can be decreased to reduce this, but then is less effective.

The fourth way is to grind the top edge of the cutter slightly over-square. This gives less of a scraping and spelching action, but obviously forms a slightly out-of-square rebate which might not be acceptable. Normally a rebate cutter is ground slightly under-square to touch only at the leading point but still form a perfectly square corner.

Scribing cutters

Scribing cutters are often fitted as separate, special-purpose cutters to the cutterhead itself. Set these slightly higher than the top edge of the rebate cutters and to project slightly more. Rebate and scribe cutters can be set on the spindle moulder, but more easily and more accurately on a setting stand. Fix a flat piece of hardwood parallel to the cutterhead arbor spaced for correct cutter projection. Grind the top edge of all cutters at a slight clearance angle tip to root and front to back. First set scribe cutters to scribe a line 15 - 20mm long when rotating the head. Set the main cutters to barely scrape the face of the timber and with the top edge mid-way in the vee-cut formed by the scribe cutters.

Purpose-made rebate cutterheads, such as some Whitehill types and special circular-heads, have scribing cutters fitted. Some have a saw-like form to give a more effective scribing action with less projection. The same setting guides apply as for single-point types.

Rebate heads are also available with throw-away tungsten carbide cutters which always align correctly, so replacing worn and damaged cutters is quick, simple and precise. With all scribed-type heads the vee shows in the corner, so use it only for hidden rebates. Where a rebate is purely decorative other methods must be used.

Rebate and plane

One way to form a spelch-free rebate is to rebate and plane simultaneously. A single cutter can be ground to both rebate and plane, but needs a square internal corner which is troublesome to grind and needs considerably more grinding from a blank than individual cutters. It is ideal for small pieces, but unusual for large rebates in door casings and similar.

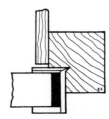

Fig. 185 Form the rebate cutter to a point to scribe whilst rebating.

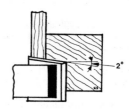

Fig. 186 Making the cutter over-square (by about 2 degrees only) reduces spelching and gives a cleaner face, but the edge is out of square, dulls more quickly and tends to burn on abrasive timber.
To prevent burning even on long runs with dulled points, some make cutters under-square so that only the point touches, see Fig. 188.

Fig. 187 Purpose-made rebating cutterblock.

Double-rebating

All regular rebating methods have a basic fault. One face has a scraping cut to give a woolly finish even with sharp cutters on good quality timber, a condition which rapidly worsens as cutters dull.

If the rebate has to be smooth for appearances sake, plane both rebate faces at separate settings. Form the rebate in the normal way then, after turning the workpiece end for end and reversing height-to-width setting of the cutterhead, plane the scraped face only at a second pass. Timber must be flat and square and cutter settings precise. If not a stepped corner forms, or the previously-planed face is scraped, or the previously scraped-face skipped. All spoil the finish and, as they are difficult to avoid, use this technique only in exceptional circumstances.

Tilted-spindle rebating

With a tilting-spindle machine set cutters to form a vee cut-out, but tilt the arbor to produce a square rebate. Feed timber in the usual way - flat against the fence or flat to the bed. This may seem an odd technique, but it planes both faces giving neither break-out nor spelching. Because of throw the edges have to be slightly curved and out-of-square, so take care in cutter development - or use a profile grinder. Setting for rebate height and depth is strange because height adjustment also alters depth; so set height first.

This method is also possible with a non-tilting spindle, but not so simply. Set the cutterhead as for a tilting spindle with an undercut rebate, but use an angled fence and bed to hold the timber at 30 degrees. With workpieces roughly square in section use a Shaw guard side pressure with a 30/60 degree vee rebate to contact the outer corner only. Oblong sections need two Shaw guards with pads having a 30 degree bevel.

To keep the wedge-bed small and the cutterhead low, this method should only be used for small rebates and relatively narrow pieces. Alternatively, use it to edge-rebate wide boards by tilting the opposite way - rebating as an overcut. This needs a bevelled support for the rebate to avoid dipping on exiting. The drawbacks are as previously detailed for over-cutting, but these are made more complex because of the angle.

GROOVING

Several different tools are used for grooving: loose cutters fitted to regular heads; a grooving, drunken or wobble saw; and specially made grooving heads.

Grooving cutters used on square blocks are normally of the reinforced or humped-back type to compensate for their narrow width and relatively big projection. Some Whitehill blocks have provision for adding cutter reinforcement when grooving, so regular-thickness grooving cutters can be used.

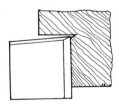

Fig. 188 Above: Form a scribe cutter to a point and with a slight angle.

Below: Set the plain rebate cutter just below the scribe mark.

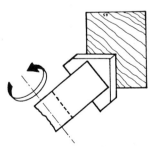

Fig. 189 An angled cutter on a tilted spindle give rebates which are both spelch and scrape-free.

By staggering the cutters, it is simple enough to vary the groove size from the actual width of the grooving cutter to slightly less than double this. Because they are no longer directly opposite they run slightly out of dynamic balance, so limit staggering with a single pair of cutters to narrow grooves only. With wide grooves use two pairs of identical grooving cutters and stagger in pairs to retain perfect dynamic balance.

If both grooving cutters are ground square-ended, feed has to be slow to avoid spelching on brittle timbers. To prevent this make one cutter with top and bottom scribes, also slightly wider than the matching square-ended cutter. As with scribe cutters used for rebating, setting has to be precise - but the effect is the same. The vee for the scribe cutter is easily formed on the edge of a square grinding wheel.

Alternatively, form both cutters to a flat and a scribe combination, one scribe up and the other down. Shape small bevels on both edges of a square grinding wheel in order to grind the main cutting edge and scribe bevel at the same time.

For wide grooves, a Whitehill head with scribe cutters top and bottom is probably the best tool. For grooves wider than the head make two or more passes. Scribe cutters are not needed when grooving and rebating at the same time.

Drunken saw

The traditional tool for grooves is the drunken or wobble saw; a thick, heavy saw clamped between double-wedged collars. The saw tilts so that the groove formed is wider than the saw kerf. This is controlled by the amount the adjusting section is twisted to the fixed section of the collars. Setting marks on the two show the saw tilt, not the actual groove width which varies with the diameter and kerf of the saw. Groove width setting has to be by trial and error.

The saw gives a poor finish as it cuts with a series of points; also the base of the groove is slightly curved. Both faults can be resolved by setting the saw to mid-position of tilt and dressing flat with a jointing stone. This can be done safely by barely breaking through a fence and using a fine jointing stone to dress. Fix the stone to a wooden arm pivoted on the outfeed fence and move the arm end up and down to pass the stone fully across the saw in dressing; this avoids ridging it. (A ridged stone rounds the upper and lower teeth.) Set the amount of dress by adjusting either or both fences. Keep hands well clear of the saw in dressing, and wear grinding goggles. Dress the saw until each point shows a witness mark as a filing guide.

Sharpen the teeth with a file held level but at a large side angle. File until the dressing mark disappears along the full tooth width at the same time to give a flat-cutting tooth. This is easier to form using a hook-tooth instead of the conventional peg-tooth so the front and top can be filed individually. Prior to dressing, set teeth outwards at the forward leading face.

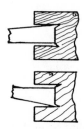

Fig. 190 Use cutters with left and right-hand scribe points for spelch-free grooving.

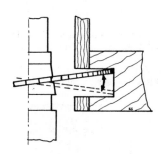

Fig. 191 A drunken saw in cross-section.

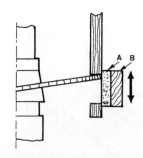

Fig. 192 Dress the saw flat by barely breaking through the fence and using a fine stone A supported on a pivoting arm B.

Plate 60 Leuco disposable-cutter type rebating head.

Plate 61 Above: Oppold variable angle head with disposable cutters.

Plate 62 Below: Oppold adjustable grooving head with disposable main and scribe cutters.

The problem with all these tools is dynamic imbalance when tilted because the two halves of the saw are not directly opposite. Vibration worsens with increase in tilt and/or diameter, so restrict tilt to within acceptable limits of vibration.

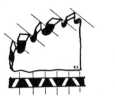 

Fig. 193 File saws with a large front and top angle to leave a flat-topped tooth.

Other types

Solid grooving saws, or those with brazed-on tips, were commonly used, but the general trend is towards one or two-piece tungsten carbide tipped cutters - because they are dependable, easy to use, long lasting and safe. All have main cutters and scribes - which must be kept at their proper heights.

One works on the same principle as a wobble or drunken saw, but uses a twisted body with hard tips instead of a conventional saw. It is similar to , but better than, the conventional wobble saw. Others use the split-tool principle in which the two halves are spaced by removable shims. These give a solid feel to the head but are messy to adjust and their many faces trap chips and dirt. Some tools have screw adjustment for infinate width variation via a setting dial. Both types retain dynamic balance regardless of width. There are several versions of the throw-away-cutter type of head for this application, but generally for wide grooves only.

CAUTION: Grooving tools project more than others and extra care is needed in guarding them, either by a guard fastened to the through-fence or an extra wide Shaw guard pad.

BEVELLING AND CHAMFERING.

These are formed using cutters mounted at an angle, and the Whitehill type is ideal for small bevels and chamfers. When forming a large angle, the cutting edge has to be slightly bowed to produce a flat face. These cuts are simpler with a tilting spindle using a simple planing block as there are no complications with cutter profile. Some throw-away heads have tilting jaws. These allow straight cutters to be tilted up to 45 degrees to form any angle whilst running timber flat against the table or fence.

MOULD PROFILES

Woodworking mouldings are traditionally based on just a few basic forms; even the most complex moulds merely combine two or more classical moulds with perhaps and extra fillet here and there. The basic shapes are ovolo, ogee, lamb's tongue (cyma recta and cyma reversa), half and quarter rounds (pencil rounds, quadrants and bull-nose) and torus, plus a few combinations of chamfers and bevels.

Moulds can be Roman type based on true quarter and semi-circles, or Grecian types based on quarter and semi-elipse, parabola or hyperbola. All these shapes can be drawn geometrically; see the examples. It is usual for all moulds combined in a single profile, part, or group, all to be either Grecian or Roman type - but rarely a mixture.

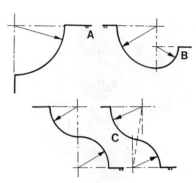

Fig. 194 Roman moulds are based on parts of circles.

Ovolos and coves at A and B are usually quarter circles. (All moulds can be viewed from either side to make two different shapes such as ovolo or cove, but geometric construction is the same).

Cyma recta and cyma reversa, lamb's tongue and ogee, are shown at C; left, as two quadrants when width is half depth or; right, as part quadrants when width is slightly less than half depth.
A bull-nose is a half-round D.

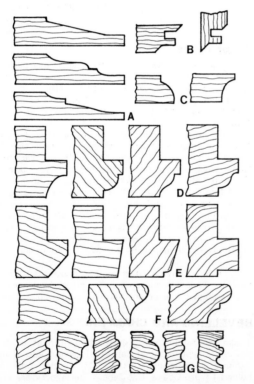

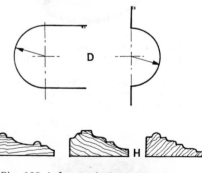

Fig. 195 A few typical moulds:
A - raised panels.
B - mitre glue joint.
C - drop table leaf moulds.
D - traditional sash sections.
E - modern sash sections.
F - edge moulds.
G - decorative moulds.
H - bolection moulds.

Fillets are an integral part of some moulds and must be in correct proportion to look right. Those who originated them had a great respect for these qualities. Cutters forming fillets parallel to the table are worked with a scraping action and may give a woolly finish or a spelched corner.

Plate 63 These Forest City tools show the many profiles available.

Fig. 196 Grecian moulds are based on quarter elipses for ovolos A and coves C, half parabolas for lamb's tongue and ogee B and bull-noses as semi-elipses D.

Proportions can be varied more than with Roman moulds and shapes are better in my opinion.

In all cases the lines are divided-up equally, then points where corresponding lines cross as shown are joined with a continuous curve.

To cure this slow down the feed or carefully break through a wooden fence to act as chipbreaker. A better cure for both is to form moulds using either a tilted spindle or an angled fence/bed. This gives a better cut and also reduces cutter projection. See section on rebates.

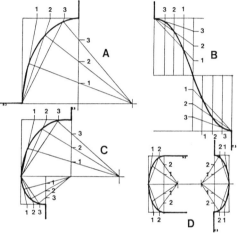

Combination moulds

With crown moulds and similar it is unusual to form the full depth with a single cutter. All combination moulds naturally divide up and can be formed by separate overlapping cutters. They could be mounted on a single cutterhead, or more conveniently fitted in sequence and the mould formed at several subsequent passes.

There are some advantages in the latter. Each cut is relatively light, and adjustment of individual cuts to match properly is a simply a matter of spindle height or fence adjustment; easier than aligning several cutters on the head itself. Combination moulds can often be formed using regular shaped Whitehill cutters, but one-piece cutters are always special. Joints between mould sections should be external corners, hard to form on a one-piece cutter, but easy by overlapping two cutters.

The disadvantages and cures of moulding as sections are: possible instability in later stages of moulding - see "deep non-symmetrical moulds"; longer running time - spindle moulder runs are short so this counts for little; and possibility of spelching on surfaces previously finished - plan so that spelching from one cut is removed by following cuts.

Fig. 197 Combination moulds are based on several shapes in combination and can be formed with individual cutters mounted on the same block - but more easily at separate settings.

Mould blending

Pencil rounds, bull-noses and similar shapes should blend perfectly into adjacent faces in theory, but this is not practical as any slight fault in flatness or squareness of the timber gives a mis-match. This looks untidy and unprofessional, especially with a high-gloss finish. Mis-matches can be sanded to blend better, but this takes time and never looks right. As a fillet-type mis-match looks very poor most operators deliberately off-set the profile, so the mis-match then forms as a wavering line which is less noticable.

These problems grow worse the nearer the cutter is to an 'ideal' shape, so don't attempt perfection. Instead, form the cutter with a lead-in angle of about 10 degrees for both face and edge. Allow 3mm projection beyond the blend line on small radii and proportionately more on large ones. The intersection lines these then form have a more acceptable appearance where planing is not perfect. When surfaces are to be face-sanded make the moulded profile slightly deeper to compensate.

If the part for pencil-rounding is relatively thin, machine the timber flat on the spindle moulder table and edge-plane and mould at the same time with a one-piece cutter. (See edge-planing). Form the edge square - a lead-in angle is not needed - and allow extra width when pre-sizing. Don't try this method with the workpiece flat against the fence to undercut the edge; it gives problems and could be dangerous.

Edge-plane whilst bull-nosing to give a clean edge. Form the cutter with a lead-in angle of between 20 and 30 degrees, or even more. A bull-nose is rarely a true 180 degree semi-circle, normally it is a smaller arc of a larger circle. The same profile is usually suitable for bull-nosing boards of slightly different thicknesses. With thick boards make the shape a semi-elipse rather than a semi-circle.

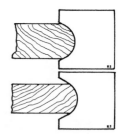

Plate 64 Under-cutting a raised panel using a through-fence and Shaw guard on a Startrite spindle moulder.

Fig. 198 Left: When corner-rounding angle the contact faces about 10 degrees from vertical and horizontal to form an acceptable mould blend.

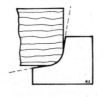 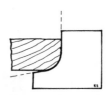

GENERAL MOULDING

There are two basic ways of forming most moulds: with the cutter above the workpiece, an overcut; or cutting below, an undercut.

An overcut is used when panel raising or when forming a deep mould on a small section of timber. A Shaw guard holds down the piece securely with its underface flat on the table so that it remains reasonably stable throughout the cut. The mould is thicknessed accurately but is prone to spoilage and violent kick-back if timber accidently lifts out of contact with the table. This is likely with a bowed piece, also with a long thin piece, if allowed to 'bounce' in feeding.

Centre: When full-depth edge moulding only angle at the under-face.

Right: Angle bull-nose cutters in a similar way. The same cutter can bull-nose boards of slightly different thickness.

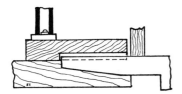

Fig. 199 Section through an overcut on a raised panel. Note the extra wide Shaw guard pad.

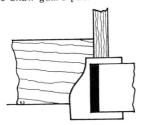

Fig. 200 Mould shallow edge cuts with the workpiece flat on the table.

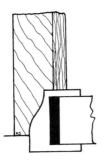

Fig. 201 Mould shallow face cuts with the workpiece flat against the fence.

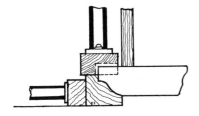

Fig. 202 Small moulds are more stable as an overcut.

Wherever practical form the mould as an undercut. This gives less risk of accident and, if the workpiece accidently lifts from the table, it simply moves clear of the cut with little danger or spoilage or kick-back. If the cut is roughly equal depth-to-width, for example, a 45 degree bevel, timber can be moulded either flat on the table or upright against the fence. Usually it doesn't matter which, although long boards are more stable if fed upright.

When depth-to-width is not equal set cutter depth (projection) to the smaller dimension and feed the workpiece either flat or upright to suit - unless there are other over-riding reasons not to. By keeping cutter projection small the fence and bed gaps are also small and the operation safer. This may involve edge-shaping long, thin boards flat on the table. The weight from the overhung parts may possibly spring it away from the table at the point of cut. To avoid this use outrigger supports at infeed and outfeed.

Setting pressures

When forming a wide mould, make sure that the Shaw guard for side pressure is longer than the gap width, otherwise parts fed singly can be forced into the fence gap when entering or leaving, to kick-back or snipe. (Some allow more length than really needed so that these defects can be trimmed off.) It is common practice and safer to fit a side pressure in line with the mould to reduce chattering at this point. Use a deep pad to cover the exposed cutter gap and apply pressure mainly opposite the solid part of the fence.

A small section may become unstable for the last few inches on leaving the infeed fence, and which normal pressures may not control. This can be lessened by pushing each piece through with the following piece rather than moulding short lengths individually.

Small sections

Avoid moulding small sections, if possible, as they smash and break too readily. If unavoidable run as an overcut with the underface flat on a support and hold down with a top pressure. Set a Shaw guard so that the cut-out just clears the cutters. This keeps full-length contact with the mould top face and avoids a possible jam.

If the workpiece is small in relation to the cut, vibration problems increase dramatically, so small pieces need pressing down on the table and against the fence by two Shaw guards. Where the section is to small to use this particular combination, rebate out the continuous edge of a Shaw guard pad, and round-in from each end for easy entry and exit. Set the rebate on the outer corner of the timber, and apply light vertical and horizontal pressure before securing. For regular use twist the pad the opposite way round so that the rebate faces out.

Leading and back up pieces

Even with all these precautions the Shaw guard may tilt and deflect timber into the fence or bed gap when entering the first section and when pulling-out the last. Keep the Shaw guard level by using scrap pieces to lead and back-up the moulds. Make them the same thickness as the mould if using only one Shaw guard, or the same section if using two.

Before starting the cut grip a scrap piece with the Shaw guard at the outfeed but clear of the cutterhead. This keeps the pad level as the timber is first fed in, and is pushed out by the first piece. The same piece can also push the last part completely through to leave a cleaner and smoother cut, or stop just short of the cutters allowing the last piece to be pulled through from the outfeed.

Make sure that the follow-up piece it is close to hand when moulding, otherwise the machine is left running with the piece in the cut as you hunt around.

Spacer guides

Where an undercut leaves little fence and undersurface on the mould it can become unstable on leaving the infeed fence. Outer guides and pressures help to control this, but for the best results use a spacer guide beyond the cutterhead to steady the deepest point of the cut. Setting and alignment has to be absolutely accurate, of course, and this isn't easy if the spacer fits directly on the fence. Instead fix the spacer guide to a wooden bed to allow fine independent setting. Use this with a through-fence, leaving a gap beneath for the bed support and spacer guide. With a spacer guide it is practical to fit a Shaw guard directly opposite the cut - but use a follow-up piece and take all precautions previously outlined.

Deep moulds

Deep mouldings need excessive cutter projection when a single cutter forms the whole mould, but cutter projection should be small. A single cutter also gives a heavy and dangerous cut for hand-fed operations and has to be specially shaped.

With deep moulds it is better to divide up the profile into individual cuts moulded at separate set-ups. This reduces weight in all cuts. It also reduces cutter projection beyond the cutterhead and by 'sinking' the head into the mould it narrows the fence gap.

Complex moulds usually combine several different shapes which can be formed as individual cuts using regular, shaped Whitehill cutters. The cut can be made as a series of deepening steps, each new cut registering against the spacer guide, but this needs many different settings. A better way is to form the deepest cut first from the opposite face as a shallow cut, then turn the moulding end for end for following passes. Run the mould section formed at the first operation against the spacer guide for all remaining cuts.

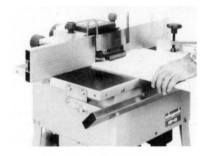

Plate 65 Over-cutting a raised panel on a Scheppach machine, with this clamped to a sliding table. The guard is raised for clarity.

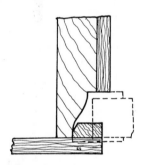

Fig. 203 Use a spacer guide on the wooden bed to support the deepest point of the cut.

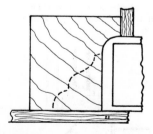

Fig. 204 The first cut on a large cove should be full depth but shallow.

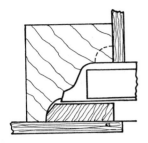

Fig. 205 Second stage, using a spacer guide to support the mould fully across the fences.

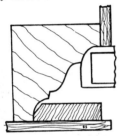

Fig. 206 Final stage with the spacer guide in the same position.

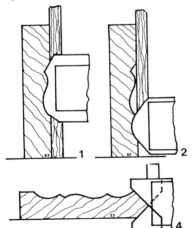

Fig. 207 Stages in forming a crown moulding from a flat section, showning sequence 1 to 4. Right: Showing in dotted outline the waste if moulded from a square.

Form each section from the nearest face so that the cutter never projects more than half mould depth. If the shape is one continuous curve there could be a problem in matching cuts where they merge, as timber rarely runs the same twice. In most cases cutters can overlap at the external corners. Because of this the two cuts can vary to one another without destroying the profile and, in addition, a perfectly sharp corner forms without need of grinding tricky internal corners in the cutter.

Tilting spindles

On machines with a tilting spindle, deep moulds can be formed without excessive projection by tilting to give roughly equal cutter projection top and bottom. Moulds can be machined from the squared-up section, or can be partially relieved by pre-bevelling or rebating. In both cases feed one flat face down and the other against the fence using regular pressures for control. If a large relief cut is made, fit a matching support on the infeed fence. Matching is easier if the pre-cut is a rebate. Use a spacer guide on the outfeed fence.

The same technique is possible, but more difficult, using a vertical spindle and angling the timber. Form a bevel on the surfacer or, for greater accuracy, by feeding on a vee-shaped bed on the thicknesser, then place this face-against the spindle moulder fence.

Crown moulds

Crown moulds are often formed from a flat, wide section rather than a square piece. This saves timber as a smaller section is needed, less is cut to waste and cutter projection is smaller to make operation safer. Mould it with the wide face to the fence which, being planed, is truer than a relief bevel. It leaves a triangular gap when in position for easier bedding.

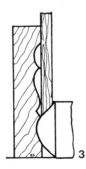

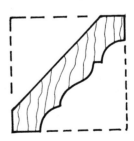

Surface and thickness the board to leave as a square-edged section. Draw out the profile on both ends to avoid error, but make sure you reverse the profile at the opposite end. If practical, first machine the centre section then work outwards to keep the mould stable against the fence. During final passes close to the edges, the remaining support may be cut away, so fit a spacer guide to keep it stable, or form high points near both edges to barely skim the face.

Finally add corner bevels, feeding mould up and back-face flat on the table. Both bevels can be formed at the same time, or individually. Always work flat-face down with an overcut for the inner bevel and an undercut for the rear bevel. Machine off the square corner to a point exactly on the edge line, or off-set the outfeed fence and plane a little off to make sure it cleans up.

When forming true rounds use a quarter-round cutter and turn at each pass so square faces go against fence and table.

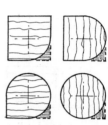

Fig. 208 Sequence in forming a round section.

EDGE MOULDING

When full-depth edge-moulding with fences aligned, the cutters may skip parts of the original planed edge if this wavers even slightly. To cure this, off-set the fences so that the spindle acts as a surfacer to fully clean up the edge and form a smoother and more consistant edge-profile. Set the infeed fence back to just clean up the edge, but leave the outfeed fence exactly in line with the deepest point of the mould.

In setting, initially have both fences in line and slightly back from the planing circle. Fit a top Shaw guard to steady the cut, then feed-in the first piece keeping it hard against the infeed fence until the leading end laps the outfeed fence by 50 - 75 mm. Stop the machine, leaving the workpiece held in place by the Shaw guard, then split the through-fence and adjust the outfeed fence until it barely buts against the moulded edge. Check the cut depth and, if wrong, adjust the infeed fence, then feed in the normal way.

The cutterblock removes timber in doing this, so allow extra width in preparation. It can also clean up sawn or rough edges and will edge-straighten bent or rough timber to a certain extent, as does a surfacer, so some preparation work can be skipped. See Figs. 175 and 176.

Plate 66 Edge-moulding on such as this sash frame is always better when using a feed unit such as this Holz-Her.

Thin beads

This technique is used for easy production of thin beads which are difficult to mould in finished size as they tend to flex, smash and jam. Instead of finish-sizing the beads, plane random width boards to a thickness equal to the bead width needed. Set the spindle to straighten, clean up and edge-mould by off-setting the infeed fence enough to remove saw marks. First mould both edges of all boards on the spindle, then saw off both beads on a clean-cutting saw and return to the spindle for further edge-moulding, sawing off, and so on, until only a thin waste piece remains from each. The beads might be acceptable if cleanly sawn, but if they are not, follow the method described under 'Thickness moulding' to plane up the sawn edge.

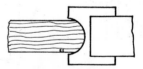

Fig. 209 Above: Set-up for edge-moulding and cleaning-up.

Below: Sawing-off the bead.

116

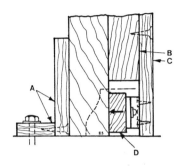

Fig. 210 Using a rigid outer guide A and spring-loaded infeed fence D. The extra-thick strip fence B is fastened to the regular fence C.

Using an outer guide

A rigid outer guide can be used to stabilise boards fed through upright. Fasten this to the table with the board a good fit between this and the fence, and use only a top Shaw guard.

Possibly fit an outward-pressing spring near the cutter-head on the infeed fence to keep timber in tight contact with the guide at this point. The spring must be recessed to project only slightly beyond the infeed fence. Projection can be altered by varying the thickness of either the spring or the wooden fence. Add a second spring at a higher point if the workpiece is deep.

With this type of set-up boards must be straight and equal in thickness, and the fences and guide accurately set. If they are not, the boards could jam or chatter.

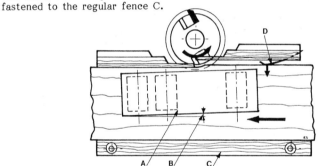

Fig. 212 When using a mechanical feed unit A for widthing, in conjunction with an outer guide C, angle this by about 6mm, B, to keep in contact with the guide.
Spring D is used for initial contact only.

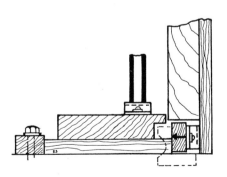

Fig. 211 Moulding drawer-sides to width using a spring-loaded infeed fence and fixed outer guide.

Widthing

Combined edging and widthing is common practice with drawer sides and similar sized parts. Prepare these by thicknessing, under-edging and sawing to width - to finally edge-mould and simultaneously width on the spindle moulder. Drawer sides could be thicknessed to width but, being thin, they tend to keel over when fed individually through a planer, or chatter when fed as a pack. Moulding to width on the spindle moulder is simple and better.

Set the outfeed fence as for edge moulding with a wood spring on the infeed fence to push the drawer side "out". A spring could be used on the outfeed fence also, but a fixed fence is more stable.

The guide should be a straight piece of hardwood fastened to the table parallel to and the correct distance from the outfeed fence. Feed the sides between the guide and the pressure, and follow up each with the next. Use a push-stick or push block for the last piece or, preferably, use a mechanical feed for this type of operation.

117

Thicknessing

It is feasible to 'thickness' thin sections using the same technique, either edge-planing or edge-moulding. This is the final part of the 'thin beads from wide boards' method described earlier. Planing rather than edge-moulding is the prefered last cut because this has a smaller and less-severe cutting action with less chance of breakage. With rebated beads the final cut is edge planing and rebating. Shape the fixed guide to the reverse of the mould to seat this better and give a steadier and a less vibration-prone feed action.

TYPES OF JIGS

Short pieces fed individually butted end to end tend to dip into the fence and table gap to end-snipe. Feed is intermittant and marks form where the feed stops momentarily. Preferably mould pieces as long strips and cut to length afterwards. When short lengths are unavoidable, grip and feed these in some form of holding jig.

The simplest jig is a block at least double the length of the piece, of the same thickness, and with a cut-out at mid-length to house the workpiece. This makes the mould virtually a continuation of the jig, so effectively increasing its length for safer handling. The jig needs handles both at the leading and trailing ends, for example large dowels or blocks, and must be wide enough for the handles to miss the top pressure. Only top pressure is needed, side pressure is applied via the handles. Fit the blank in position and feed the assembly through as a single piece, using a steady and continuous movement to give the best finish.

The jig can have a top piece added incorporating brads to grip the workpiece firmly. The brads are best driven in by positioning the jig on the workpiece and tapping home. Take care that it butts against the back fence and stops, or the part may slip in machining or be moulded under-size. To eject the finished timber quickly, drill a large hole through the top piece and tap through on a rounded handle on the machine.

The Shaw guard presses on the jig, not the part, but has the same effect. If the jig is made large and heavy a top pressure may not be necessary, but still use a Shaw guard for protection. With a fully-bradded jig a full-depth cut is possible on the workpiece, using the top piece as a template guide against the fence.

A variation of the above uses a bradded and jigged template to accurately size and edge-mould straight tapered pieces. The jig itself is parallel, but has an angled back fence and end stops. Use it both for edging and for taper-cutting blanks from wide boards. The boards are initially equal in width to the wide end, plus the narrow end, plus saw-cut and edge-planing allowance. Angle the back fence for the piece to feed with the grain, i.e., thick end first. Make sure the workpiece is properly seated against the trailing end-stop or it could shift and spoil.

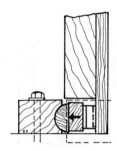

Fig. 213 Thicknessing a small bead using a spring-loaded infeed fence and shaped outer guide.

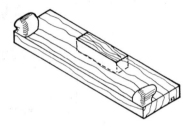

Fig. 214 Typical jig for feeding short and small parts.

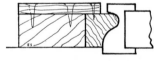

Fig. 215 Above: First cut in forming drawer pull. This could be a stop-mould if front and back-stops are fitted, or if the jig is made captive by a fixed pin through a slot in it.

Below: Second cut in forming a drawer pull with the mould seating against a rebate.

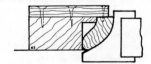

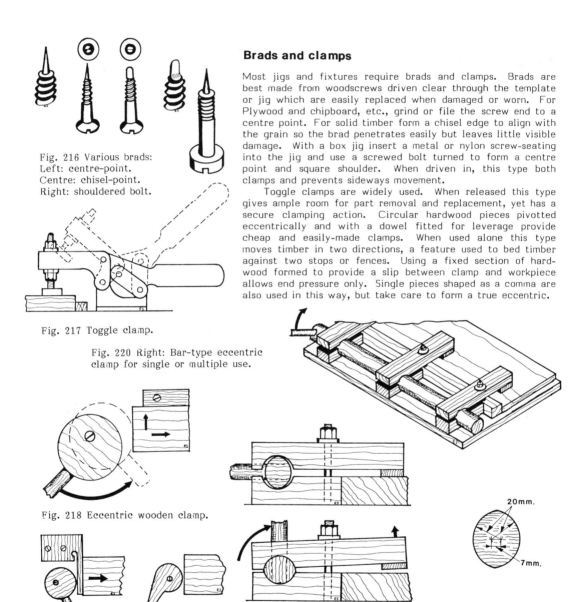

Brads and clamps

Most jigs and fixtures require brads and clamps. Brads are best made from woodscrews driven clear through the template or jig which are easily replaced when damaged or worn. For Plywood and chipboard, etc., grind or file the screw end to a centre point. For solid timber form a chisel edge to align with the grain so the brad penetrates easily but leaves little visible damage. With a box jig insert a metal or nylon screw-seating into the jig and use a screwed bolt turned to form a centre point and square shoulder. When driven in, this type both clamps and prevents sideways movement.

Toggle clamps are widely used. When released this type gives ample room for part removal and replacement, yet has a secure clamping action. Circular hardwood pieces pivotted eccentrically and with a dowel fitted for leverage provide cheap and easily-made clamps. When used alone this type moves timber in two directions, a feature used to bed timber against two stops or fences. Using a fixed section of hard-wood formed to provide a slip between clamp and workpiece allows end pressure only. Single pieces shaped as a comma are also used in this way, but take care to form a true eccentric.

Fig. 216 Various brads:
Left: centre-point.
Centre: chisel-point.
Right: shouldered bolt.

Fig. 217 Toggle clamp.

Fig. 220 Right: Bar-type eccentric clamp for single or multiple use.

Fig. 218 Eccentric wooden clamp.

Fig. 219 Left: Eccentric clamp with a slip.
Right: One-piece 'comma' clamp.

An eccentric clamp can also be made from an egg-shaped strip using half-round cutters on a piece too narrow to form a perfect full round. Use this type with a single clamp, or to operate several in-line clamps with a single movement. Adjust individual clamp pressures by means of the hold-down screws.

General purpose clamp

It is impractical to make individual holding jigs for every new part, so make a general purpose jig suitable for small parts of different width, length and thickness. One type, based on a French idea, has a wide stable base with a substantial support fastened vertically to this and with a reinforcing bracket. A large diameter hardwood disc turns eccentrically on a horizontal pivot and is operated via a lever and handle at the outside. The disc and handle are connected by a nut, bolt and bush through a slot in the support. The clamping thickness is varied by connecting the operating lever to alternative holes drilled through the disc.

Fig. 221 Left: Cutter head side of a general purpose jig.

Right: Operator's side

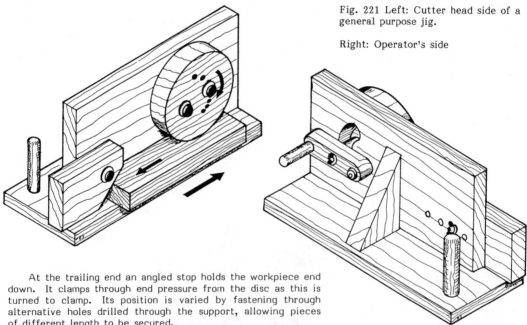

At the trailing end an angled stop holds the workpiece end down. It clamps through end pressure from the disc as this is turned to clamp. Its position is varied by fastening through alternative holes drilled through the support, allowing pieces of different length to be secured.

Narrow pieces overhang. Wide pieces are supported near the cutterhead by a strip bed against the fence (of equal thickness to the base). When feeding, the lever handle is held down and the trailing handle is used to push the assembly forward.

STOP MOULDING

Stop-moulding is moulding along only part of the workpiece by running the mould in from the leading end, starting part-way along and running out to the trailing end, or starting and stopping it within its length.

In some cases moulding may start and stop at more than one point, or even change profile at different points. Examples are the head, sills and transoms of windows which need different sections for alternate opening and fixed lights.

Stop-moulding gives a decorative effect to priory-type furniture or similar. It also simplifies tenoning of moulded window frames with mortise and tenon joints. (The mould stops short of the mortises, allowing simply-formed square shoulders to be used which do not need complicated scribing.) The practice is common on furniture to avoid difficult scribes, and to add interest to an otherwise plain part.

Use a top Shaw guard when stop moulding to steady the cut, but do not apply excessive pressure which might prevent easy movement towards and from the fence. Wax the Shaw guard pad and the table to make starting and stopping easier and safer. The points to start and stop can be indicated by guide lines, or controlled by stops. Guide lines can be clearly marked on the fence. Stops are fitted to a through-fence or the table.

First set-up the machine, then fit and break through a wooden fence. Mark prominent vertical lines on the fence where the longest point of the cutter passes through. Mark a thick horizontal line between the vertical lines, and above workpiece level, to show the effective width of the cutter.

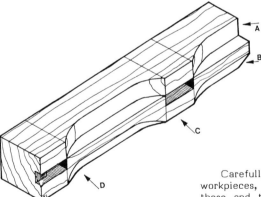

Fig. 222 In this window section the rebate and chamfer A and B are started and stopped at C and D for the mortises.

Carefully mark start and stop points on the top face of all workpieces, squaring the lines round from the mortises. Use these and the fence marks to show where to drop-on and pull-out when using a jig, or when setting the stops. With a Shaw guard fitted fence marks may be difficult to see, so repeat them on the wooden bed or table.

Running-in

Some moulds run-in from one end. These can be worked quite safely by feeding forward as normal then, after first slowing-down to a crawl so that tear-out reduces, simply stopping forward feed where needed. Without stopping the machine, lever the workpiece out of the cut simply and safely, pivotting on the remote end by pushing the trailing end outwards. Take care not to feed the workpiece forward in doing this.

If the mould has to be stopped precisely use a stop block. Fasten this to the outfeed fence or table. Position it against the end of the workpiece when the stop-line on the workpiece is opposite the right-hand vertical mark on the through-fence. Extend the through-fence if necessary.

Parts are often machined in pairs. When these have a symmetrical mould running in from one end, for example an ovolo, 45 degree bevel or quarter round, both cuts can be run-in. Feed one face down and the other face against the fence so that the mould runs-in from the leading end regardless of hand. Not all moulds are suitable as the sweep-out appears slightly different on the two pieces.

When the form is not symmetrical, for example a mould such as a lamb's tongue, both halves of a pair can still be run 'in' by using two pairs of opposite-hand cutters. Set one for an overcut and the other for an undercut. Run-in both from the leading end to give matching sweep-outs. Alternatively, both can be formed as an undercut by using cutters with the profile turned through 90 degrees.

Making opposite-hand cutters or different cutters just to do this, though, is hardly justified. The simpler alternative is to run one mould 'in' and the other 'out' after dropping-on - in both cases using the same setting.

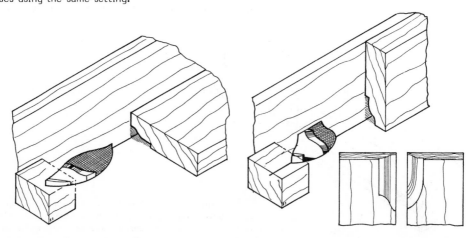

Fig. 223 Non-symmetrical moulds on pairs of parts can be stopped by running-in with an undercut from the same end (if the cutter profile is changed) - but the sweep-outs do not match.

Dropping-on

When the mould starts part way along the timber it has to be 'dropped-on', that is moved into the cut at the appropriate point before being fed forward. Moulding may run out to the trailing end, or run only part way involving dropping-on, feeding, then stopping and drawing-out. Some may require stop-moulding at more than one section.

With very small mouldings on heavy workpieces, for example, a pencil-round on a newel post, dropping-on can be safely carried out by an experienced spindle-hand using only a holding jig and a top Shaw guard. Taper the Shaw guard pad upwards away from the fence for easy entry width-ways. With larger moulds or lighter pieces take great care, and use aids such as a back stop, or cam and template.

Operation

Never drop-on by attempting to move the workpiece up to the fence in a parallel movement. Instead set the workpiece under the Shaw guard pressure so that its leading corner contacts the outfeed fence, but angled to clear the cutterhead. Securely hold the workpiece with both hands, preferably to the right of the cutterblock, and, using the opposite end as a controlling lever, carefully swing it towards the fence by pivotting on its leading corner in a gentle and controlled movement. Take care to avoid snatch, and do not to allow the piece to move back when starting the cut. Preferably feed slightly forward to make sure neither happens. Once in full contact with the fence, feed forward in the usual way.

Always use a top Shaw guard and make sure that the table surface is clean so that movement is smooth. If the table is slotted use hardwood strips to fill-in the slots level with the table top. Always start with both hands to the right-hand side of the cutterhead so that they are thrown clear should a kickback occur. By gripping at this point they also have better control in dropping-on.

The correct starting position for dropping-on is with the start mark on the timber and the left-hand mark on the fence or bed in alignment. It isn't easy to hit the correct position because the two marks are initially separated by a gap - and may not correspond when in contact. Preferably start slightly forward, but make no attempt to draw back once in the cut as this will kick-back. Instead move the timber clear of the cutters, draw back slightly, then drop-on a second time.

Back-stops

Dropping-on is dangerous because kick-back is likely, i.e., cutters can grab timber and throw it violently back at the operator. A Shaw guard helps to steady the part but preferably use a back-stop. Using a back-stop is not only safer, but quicker and more accurate. Most authorities recommend using a back-stop, even for small cuts, as does the writer.

The obvious place for a back-stop is secured to the table. It can be fastened to the infeed fence, but must extend from the fence, and both fence and back-stop must be secure. Fix the back-stop against the end of the workpiece when the start mark on it aligns with the extreme left-hand mark on the fence. The stop must be securely held, as a kick-back on dropping-on too quickly could shift both this and the workpiece.

Sometimes chips get trapped between timber and fence when dropping-on. After the first contact draw the timber clear so that chips are blown away before dropping-on a second time. Leave a small gap between back-stop and fence so that chips blow clear.

The back-stop must extend well away from the fence so that the workpiece is in full contact with it when in the drop-on position: i.e., angled to touch the outfeed fence but well clear of the cutterhead. In this way the timber is under control before the cutters start to grip. The Shaw guard pad should grip the workpiece when in the start position so that no sideways resistance is met in actually dropping-on.

A front-stop limits forward movement to prevent over-run, but need not extend much from the fence. When in contact with the front-stop draw out the trailing end of the workpiece, pivoting its leading corner on the front-stop.

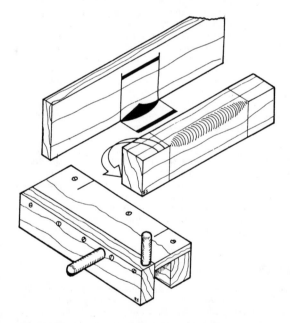

Fig. 224 Left: Mark vertical lines on the fence where the extreme points of the cutter break through. Mark the piece all round for the start and stop positions.

Below: The recommended sequence of dropping-on and stopping using front and backstops.

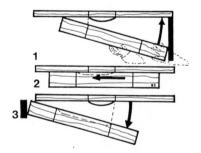

Left: Alternatively, use a holding jig and work to marked lines. Make the jig wide with an outer support and control handles.

Cam stops

With long workpieces a back-stop may not be practical, so nail or screw a 25mm thick hardwood template to the top face of the timber for use with a cam on the fence. Form a 45 degree trailing bevel where the mould begins - with the heel where the mould actually starts. Form a similar bevel at the mould stop point, but facing forward.

Securely fit a cam with 45 degree bevels at both ends to the fence, barely clear of the timber and to contact the template. The cam should be fractionally wider than the effective cutter width at furthest projection, just outside the vertical lines drawn on the through-fence, and project slightly more than the cutters. Thickness can be about 25mm.

The cam and template control both start and stop positions. Place the timber at an angle so the end contacts the outfeed fence, with the template edge in contact with the cam so that the cutters are clear of the timber.

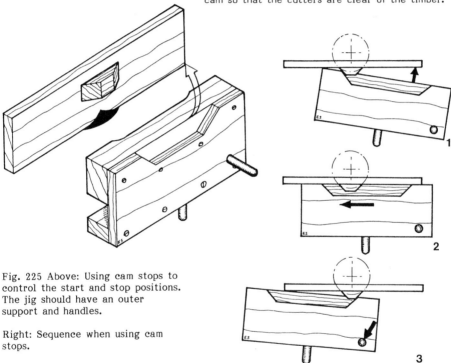

Fig. 225 Above: Using cam stops to control the start and stop positions. The jig should have an outer support and handles.

Right: Sequence when using cam stops.

Start the cutterhead and move the timber forward and in so the start bevel follows down the angled slope of the cam. This commences the cut safely and without chance of kick-back. It helps if the angled faces are smooth and polished. The stop cam feeds the piece out automatically and smoothly at the proper point. This method allows several stop moulds to be made on a single piece simply by adding start and stop bevels where needed on the template.

It is tedious to repeatedly nail the template in place if several workpieces are to be identically stop-moulded. Preferably make the template as part of an open-sided box fastening parts by a clamp at the leading end.

Moving table machines

Machines with a moving table offer a safer alternative to any of the above - and, in fact, the safest method of machining stopped moulds. One example is the Robinson spindle moulder with a swivelling table, lock and screw-adjusted movement. Set-up is made as previously described, then move the table clear of the cutterblock. Fit the workpiece against the fence and end-stop, and under the Shaw guard.

To drop-on, start the cutterhead, then release and move the table back into the operating position. Feed the workpiece forward in the usual way until against the stop block, then move the table out. The operation is under full mechanical control with the workpiece against the fences throughout.

Fig. 226 A box jig for stop-moulding with the template as part of the box top.

Plate 67 The Robinson EN/T spindle moulder table swivels, and has a screw-adjusted movement.

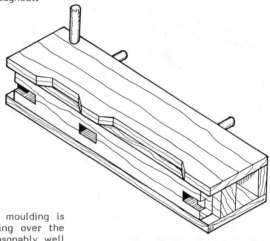

Most moulding is with the grain, but sometimes moulding is needed across the grain, for example, in rounding over the tops of uncapped newel posts. Cutters work reasonably well either with or across the grain, though a slower feed is needed for cross-grain moulding. Most end-grain work is on a narrow face, so certain precautions are essential as workpieces are unstable and prone to back-spelching as the cutters break through the trailing face.

Preferably use a tenoning attachment, or the spindle table itself if of the rolling type. With these the traverse is under mechanical control and one or more pieces can be clamped firmly in position to back-up one another. This gives a better cut than any other method, and much safer working conditions. To reduce break-out, use a backing piece to initially project slightly beyond the moulding line.

The full depth can be safely formed at a single pass because the clamp holds the timber firmly. Make the pieces slightly over-long for moulding and length trimming at the same time. On double-end trimming, gauge the first position from an end-stop, and the second from a sprung shoulder stop.

When moulding one end only, use a fixed stop to locate the opposite end. (See section on Tenoning.)

Plate 68 The table position of the Robinson EN/T is clearly seen from the front.

END GRAIN MOULDING

If the workpiece has a large cross-section it remains reasonably stable when end-wise against a through fence; examples are large newel posts or short, wide boards for pencil-rounding only. With these a large block-type back-up piece is all that is needed to keep the workpiece square and stable, provided the two are clamped together in some way and an undercut is used to mould only part of the depth. It is essential to use both a through-fence and wooden bed to give the smallest possible gap and continuous support to the parts. Grind the profile near to the top edge of the cutters, to leave the maximum amount of fence above the cutters.

Use the back-up piece to steady the cut and prevent spelching by feeding the two together underneath a top Shaw guard. Make sure the back-up piece is tightly held against the workpiece during the complete movement, perhaps 'G' clamping them together or fitting brads in the back-up piece to drive into the workpiece and lock the two together. Nail a replaceable facing to the back-up piece to allow a quick change for any profile.

Plate 69 Using a sliding table on a Startrite spindle moulder to end-mould parts safely. In addition to a Shaw guard a through-fence is needed. Edge moulding is a following operation with timber fed in the normal way to remove any spelching.

Fig. 227 Back-up block for end-trimming large sections or wide pieces. The face provides back-up to prevent spelching, and is a loose piece which can be replaced. Hold the workpiece to the back-up block securely using a clamp or brads.

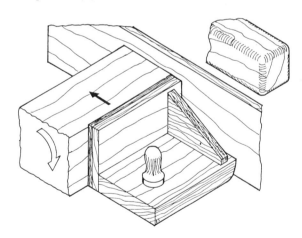

Plain table machines   Jig working

When dealing with narrower pieces that are less end-stable, make a wide jig with a large piece of plywood as a base to ride against the fence, and screw a back-up block to the right of centre. Grind the cutter narrow to cut the least amount from the jig base. Push the timber and the base against the fence to properly end-align them, then clamp firmly to the back-up block or base by any suitable means such as eccentric wooden or toggle clamps.

By using a sliding jig several pieces can be clamped horizontally and end-moulded together. This is an advantage as the set-up is more stable and each piece is firmly supported by the piece following, so there is less break-out.

It is impractical and dangerous to mould the full depth at a single pass with this set-up. Mould only a part of the depth as an undercut so that the unmoulded section remains supported by the through-fence. Mould the rest at a second set-up, preferably using a reverse-shaped support for the previously moulded profile.

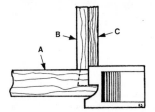

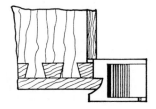

Fig. 229 Above left: Rebating and rounding drawer front A flush with side B by running against strip fence C.

Above right: Rebating and rounding the drawer front top edge by running the drawer side top edges against the strip fence. The drawer tops are usually down slightly from the frame underside.

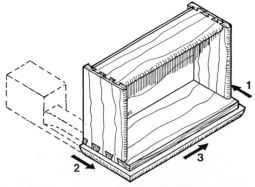

An example is when forming a full bull-nose. First form slightly more than half the bull-nose as an undercut quarter round. The second pass uses the same set-up, but with a shaped strip fence added to the through-fence to match the quarter round already formed. The pieces ride against this support for the final cut.

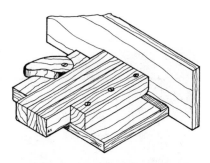

Fig. 228 Above: A sliding jig running against a through-fence and with several pieces clamped together against a square fence.

Below: The two stages in forming a complete end-trim. The first stage is shown on the left. The second stage is on the right. In the latter, the profile previously formed, now uppermost, rides against a reverse-shaped strip fence. Use a Shaw guard.

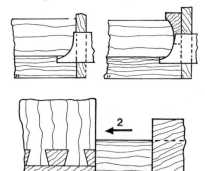

Fig. 230 When making the cut for the left-hand end, use a follow-up block against the drawer underside to prevent break-out.

Fig. 231 Left: Sequence of cuts to prevent spelching.
1 - Right-hand drawer end.
2 - Left-hand drawer end using the back-up block.
3 - Drawer-front top at a separate set-up.
Arrows show the direction of feed.

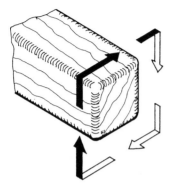

Fig. 232 Top-easing a newel post. Arrows show the sequence of cuts, so rotate the post the opposite way. Use a clamped follow-up block.

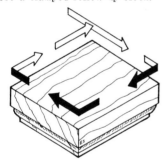

Fig. 233 Forming a newel cap. Arrows show the sequence of cuts, so rotate the cap the opposite way. With small parts it is essential to use a holding jig.

Another example is in rebating and rounding the ends and the top edge on the fronts of assembled kitchen drawers. The fronts are first sized marginally over depth and over length. The set-up has a strip fence fitted to allow the drawer front to pass underneath when face down on the table. The rebate and round are best formed at a single pass. Initially, set the rebate cutter in line with the strip fence to rebate the drawer front ends flush with the drawer sides. Use a follow-up block to back up the drawer under-edge to prevent break-out. Reset the fence to give the usual step between the top-edge rebate on the drawer front and the drawer side top edge.

Form the drawer top edge by running the drawer side top edges against the strip fence. Make sure the strip fence has a clean, flat and damage-free face, or the top edge will mould unevenly. This final cut removes any break-out at the top edge resulting from the end-moulding cut.

Operating sequence

When workpieces are moulded on three or four corners using set-ups such as this, the sequence has to be correct or spelching results. The correct sequence is to work so that any spelching is machined-out by following cuts.

When forming a bevel or quadrants around the top and long edges of a capless newel post, mould all these using an undercut head, through fence, Shaw guard and follow-up block.

First form the mould around the top with the newel post flat on the table, end against the fence and steadied by using the follow-up block. When turning for the next cut, rotate the newel post clockwise (viewed from the lower end) so that the next cut starts where the previous cut ended and might have spelched. This cleans up all corner spelching bar the last cut, which should be fed slowly to keep spelching to the absolute minimum. Finally, make cuts along the grain for the four remaining long corners using the same set-up, but feeding in the usual way. The sequence in this case is unimportant. If end-grain moulding a square or similar workpiece on all edges, turn between cuts to give the same cutting conditions as above and for the same reason.

Template sizing

The spindle moulder can be used very successfully to dress and edge-mould to size shapes having straight sides, by using a tenoning attachment, or a sliding table. A template serves the same purpose, though, and is quicker in use, keeps a constant overal size and allows all cuts to follow one another in proper order to complete sizing at a single handling.

The template should be a piece of plywood or similar, trimmed exactly to the overall size wanted, i.e., to the outside dimensions of a square-edged workpiece, or the overal size measured to the outside point of an edge-moulded part. Fasten the template to the workpiece by nails (which want extracting individually) or use brads which keep in place when the template is sprung-off.

Fasten a strip fence (which is thicker than the amount to be trimmed off) to the through-fence, positioned to allow the untrimmed workpiece to pass beneath. Set planing cutters exactly in line with the outer face of the strip fence and to project only about 2mm above the workpiece (so the least amount is pared off both strip fence and template). For the same reason grind the mould close to the top edge of the moulding cutters. Set them so that the deepest point of the mould aligns with the strip fence. Make the template thick enough to leave a deep contact face when the cutter breaks through the fence, or use a spacer between workpiece and template.

Place the workpiece flat on the table and fasten the template to it. Run each end or side in turn, with the template riding on the strip fence, to size and mould at the same time. Rotate counter-clockwise between cuts to prevent spelching. The operation is similar to shaping using a ball-bearing collar or ring fence, but a straight fence makes the operation steadier and safer.

The method is ideal for squares, oblongs and other shapes bonded by straight lines, either as individual pieces or part-assemblies. Use it, for example, in sizing and edge-moulding window sashes. These are machined and assembled with the outer face square for easier and less critical manufacture. Precise overall size is difficult to guarantee when fully machining in small lots, but no problem when sizing is the final operation.

There is an additional advantage; it gives a uniform and cleaner appearance at the corners without complicated tenoning to end-profile, which might not match in final assembly anyhow.

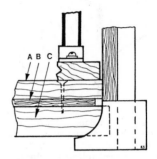

Fig. 234 Sizing-template A to form a quarter-round on the part C.
B is a sandwich piece to ensure the template fully contacts the strip fence.

Type of template

Either an over or under template can be used; there are pros and cons for both. An over-template allows guards and handles to be fixed to the top surface for safer and easier feeding. This type also protects the user better because cutters are below the template. On the other hand, when machining open frames, the assembly needs flipping-over before use then flipping back to unload and reload.

Brads aid in locking template and workpiece together, but with open frames fit location strips and inside eccentric clamps to firmly lock the assembly. These also support thin sections which might otherwise spring or vibrate.

Machines set for an overcut are more convenient and quicker for open frames. The operator can also see the cut and better judge the correct feed speed needed. The main disadvantage is that the cutterhead is more exposed and needs extra guarding which with these set-ups is always poor.

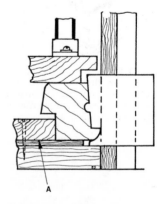

Fig. 235 Sizing a frame using an under template.
Block A locates the frame in position and makes it secure.

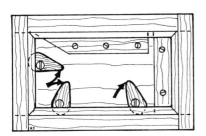

Fig. 236 Top view of a jigged-template for sizing frames. The frame is locked by eccentric clamps which in tightening pull the frame against blocks.

Reducing spelching

Regardless the type of template, correct operating sequence is essential to reduce spelching on frames. To do this rotate the assembly counter-clockwise to mill-out spelching from the previous cut. There is one additional and important factor with plywood and assemblies such as window frames. If each side is fully machined in turn, a following clean-up cut is made at each corner except the last. This can only be supported (to avoid break-out) by using a complicated, reverse-shaped back-up piece, but this is never entirely satisfactory.

To resolve this without using a back-up piece, simply start and finish the cut about half-way along one long side. Start the sequence of cuts by dropping-on, follow-up as through cuts after turning counter-clockwise, with the first and final cuts matching-up at the drop-on point. This gives better corners than the best back-up piece.

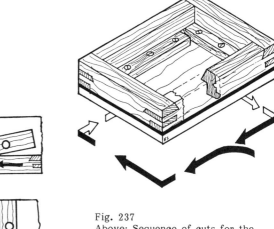

Right: Use a wide back-stop swung from the fence which pushes clear when through-feeding.

Fig. 237
Above: Sequence of cuts for the frame. Arrows show the cuts, so rotate in the opposite direction. Make the first cut part-way along one long side to avoid end spelching.

Take all the basic precautions detailed earlier for dropping-on using a back-stop. The latter must flip or swing clear after the first cut as the remaining passes are through cuts. Because the work is a series of four following cuts these can be interrupted to shift the stop, but a swing-away stop is more convenient. Starting position is not critical, but should be about mid-length of one long side to give a suitable leverage when dropping-on.

TRIMMING OPERATIONS

Box corners

Another example is trimming fingers and corner-rounding corner-locked boxes. A strip fence is again needed with an under-gap slightly more than the thickness of the box sides, and a wooden bed with a similar gap along the fence line. Align the quarter-round cutter to the faces of the strip fence and the bed. When the boxes are placed face down on the bed and end against the fence, the fingers and excess glue project into the gaps so that the cutters remove the projecting fingers and round the corner at the same time. Use a clamped follow-up block and Shaw guard.

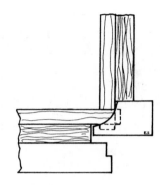

Fig. 238 Corner-rounding and trimming finger-jointed boxes using a gapped fence and bed.

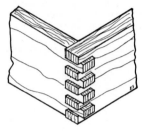

Fig. 239 Make the fingers protrude slightly on assembly.

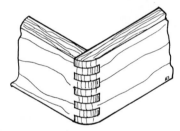

Fig. 240 The same joint after trimming and rounding.

Skins

A narrow strip fence can be used for trimming frames clad in plywood, veneer or plastic. Usually the frame is made to size, or sized after assembly, then skins are trimmed down flush with the frame after fixing. (It is impractical to pre-trim skins to a precise size and expect them to align perfectly with the frame).

Use a full-length strip fence marginally thinner than the frame, together with a double grooving head spanning the strip fence and with cutters precisely aligned to it. In use, simply feed the assembly with the frame riding on the strip fence, so that the skins are trimmed level with the frame.

If the corners need chamfering or rounding this is possible either as a following operation or at the same time. Whichever way is chosen, preferably form as an under-cut only, turning the assembly over for the second cut. A dual cut could be used to form upper and lower cuts at the same time, but the danger is that any slight springing of the frame could dig the cutter into the top surface and spoil it. To avoid spelching at the last corner when sizing all round, drop-in part way along either long side.

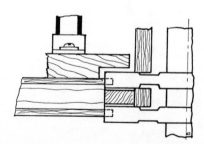

Fig. 241 Trimming skins to the frame overall size using a strip fence.

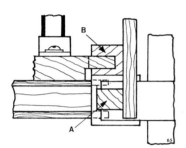

Fig. 242 Trimming skins and frame simultaneously using a strip fence on the infeed and an in-line outfeed fence. The original edge rides against strip fence A, and the finished edge on outfeed fence B.

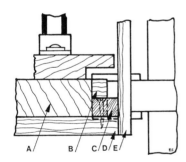

Fig. 243 Right: Using a sliding jig to trim frame ends. The frame is locked against a guide on the sliding jig in line with the planing cutters. To trim, move forward against a stop, then flip and repeat.

Above: Section through frame end trimming set-up showing:
A - door rail.
B - projecting frame end.
C - guide strip.
D - sliding base.
E - fence.

Facing

Regular edging trims down to the frame but doesn't clean-up the frame edge itself. This is possible using a planing block aligned to the outfeed fence. A strip fence is needed only at the infeed fence, and must be set-back by the cut-depth needed. The frame first rides on the infeed strip fence, then on the outfeed fence. The operation is equivalent to surfacing or mould edging.

Only a single pass is permissible; if further passes are made extra is planed-off in the same way as when surfacing. Use a back-up block, but never start the cut part way along.

It is essential to control movement firmly, particularly when machining the ends of long but narrow workpieces, otherwise side ways rocking is likely to form an uneven edge which takes a lot of making good. As this set-up also needs a fence gap there is always the chance of dipping when starting or finishing the cut.

These problems are best resolved by using a template as described earlier, but the strip fence is quicker to use and less troublesome. It gives acceptable results if workpieces are of about normal cupboard door size.

Ends and tenons

With mortise and tenon frames, it is difficult to machine them so precisely that, when assembled, the tenons and ends are perfectly flush with the frame. Doing this is rarely successful - tenon ends and horn invariably either sink or protrude. Preferably machine them to project slightly, then trim flush after assembly.

One set-up for frame end or horn trimming has a base sliding on the table to bear edge-against a through-fence. A narrow guide screwed to its top surface and flush with the fence edge extends fully across, but with a working gap at the cutterhead. Stops limit the movement of the base so that the guides stop short of the cutterblock in both directions. Set planing cutters to just clip the top edge of the base and to align precisely with the outside edge of the guides when the base is against the fence.

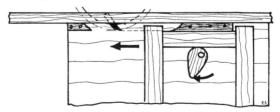

Fit the frame edge-against the guide and with the end for trimming leading and central in the working gap. To make the frame more stable fit inside eccentric clamps to lock it or fit a second close-fitting guide inside.

Draw the jig clear of the cutters before starting up, then feed forward so that the cutters merely plane off the projecting ends flush with the frame.

The position and size of the guides is governed by the size and construction of the frame. It could, in fact, simply be a series of separate blocks leaving gaps for untrimmed ends. A simpler form uses the same basic principle but with a loose spacing piece to ride against the fence and move with the frame. This is quicker to use than a sliding base, but is less stable and could allow the frame to dip into the fence gap.

For tenon trimming use upper and lower strip fences, or groove-out a wooden fence, so that the tenon projects into the gap. The cutter operates between the strips (or in the groove) and is flush with the outer face. To trim tenons flush with the frame simply feed the frames across the fence gap.

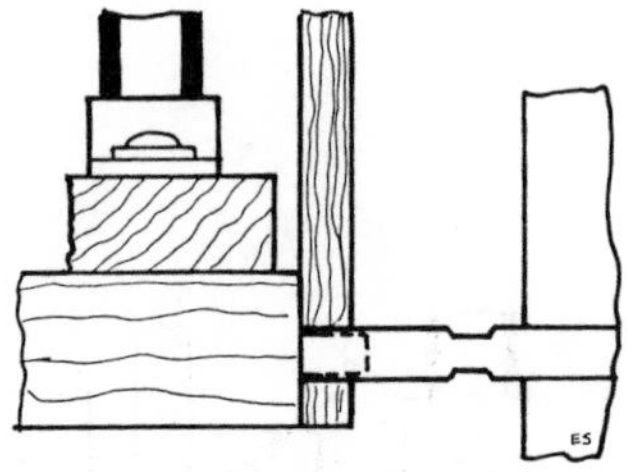

Fig. 244 Strip or slotted fence for tenon trimming.

CORNER ROUNDING

Frames can be corner-rounded by shaping with a template as described later, but if the round is a quarter of a true circle it can be formed using a pivotting jig. This is screw-pivotted to a wooden base fixed to the table, and to trim through 90 degrees. The pivot screw must be in line with the spindle arbor, and spaced from a planing block cutting circle a distance equal to the radius of curvature. The jig needs side guides to locate the workpiece at the correct distance from the pivot.

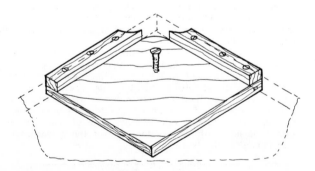

Fig. 245 This jig for corner-rounding has a wooden bed which pivots directly opposite the spindle cutterhead.

Set the spindle fences to control the 90 degree movement needed to form the quarter-round. The distance that the fence is set back from the cutting line equals the width of the side guides. To protect the cutterblock, fix a block across the fence gap immediately above the workpiece, or use a front guard.

Swing the jig against the outfeed fence. Fit the workpiece, clamping it if small or unstable, then simply rotate the two together counter-clockwise through 90 degrees to form the rounded corner.

Fig. 246
Left: Start the corner-round cut with the jig against the outfeed fence.

Right: Finish the corner-round cut with the jig against the infeed fence. The arrow shows the direction of movement.

Clamping isn't absolutely vital, and for faster operation the frame can be held up to the guides by hand pressure - but use a top Shaw guard. Make the cut with the grain by positioning the workpiece with the grain parallel to the fence when in the start position.

When the workpiece is a frame with cuts against the grain regardless of how it is machined, for the first cut rotate through only about 45 degrees before drawing clear out. Flip it over, then re-insert and finish-off the same corner to meet the first cut part-way round.

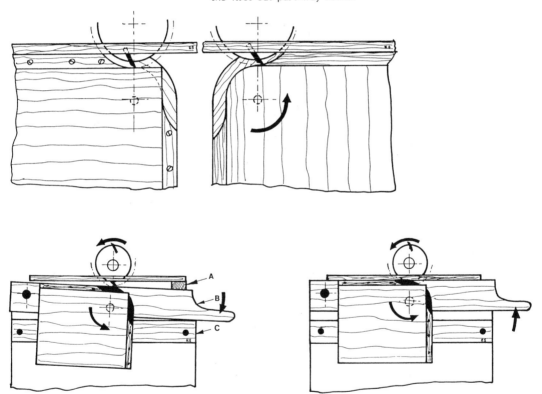

Fig. 247 If the cut is a heavy one, mount the corner-rounding jig on a pivot and swing out to insert a spacer A, then make a roughing cut. The jig is moved by handle B. Bed strip C remains fixed to give support.

Fig. 248 Final position with the spacer removed for the finishing cut.

If the radius is large and formed from a squared corner, relieve the main cut with a pre-cut. To do this pivot the jig on a base which itself pivots near the end of the outfeed fence. The technique in this case is to draw the jig away from the fence using a lever handle at the right-hand end and fit a spacing block to restrict movement towards the fence.

Fit the frame in position and make the pre-cut. Then move the assembly out, remove the spacing piece and repeat, this time machining the full depth. In addition to allowing a precut this alternative method also also allows the workpiece to be fitted and removed when well clear of the cutters, so it can be an added safety factor even when no pre-cut is needed.

EDGING CIRCLES

This uses a jig sliding between guides on a base fixed to the spindle table. The jig has a number of holes drilled in it for pivot centres to locate a turntable at various distances from the fence. Final size is controlled by the distance of the base from the fence.

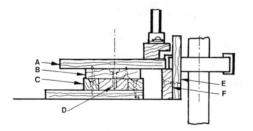

Fig. 249 Section through a sliding jig for making circular parts showing:
A - workpiece.
B - turntable.
C - fixed slide guide
D - base slide mounting the pivot.

The whole unit moves towards or away from the fence to give different diameters, and also has extra pivot holes.
The through-fence E is a necessary safety feature, and F is a support block fastened to the fence.

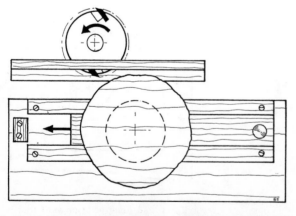

Fig. 250 Top view of the circular jig in the start position. The arrow shows the initial movement.

The turntable supports the piece being machined and holds it via several brads driven-in from the underside. A stop-block prevents further forward movement of the jig when the pivot is directly in line with the spindle. The spindle can have an edging or moulding head, and is broken through a fence in the normal way for a slightly deeper cut than the maximum amount needing trimming-off the rough parts. Use a top Shaw guard.

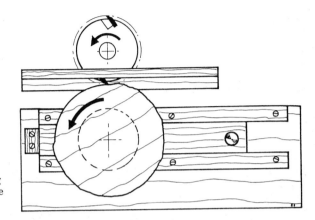

Fig. 251 Top view of the circular jig when rounding. The arrow shows the direction of movement.

Draw-back the jig so that the part can be positioned on the turntable whilst clear of the cutter. (Guide lines drawn on the base can show the proper position for the workpiece, or fix a shaped guide piece and jig stop at the infeed for more precise setting). Move the jig forward against the front-stop, holding the part steady and rotate the part counter-clockwise to trim it. Draw back before removing and reloading.

Plate 70 Profiling and sizing a sash frame on a Wadkin Bursgreen BEL/T spindle moulder provided with a rolling table and front support rail.

Plate 71 Edge moulding a sash frame on an SCM spindle moulder. It is also practical to use a template for sizing.

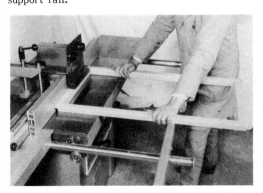

Plate 72 Whitney heavy-duty
spindle moulder for complex
shaping. Spindles run in opposite
directions and the assembly is
transferred between them.

Plate 73 An example of a good
jigged template for edge profiling
and moulding. The ring is slewed on
this Startrite spindle moulder to
give more support to the assembly.
Note the hand-holds well clear of
the cutters.

CHAPTER 12

SHAPING

Shaping is square-edging or edge-moulding solid timber, a frame, or a laminate to an outline shape. A follower, on or near the cutterhead, contacts a template fastened to the workpiece to control both shape and overal size, whilst the cutterhead edge-planes or moulds it.

Many different heads can be used for outside shaping. For inside shaping the cutterhead must be much smaller than the smallest curve to avoid snatch; also small cutterheads are easier to guard and safer to use on what is a dangerous operation.

The French Head was once popular for this, but it has a poor cutting action and is used only where no other head is suitable. Slotted collars are widely used in combination with a ball-bearing follower. Whitehill and circular planing heads are excellent, and matching ball-bearing followers are available. Solid profiled heads can be used, but there is a problem in matching them to a ball-bearing follower because their diameter grows less as they are ground down. Tipped profile heads reduce less and are better, but not ideal. Both can be used with a ring fence.

Square heads are not really suitable because they have a big bite and could snatch, particularly when cutting against the grain. Because the cutting circle is large they are difficult to guard and dangerous in use.

Disposable cutter type heads are fine for shaping as they have a small bite. Chip-limiting heads are exclusively used in Europe for all spindle moulder work and because they do not kick back they are very safe for shaping. They are rarely used in the UK as they are higher in cost and are more difficult to maintain than other types.

FEED DIRECTION

Feed must be against the rotation of the cutterhead when shaping. Never attempt climb or back cutting as a kick-back will almost certainly result. Take particular care when dropping-on or starting, as a shaped workpiece/template combination is more difficult to control than a straight mould.

It is possible with most outlines to shape and edge-mould at the same time. Alternatively the part can first be edged-planed to outline using a template, then the mould added as a second operation. (The jigs and templates all show shaping and edge-moulding at one operation, but all could be separated).

Shaping first, then edge-moulding later, divides the cut; it is a safer way of working because both cuts are lighter so there is less chance of kick-back; also the moulding cutters dull less because they remove less. Against this, of course, there are two separate operations. In moulding, it isn't essential to use the jigged template, instead the follower could contact the edge-planed section of the part. A deep enough section must remain against which the follower can run, or if not, moulding can be split into two operations. It is possible to make the second cut running the follower against the first mould; preferably a square cut such as a rebate. Where this is not practical, use the template both for initial shaping and later edge-moulding.

When edge-moulding without a template, it is essential instead to use a holding jig with secure handles. A holding jig, for example the general-purpose holding jig shown earlier, can be simpler and quicker to use than the original jigged template. Perhaps the easiest way, though, is to again use the jigged template, but not necessarily following the template outline against the follower.

TEMPLATE FOLLOWERS

The follower used in shaping, against which the template bears, can be one of three types: a table ring, a ball-bearing follower mounted on the arbor, or a ring fence.

Plate 74 Using a ring fence and cage guard on a Wadkin Bursgreen spindle moulder.

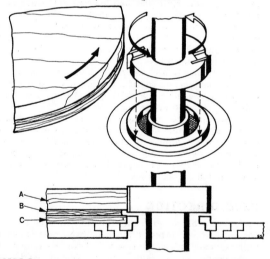

Fig. 252 Using an inverted table ring as a follower, showing:
A – the workpiece.
B – spacer.
C – template.

The upper sketch shows the cutterblock and jigged template raised so the ring is visible.

Guards are not shown but are essential for all work of this type. They are ommited from most sketches solely for clarity.
Use a bonnet or cage guard to enclose the cutterhead from table level, leaving a working gap wide and deep enough only to admit the workpiece and template.

TABLE RINGS

Most spindle moulders have table rings to fill in the gap between cutterhead and table. Some turn over so that a raised flange on them projects above table level to use as a template guide for an under-template. As the rings are absolutely concentric with the spindle, in theory, contact is possible from any side. In practice, however, there could be some slight eccentricity to produce slightly different cut depths at different points of contact. Planing cutterblock diameter must match precisely the ring diameter, and the template (or template plus spacer), must always be slightly thicker than the ring flange.

Fig. 253 Using a starting block with a slotted collar and ball-bearing follower. The block has a projecting section opposite the template, perhaps with a wear strip fitted.

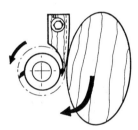

Fig. 254 Starting position when shaping using a ball-bearing follower and a starting block. Follow around the starting block to ease-in the cut.

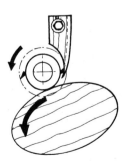

Fig. 255 Operating position, contact can be made at any point.

BALL-BEARING

Plain followers are not recommended as they give a rough feel to the work and tend to grab the template. A ball-bearing follower is commonly used and fits on the live spindle. Initially it spins with the spindle when started-up, but slows down to roll with the template when the two are in contact. This gives smooth and frictionless movement, probably the most sensitive of all the types used. The ball-bearing follower is absolutely concentric with the spindle so can be used from any direction without altering cut depth. This allows difficult shapes to be followed more easily than with a ring fence, for example, because contact does not have to be maintained at a precise point.

As with the table ring, cutterblock planing diameter must correpond with the ball-bearing diameter. This limits the heads that can be used to those with loose, adjustable cutters and disposable-cutter types. Most ball-bearing followers are used above the cutterhead with an over-template, but there is no reason why this could not be reversed.

Safe starting

Both the table ring and ball-bearing follower need a run-in to start the cut, otherwise the head snatches on first contact. With a part-outline template, a safe run-in is possible simply by extending the leading section of the template. Add pieces underneath at the leading and trailing ends and the side of the same thickness as the part to give stability. With a full-outline template, or when a part-outline template has no lead-in, use a starting block, the normal form of which is a comma-shaped piece of hardwood. This is fastened to the table to curve into the cutterhead level with and close to the follower. To fit close it may be necessary to pare the starting block away with the cutters.

The starting block should have a projecting wear strip to bear against the template. With this, rough timber makes no contact with the starting block, so movement is smooth when first starting the cut.

The block is normally fixed to the right-hand side (with counter-clockwise rotation) so that the cutterhead is accessible at the normal working position. The leading end of the template first contacts the block well clear of the cutterhead, then feeds clockwise around the curve to enter the cut in a controlled and safe manner. In a similar way, full outside shapes first contact the block and follow around the curve, without actually rotating, to enter the cut safely. Once fully in the cut the workpiece is rotated in the usual way.

An alternative is to use a loose nosing on the template to start the cut, but which easily pulls off during the shaping operation.

Inside shapes are a little more tricky. When working inside bull's eye windows and similar, the starting block must be small enough to avoid fouling the workpiece in operation. The template first contacts the starting block, and is then shifted around the curve towards the head and rotated against the cut at the same time. This is not as easy as it sounds because grip on the assembly has to changed, and this could lead to a kick-back. Don't simply try to swing the assembly on the starting block, you must feed forward at the same time.

Fig. 256 Sometimes a loose nosing can be fitted to start the cut as an alternative to a starting block or ring fence. This must be secure in use, but easily pulled off during shaping.

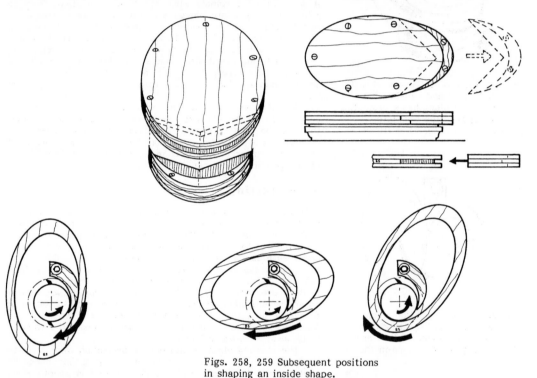

Figs. 258, 259 Subsequent positions in shaping an inside shape.

Fig. 257 Using a starting block with an inside shape.

There is a good case with inside shaping for an extra, rear starting block on almost the opposite side of the spindle, leaving working space between the two blocks. First contact the rear block at an angle to clear the cutterblock. To enter the cut, move the assembly across the cutterhead right to left, without rotating it, whilst retaining the same grip. The front block prevents the workpiece contacting the cutterhead except when intended.

An alternative method of safe starting with inside shaping is to fix a starting strip partially across across the outline which can be swung clear as the assembly is rotated.

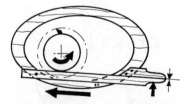

Fig. 260 Another way of starting an inside shape using a swivelling start strip. In starting the cut the strip is clamped manually against a fixed handle.

142

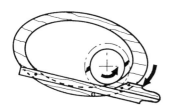

Fig. 261 Once in the cut the workpiece is rotated as normal.

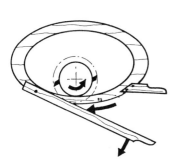

Fig. 262 The start strip is swung clear to complete shaping.

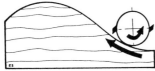

Figs. 265 In using a ball-bearing follower the point of contact doesn't matter. The template can be shaped without swinging it, so it is easier to use and there is little chance of inaccurate shaping.

RING FENCE

This is a ring surrounding the spindle and mounted on a support fastened to the table. The ring is eccentric, and with an operating point furthest from the support perhaps 5mm wide. This point is marked to show where template contact should be made. Set the ring eccentrically to the spindle so that cutters project the correct depth beyond the ring only at this point - at all other points cutter projection should be less or none at all. Because the ring is set to the cutterblock, whatever its diameter, any type of cutterblock can be used, and diameter reduction through wear is no problem.

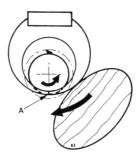

Fig. 263 Starting position with a ring fence; work around the fence without rotating the workpiece until opposite the operating point A.

The ring fence can be fitted above or below the cutterblock and is used as a ball-bearing follower combined with with gap-free starting blocks at both sides.

Start the cut by working around the infeed curve but, unlike a ball-bearing follower, once in the cut the template must contact the ring fence only at the marked point. If contact varies the outline will be wrong.

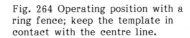

Fig. 264 Operating position with a ring fence; keep the template in contact with the centre line.

As contact must be maintained at the marked point, complex profiles are difficult to follow because the template has to be continuously swivelled. One example of a difficult shape is a serpentine or wavy-edge form. With a table ring or ball-bearing follower the assembly is fed roughly in a straight line whilst allowing the template to swing in and out to maintain contact, though at a constantly changing point.

STRAIGHT FENCE SHAPING

When forming outside curves it is practical and preferable to use a rigid hardwood strip fence across the false fence instead of using either a ball-bearing follower or a ring. Mark the fence with a clear vertical line directly opposite the spindle. Set cutters to this, and work against it, as with the centre mark on a ring fence.

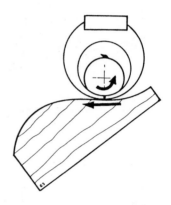

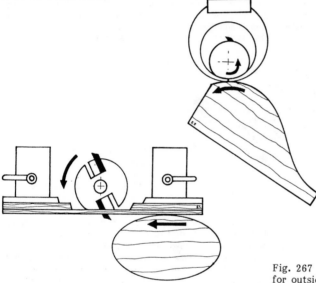

Fig. 266 In following a shape similar to this on a ring fence, swing the template around always to keep contact at the marked point – otherwise shaping will be inaccurate.

Fig. 267 Using a thick strip fence for outside shaping.

Above: Start the cut by feeding the assembly parallel to the fence without rotating it.

Below: Rotate when opposite the centre mark shape – as with a ring fence.

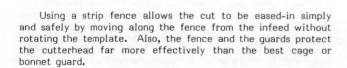

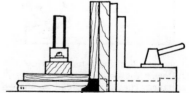

Using a strip fence allows the cut to be eased-in simply and safely by moving along the fence from the infeed without rotating the template. Also, the fence and the guards protect the cutterhead far more effectively than the best cage or bonnet guard.

Fig. 268 Section through strip fence for shaping.

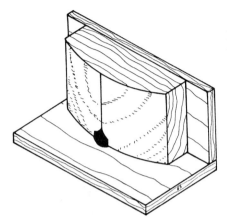

Fig. 269 Fence saddle and bed for true-circle inside curved work.

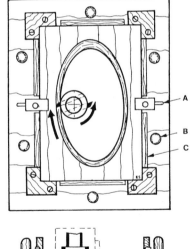

Fig. 271 A jigged template for an inside shape can be made large. This shows an under-template with clamps to hold down the workpiece A, push handles B, and finger guards C.

For the same reasons a fence saddle is better on shallow internal curves which form part of a true circle. Make the template to exactly the same curve. In this way both keep in full and stable contact as the template follows round, giving the same control as when straight moulding.

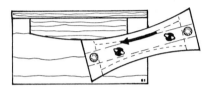

Fig. 270 The saddle should match the template to give stability in feeding.

TEMPLATE TYPES

There are two basic types of template; full-outline templates used to form the complete outer edge of a table top or an opening in a panel, for example, and part-outline templates used where only part of the outline is formed, examples are shaped chair legs and arms. Sometimes a full outline is formed at two separate set-ups using two templates. An example of this is the outer curve of a table leaf at one set-up, with a following set-up to form the straight folding bead on the matching edge. Each template in the latter case is a part-outline template. Templates can be used either above or below the workpiece. There are pros and cons for both, as explained later.

Full outline

These, used for forming a complete outside profile, are often flat templates fastened to the workpiece by brads. The template is made exactly the same shape and overall size as the part wanted. Any moulding on the workpiece must be inside the template outline with outside shapes, and outside the template outline with an inside or negative template (as used for the inside of porthole windows or an opening in a panel). Avoid the mistake of forming the template to the outline of the mould at it s full cutting depth.

Templates can be made from plywood or durable, rigid plastic. They must be perfectly flat, and thick enough to give full contact with the ball-bearing follower or ring fence when the cut is made. Allow the minimum overlap for the cutter so that it pares away only a small portion of the template edge, or fix a spacer between template and workpiece to allow more overlap. Fit handles and finger guards to aid feeding and to protect the operator. Make templates for inside shapes well oversize for stability and ease of handling.

Template size

A large template can become unstable when used on a spindle moulder with a small table. Before starting the cut make a trial run over the full movement (with the machine stopped) to check that the template does not overhang so much that it becomes unstable and tends to overbalance at any point. A ball-bearing follower needs less swinging about, so movement can be planned to avoid this, but take care in shaping to follow the same path each time. More template movement is needed with a ring fence, so check thoroughly before use. In some cases it may be an advantage to re-position the ring fence to give better support to the template assembly.

Make the edges of all templates accurate and smooth as even the smallest lump or notch repeats prominently on the finished workpiece. Fasten the template to the workpiece by brads. Make these from screws driven through the template and ground to a point so removal for sharpening and replacing is quick and simple. With solid timber, sharpen brads like a chisel and align then with the workpiece grain for ease of driving and so that the cut they form is less noticeable.

Fasten the workpiece and template together by tapping with a mallet when positioned; i.e., with the workpiece projecting beyond the template by an equal amount all round. For accurate registration use a fixed register block to locate both template and workpiece to one another. Take note that brads are not absolutely reliable in securing the workpiece. With very heavy cuts use two part-outline templates instead which allow toggle clamps to be used.

Small and medium workpieces with a full outline should not be worked individually, it is dangerous. Preferably handle them two or more up using a much bigger template, forming only two sides at one pass on a multi-station jigged template rather than the whole outline. This makes the whole thing safer and allows easy fitting of handles and guards on both over and under templates. See multi-station jigs.

When the jigged template needs unloading and reloading on machines with small tables, move the assembly to workbench alongside and at the same height by sliding it along. Doing this is more convenient because there is more room, and safer because it is clear of the cutterhead which is usually left running. (The guards used in shaping rarely give complete protection when the template is out of position).

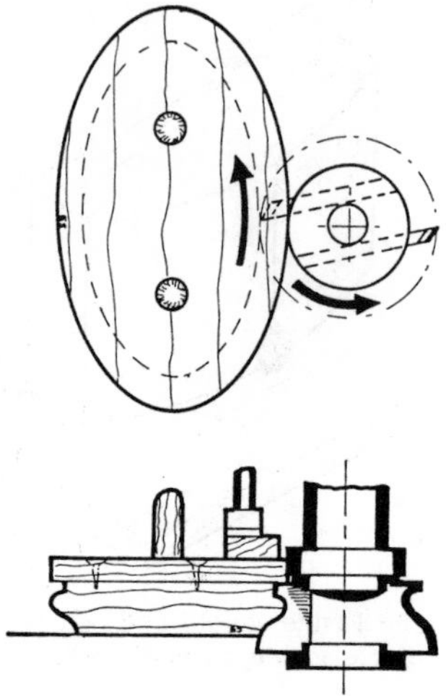

Guards

Set a Shaw guard at the point of cut with pressure light enough to keep control without making movement difficult. Preferably wax the the table to make movement smooth, also the underside of the template if used template-down. The Shaw guard should only make contact outside the maximum cutting circle with top templates, or it could tip the assembly during the final cut to snatch and possibly throw-back.

Fig. 272 Using an over-template fitted with handles.

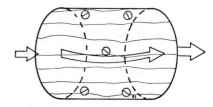

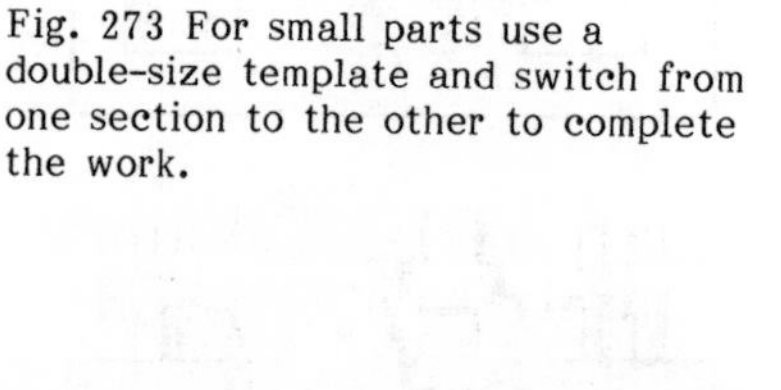

Fig. 273 For small parts use a double-size template and switch from one section to the other to complete the work.

Plate 75 Edge sanding a part on a Scheppach spindle moulder prior to adding the moulding.

Plate 76 Inside shaping on a Delta light duty spindle moulder with a Safe Guard 11 mounted directly on the spindle arbor. This gives protection together with an excellent view of the work.

With a top template fit handles to the top surface for grip, also finger guards in case of slippage, but both must clear the Shaw guard. Handles are an essential safety feature with all templates. They should afford a firm and dependable grip for the user, well clear of the cutters and guard in case of kick-back. Position them to give proper and complete control in shaping, fitting more than two on a full-outline template to allow easy grip-change during the cut. Never hold the toggle clamps to control the jig; they are uncomfortable to grip and could accidently release during the cut if the user is distracted. Fit and use control handles.

A cage guard is essential with all shaping operations. This should neatly fit around the cutterhead down to table level except for a small working gap, also above template level at this point. Make sure the cage guard gap is only wide enough to allow the assembly to be swept around comfortably without fouling. This is especially troublesome on internal work.

A cage guard restricts the cut to a small segment of the head, but this is normal practice in any case with a ring fence. A ball-bearing follower and table ring can both be used through 360 degrees in theory, but this is only theory. In practice, contact is always made roughly within the same small arc for ease of operation, so again this is not too restrictive.

Before starting the cut with any shaped work make a practice run with the machine switched-off to make sure nothing interferes with smooth movement. Take care to repeat exactly the same path in shaping.

Because guards restrict sight of the cutterhead, the spindle is sometimes worked without a guard when shaping. The reason usually given is that the cutterhead can be seen more clearly without a guard, taking the view that something dangerous has to be watched. Older guards were poor in this respect, but modern ones have clear protective panels which allow viewing but still provide good protection. Shaping is a dangerous operation, much more than straight moulding, so don't attempt to shape unless both a Shaw guard and a cage guard are fitted, even when making a trial cut in setting.

Template position

A template above the workpiece partially guards the cutter-block to make operation safer, and allows handles and finger guards to be easily fitted. When the cut is deep and the work-piece small the assembly may not be stable when fully machined, so use an under-template as this has a larger bearing area. Make sure that the template is flat on the table before contacting the follower, or it could ride over the top with disasterous results. As a protection against this it is absolutely essential to use a Shaw guard.

An under-template must be truly flat and with its top face absolutely parallel to the underside, otherwise the mould face-alignment varies. It isn't possible to use any form of handle or guard when working template down (except when shaping an open frame or a part-outline template), so grip and guarding is much more difficult. Only use these with large parts that allow hand-grip for proper control well clear of the cutterhead - in case of kick-back.

Part outline types

Part-outline templates are used to form workpieces along only part of the outline at a single pass. They can be similar to full-outline types as a simple brad-held template, but it is better to use a jigged form of template. These are much safer to use because the jig can be physically bigger than a simple outline jig and easier and safer to handle. Also finger guards and handles can be fitted with less restriction. The simplest form has an over-template with spacers underneath level with the workpiece so that the assembly lies flat and stable when starting the cut.

It is possible to fix the workpiece simply by brads - after projecting it the proper amount beyond the template. As width can vary doing this, preferably fit back and end blocks to quickly and precisely locate the part. A full-length back fence can be used, but blocks near to each end and against the ends are usually enough. If the ends of the workpiece are square it may be possible to use a toggle type end-clamp against one end with the opposite end against a block and with brads in both.

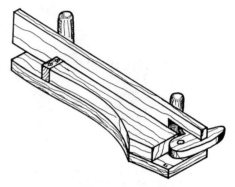

Fig. 274 General view of a typical jigged template for a part-outline shape, fitted with handles and finger guards.

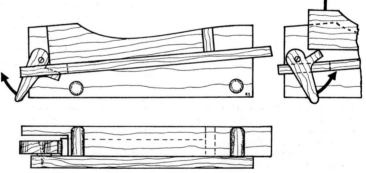

Fig. 275 Sketches of the template jig shown above. The eccentric clamp pulls the part back against the fence in fitting, then kicks it clear when shifted the opposite way. Use the handles to move the jig, never the clamp.

The assembly can be made as a jigged template on a substantial base with the workpiece sandwiched between base and template. In this form it is normal to fit toggle clamps against the ends or to act vertically through cut-outs in the template. An alternative form has the base as template with back and end blocks fitted to the topside where the workpiece sits clamped in place. This type is easy to load and can have top toggle clamps for speedy operation. Make sure any gaps at the ends of, or between, parts are filled-in, and with finger guards for protection when the jig is not fully loaded. In this way the cutterblock is never exposed when the jig is in position.

Allowance for lead-in

When the template is the same length of the workpiece the cut starts at the full depth, so use either a ring fence or a starting block to enter the cut. It is easier and safer to extend the template at start and finish to allow run-in and out with the template in full contact with the follower, but with cutters clear of the workpiece. Make end blocks with an over-template the same thickness as the workpiece to make the assembly stable. Project them slightly beyond the cutting line as a support to reduce break-out when cutting against the grain or working brittle timbers.

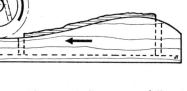

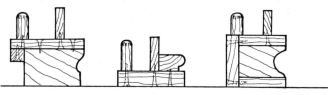

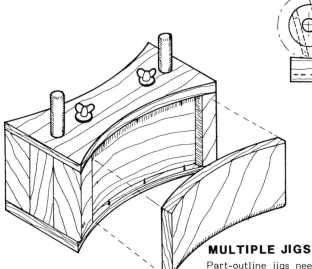

Fig. 276 Various types of jigged template to the general form shown below. The template itself is extended to lead in and out safely.

The sketches above show:
Left: Template above.
Centre: Template below.
Right: Box-type jigged template.

Fig. 277 Double-sided template for moulding chair rail corner-rounds using the fence saddle shown in Figs 269 and 270.

MULTIPLE JIGS

Part-outline jigs need not be for a single profile only. It is practical to form two or more profiles on the same jig using two or more work-stations. If a narrow workpiece needs two edges moulded it is safer and more efficient to mount both on the same jig and edge-mould both in following passes.

An example is a narrow table leg moulded both edges. A simple double-edged template could be used for this, but could be unstable. Also the leg must be carefully positioned or the shape and edge-planing many not marry.

An alternative way is to form a double-width template with opposing edges formed to the two outlines wanted, which need not be the same profile. Separate back and end blocks should precisely locate both workpieces for each cut. Both legs are fitted, one in one station and the second in the other, then the two outer edges are formed at consecutive passes without stopping the machine.

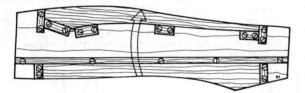

Fig. 278 Double-width jigged template for inner and outer leg profiles.

Where the edge-profile is formed along the full length, seat this against shaped blocks in the second station. In making the initial first pass fit legs at both stations, but only edge-mould that in the first station. Remove the part-finished leg and fit in the second station, fit a blank in the first station then edge-mould both. Repeat this sequence for the full run. To keep the final cut stable re-fit a finished leg in the first station but do not shape it.

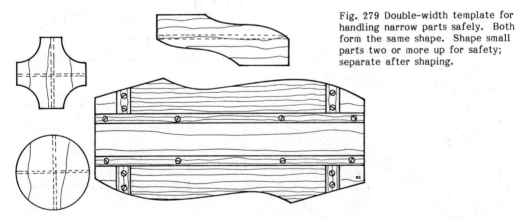

Fig. 279 Double-width template for handling narrow parts safely. Both form the same shape. Shape small parts two or more up for safety; separate after shaping.

Templates of this type are stabler because they rest either on a wider base when template down, or on two parts side-by-side when template up. It is also easier to fit finger guards and handles. Because parts locate against blocks replacement is quick and alignment precise. When used for handling parts too small to fully shape individually, part form at one station, then transfer between stations to complete. Where parts are very small, shape them two or more up for safety, then separate later.

CUTTING AGAINST THE GRAIN

Shaping often involves cutting against the grain at some point because grain never follows the profile wanted. Wherever possible timber should be chosen, prepared and worked so that most of the cut is with the grain. In this case a normal hand-feed speed is used for most of the cut, slowing down only where against the grain to reduce tear-out to an acceptable level.

Fig. 280 Using separate jigged templates to cut always with the grain when forming an oval shape. Arrows show the cut directions.

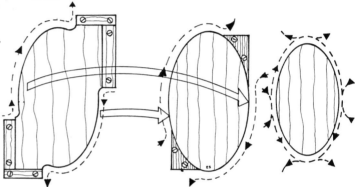

Where workpieces are moulded both edges and the finished product is wedge-shaped in overall appearance; for example, the tapering sides of a magazine rack, it makes sense to form the two edges at separate operations rather than forming both at a single handling where one cut is always against the grain. On a part-outline form for either square-planing or a symmetrical edge-moulding, such as a bull-nose, there are two choices: either use two single-edged templates arranged to cut with the grain and switch the part to complete it, or, a single jigged template switching parts edge for edge and inserting loose spacers for position.

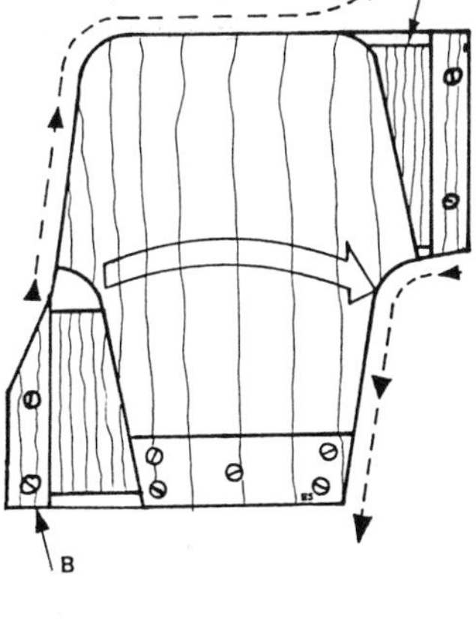

Stacked jig

A stacked jig can be used to shape workpieces two-up and back-to-back forming opposing cuts on both pieces at the same time. A double-depth cutterhead is needed with a jigged template on a wide base. Use toggle clamps to secure the workpieces in place, with double-depth back and end blocks or fences. Make the template profile to feed mainly with the grain. Fit side and end blocks to locate for the second operation directly on the base, with blocks for first operation fixed on these.

Make two cuts at a single pass and remove both pieces. Re-fit the first cut (top) part directly on the base after flipping, fit a blank on top, then clamp and shape. Repeat as needed. The same method can be used as an alternative to the double template, but is more trouble to load and unload.

Fig. 281 Arrows show the cut directions to mould with the grain using a single jigged template. Flip the part to repeat the same cuts on sections not previously shaped. Mark the template for second-cut position, or use loose spacers A against side guides B.

The method is fine if the workpieces are consistant in thickness and perfectly flat. If there are any irregularities in the bottom piece, the top part miss matches even if the piece itself is perfect.

Paired shapes

A simple template with brad fittings to fit either face can produce shapes in true pairs. Use one way up for one hand and complete the initial run. Flip the template and reverse the brads to the opposite face for the opposing hand, and complete the opposite hand workpieces. By doing this, cuts are with the grain in both cases. This is no problem with brads made from end-sharpened screws, simply screw these out and insert from the reverse face after flipping. End blocks must also be fitted on the reverse face.

All the above jigs assume that most of the cut is with the grain and that slowing down the feed is enough to avoid tearing-out on those sections when feed is against the grain. On some timbers and certain outlines this method does not give acceptable results, so possibly use a sandwich template.

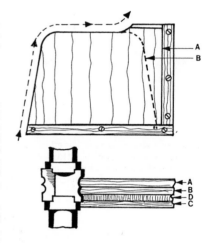

Fig. 282 Forming cuts with the grain on a stacked template. The part for the first cut is A, for the second cut B, whilst C is the template and D a spacing piece.

Fig. 283 Sequence of cuts on a sandwhich template showing one template A, the second C, part B and locating fence D by which the two halves are locked together.

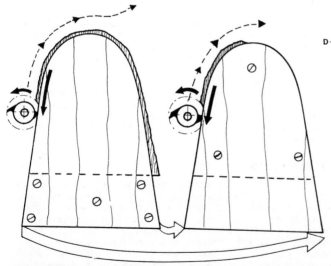

Sandwich template

This is a double template with the part sandwiched between. First shape all sections where the cut is with the grain by dropping-in and running out, then flip the template and run in the opposite direction to complete those sections of the outline where the cut is now with the grain.

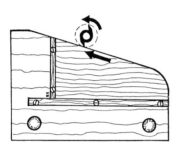

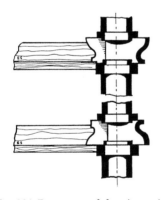

Fig. 284 Two ways of forming paired parts both to cut with the grain. The upper sketches show separate settings for each, and the lower one a double set-up with stacked parts.

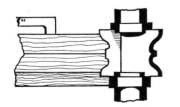

An example is when shaping an oval table leaf to a bull-nose. The first cut is made from the centre towards the trailing end. The assembly is then flipped over to repeat the cut from the centre towards what originally was the leading end but which now trails. The same applies with a part-circular cut-out on, perhaps, an inwardly-curved dressing table top. In this case, start the cut at the leading end and finish at the centre, then flip and repeat.

Absolute alignment of separate full-outline templates can be difficult in regular workshop practice because they must separate completely. One method is to use a register block fixed to a bench and shaped to the reverse of the template outlines and rough workpiece. The rough workpiece and both templates are pressed against this to align them before fastening together with brads. However, alignment can easily be out to show prominently as a mis-match. Alignment also needs repeating precisely and individually for each part. Being made-up of three separate pieces the various parts can shift in used. For safety's sake use a full-outline sandwich template only on light cuts and with any open frame through which screws can clamp both halves together.

With heavy cuts preferably use a part-outline sandwich template which can have secure toggle clamps, and form the outline at two passes. Part-outline templates align precisely because the two halves fasten together via the back fence and blocks. Regular fixed brads cannot be used, so use screw-in brads which are flush with the surface when driven in. Brads must be screwed bolts with precise, turned centre-points, otherwise they shift the workpiece on fixing. There is no need for brads at both sides, simply fit the workpiece when the brad screw heads are uppermost for fitting, then flip as needed.

The templates need not be identical, so it is practical to automatically feed in or out where cut-direction changes by slightly modifying the two outlines. This type is easy to use, simply follow the profile. Operation is quick as there is no danger of cutting against the grain accidently. Take care that the template not in use is well clear of the cutters, or other parts where it could foul, during the full shaping movement whilst using the other template.

A serious problem with sandwich templates is that control handles must be screw-in types that can be switched quickly from one face to the other when flipping the template. This adds considerably to the cost of making, and is a nuisance to the user however easy change-over might be. But handles are an essential safety feature - do not shape without them.

Single-sided types

A single-sided part-outline template can be used to form opposing cuts if the shape is symmetrical both in outline and profile. An example is a full table top moulded to a bull-nose profile. With non-symmetrical moulds use two set-ups, or stack parts and use a double-depth cutter.

TWO-SPINDLE OPERATION

The traditional way to cut with the grain regardless of outline is to use a two-spindle machine, one spindle rotating in one direction and the other in the opposite. Both spindles mount identical cutterheads when the cut is symmetrical, but need opposing profiles with non-symmetrical moulds. Both can run at the same time, though it is safer to run only one, and the workpiece is transferred between them as needed so that all cuts are made with the grain.

This technique easily gives the best results and the shortest handling times, but there are some disadvantages. Apart from the obvious one that a two-spindle machine and two sets of cutters are needed, opposing cuts are in opposite directions so extra dexterity is needed on the operator's part to work alternately right hand or left hand without error and with a smooth feed movement.

With a double spindle, the second spindle creates an extra hazard even when not operating; so take care not to swing the assembly to foul it. Regardless of profile, a one-piece template is normally used. Clearly mark this to show points between which opposing cuts are made. The operator then enters and exits the cut as needed. Some form of lead-in is essential using either an eccentric ring fence or a starting block.

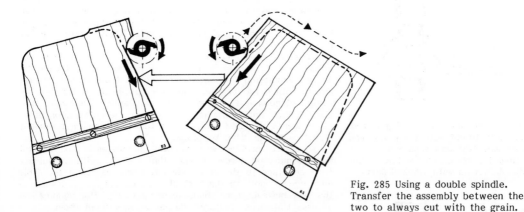

Fig. 285 Using a double spindle. Transfer the assembly between the two to always cut with the grain.

To make operation safer and error impossible set the two template followers at slightly different heights to each contact a different level of a double-stacked template. Make each template to a slightly different profile to incorporate automatic feed in and out where needed. At the change-over positions where both cuts are parallel to the grain the two templates are level, but could cross mid-way at a slight angle to merge better.

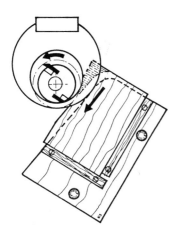

Fig. 286 Easing a heavy cut by first shaping against on off-centre section of the ring fence, above. The final cut is shown below.

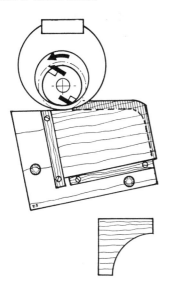

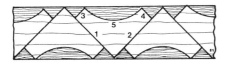

CUT-RELIEVING

Where sweeps are gentle the full cut depth can be shaped at a single setting, however, a deep cut chances a kick-back and it is better to cut-relieve before the final pass, perhaps in a pre-shaping cut, using a ring fence. If making a rounded corner from a square, for example, first mill-out the weight by feeding whilst in contact with the ring well clear of the centre mark. Then move nearer to repeat, and so on, until only a light cut remains for the final cut. An alternative is to make the full cut at two passes, setting for a smaller first cut by using a larger diameter collar, or resetting the ring and handling the workpieces twice. The method is rather messy and takes much longer than normal, but it is okay for short runs.

A common way to cut-relieve prior to shaping is to band-saw into shaped blanks which previously have been outlined in pencil using the template or finished part as a guide. Cutting blanks first into regular squared shapes might seem a nice tidy way of doing things but it can be uneconomical. Complex shapes could well interlock and save timber if marked directly-on a wide board. Don't simply place the template guide always in a regular pattern; move it around or even flip it to get more pieces out; it doesn't usually matter provided the run of the grain is correct. Mark around the template or guide using a thick pencil to allow enough overlap to clean-up fully on shaping.

In bandsawing, the drawn outline is followed only roughly, taking care not to cross the line. It is also possible to first divide-up the board roughly into blanks each with a single piece, then fit to a template and use as a bandsaw guide. Fit a small pin to the guide in line with the bandsaw teeth and about 3mm to the right-hand side. Move the template around to always line-up with the next immediate section of cut and feed to keep template and pin in light contact.

Fig. 287 Left: The correct grain direction.
Centre and left: Incorrect grain direction which allows sections to readily break off.

Set-out as shown at the extreme left to bandsaw.

It is essential to get the grain direction right with solid timber, or the parts may be short-grained, i.e., with corners that easily break-off. Generally, the curve should by tangential to the grain, roughly to follow the grain at the centre point of the curve. Curved parts often interlock when cut from a board.

155

Thin plywood gives no problems in grain direction. Often several pieces can be bandsawn and shaped at the same time by nailing from one side, then nailing the template from the reverse face to make the pack secure. If curves are part of a true circle a pivotted jig can be used in bandsawing.

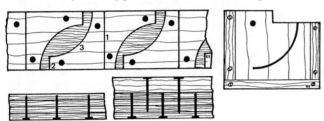

Fig. 288 There is more layout scope with plywood. Nail several sheets together for bandsawing and shaping as a single piece. Nail on the template from the opposite side.

When shaping fragile parts such as glazing beads for a decorative door opening light, use the same jig for shaping and bandsawing as following operations. Make the blanks over-long, and clamp vertically, between side guides. Use a simple gauge to project the sawn piece the proper amount to cleanup in the shaping operation. Following the sequence shown makes the beads absolutely parallel when bandsawn. Finally sand flat the seating face using a bobbin sander.

CURVE ON CURVE WORK

The most intricate and dangerous work on a spindle moulder has curves in two planes. It could be assumed that with CNC and floating head routers now used for this, hand work is no longer needed, but this is not always the case. If proper jigs and fixtures are made it is possible to operate curve on curve work in reasonable safety. The methods that are used are not always theoretically correct, but give acceptable results. Three specific points need noting:

Firstly, do not use square-in cutter profiles, such as rebates, as the cutters score the surface at other points. Always form cutter shapes at an angle to avoid fouling other parts, See Figs. 312 and 315 relative to simple sweeps.

Secondly, when forming curves to the top or under faces blend them with the same angle to level. This moulds an acceptable junction line even though a true blend isn't possible. Do not attempt a perfect blend, the result will disappoint.

Finally, to reduce errors to the minimum, use a small diameter head and a large diameter saddle, curve or ring fence.

Fig. 289 Left: Jig for bandsawing curves on a pivotting jig.
Right: The initial square-in cut .

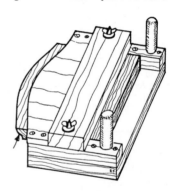

Fig. 290 Above: Jig for shaping, then bandsawing, narrow glass beads and similar. The arrow shows a moulded bead ready for bandsawing off.

Below: The upper sketch shows the moulding operation. The lower sketch shows the following bandsawing cut. Note the bandsaw guide pin at A.

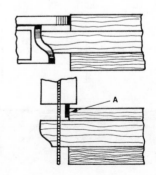

Fig. 291 The base saddle for curve on curve work fixes to the machine table with the cutterhead opposite the lowest point of the sweep.

Chair backs

Some chair back rails are typical of curve on curve work. The first process is to square-edge shape the rail, but without the mould. (To combine edge-shaping and moulding is difficult in the extreme and makes the operation unnecessarily dangerous. Whether bentwood, laminate, or shaped, the rails rarely match one another exactly, nor do they form part of a true circle. Any template would be very complicated for this reason and never satisfactory.)

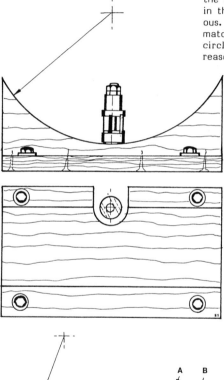

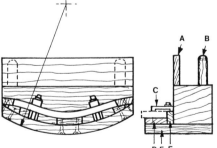

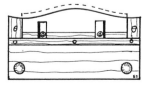

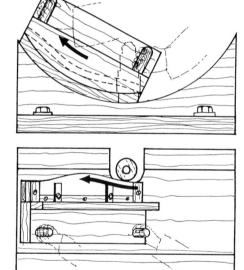

Fig. 293 In rocking the jig, keep it parallel to the base edge whilst following the ball-bearing.

Fig. 292 The rocking carriage seats the chair rail on blocks D, held down by clamps C and back against rear fence F. The curved base E is also the template. Handles B and a finger guard A are essential.

To edge-shape and plane use a rocking jig which roughly follows the chair rail curve. Make the contact face of the jig a true part-circle. Support the chair rail on blocks and against end-stops so that it lies more or less evenly, then clamp in place. The underside of the jig is also the template and must be edge-shaped to the required rail profile. Fix a finger guard and handles to the outside.

The jig rocks on a shaped seating formed in a base fixed to the machine table. The base should partially wrap around the cutterhead at the deepest point of the sweep. Use a small-diameter cutterhead with the follower beneath the head and level with the template of the rocking jig.

The jig is moved around the curved seating and simultaneously in and out to keep the template against the ball-bearing follower so that the cutters edge-mill the rail to profile. Before starting the cut make a dummy run to ensure that the template can maintain full contact with the follower. The jig must not swivel in any way in rocking, it must always move in and out, parallel to the base edge. This is why a ball-bearing follower is needed; a ring fence would not give the proper outline. Cutters must be much deeper than the thickness of the chair rail and perfectly square to the table because the rail edge height varies in shaping. Wax both jig underside and base topside to keep movement smooth.

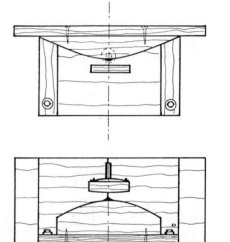

Fig. 294 Top and front views of a bed and fence saddle used for moulding chair-back rails.

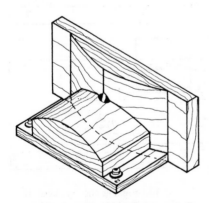

Fig. 295 General view of the fence and bed saddle set-up.

The second operation is to add the mould using a very small diameter cutter such as a router cutter. Shape a bed saddle to a curvature side to side but level front to back. The curve should be slightly less than the smallest internal face-curve in the rail. Fasten it to the table with the top dead centre of the curve directly opposite the cutterhead. Also fix a saddle to the fence to match the smallest edge-curve and with the highest point central to the cutterhead. Break through the bed and fence saddles by raising the cutter to line up as shown. Mark the contact point clearly on the fence saddle. Fit a top Shaw guard pad with a curved undersurface.

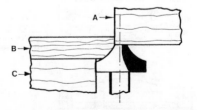

Fig. 296 The rounding cut on the rail at B is made on a bed saddle C and a fence saddle A.

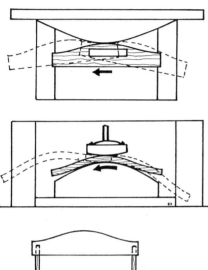

Feed the rail inside-curve down on the table saddle, always so that the section opposite the cutterblock lies level. Swivel it to keep the template in contact with the highest point of the fence saddle, as with a ring fence. It is technically wrong to swivel the rail as shown, but there is no other choice, and the distortion this gives is of little consequence.

Fig. 297 In feeding keep the rail curve-down, level with the table at the contact point and touching the contact point of the fence saddle.

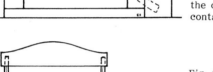

Fig. 298 If the chair-back is pre-drilled for rods, drive dowels into these and use them to control the movement.

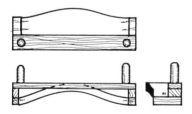

Preferably a holding jig should be used to control the chair back, having clamps or other fastening means and control handles. Allow extra length for screwing or driving-in through brads from end plates on the jig. Alternatively, if the rail is pre-drilled for chair rods, temporarily insert control handles in these holes. A holding jig should be made so as not to foul the saddle - unless under-profiled to the same shape of the chair rail, in which case it could add stability to the operation.

Stair handrails

Fig. 299 Screw-on holding jig. Use the turned screw shown in Fig. 216 to end-clamp and pierce the part with the brad point to give extra holding power.

These are amongst the most difficult parts to machine and often caused accidents when they were regularly produced on badly-guarded machines. The twisted section of handrail joining two handrails square to one another on a kite-tread turning is probably the worst type, as each is individual according to the stair layout and distance in from the fulcrum of the kite treads.

It should be a quarter turn in plan view, but from any other viewpoint the finished handrail appears twisted. Plan for a quarter turn which is not too tight, then vertically measure the height from the joint of the lower handrail to that on the upper handrail.

The first process is to bandsaw the vertical inside and outside faces to the quarter turn shape shown in plan view. Use a pivotting jig for this. Make two cuts in it as a guide to size and to position the block.

Fit a support to angle the block to the height measurement taken, allowing overhang for later trimming. It is difficult to be certain of the proper size without complex geometry, so make trial cuts in scrap pieces before cutting the piece selected.

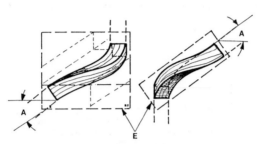

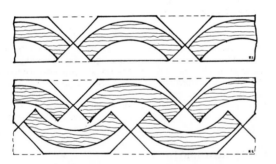

The grain on the block should be diagonal to generally follow the handrail curve. Cross-cut the board at about 45 degrees to produce either true squares or, to use less timber, squares but with inside and outside diagonal corners missing.

Fig. 300 Sketches of a curved handrail showing:
A – stair rake angle.
B – handrail width.
C – inside radius.
D – distance from lower to upper handrail.

The left and centre sketches are horizontal views in the direction of the arrows on the right-hand sketch.

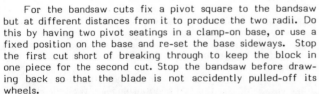

Fig. 301 Typical layouts for cutting handrails from wide and narrow boards.

For the bandsaw cuts fix a pivot square to the bandsaw but at different distances from it to produce the two radii. Do this by having two pivot seatings in a clamp-on base, or use a fixed position on the base and re-set the base sideways. Stop the first cut short of breaking through to keep the block in one piece for the second cut. Stop the bandsaw before drawing back so that the blade is not accidently pulled-off its wheels.

Separate the parts, then replace the handrail alone on the bandsaw jig in its original position and carefully mark out the angle and depth of the matching stair rail at top and bottom along the inner curve. Join the lines with fair and parallel curves to blend into the drawn angles. The curves vary considerably from one staircase to another so only general guides can be given.

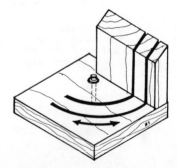

Fig. 302 Pivotting jig used in bandsawing.

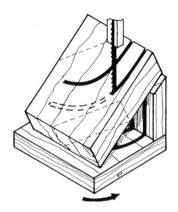

Fig. 303 Support the block at the correct angle. Follow the plan view of the curves in bandsawing by setting the pivot square to the bandsaw blade.

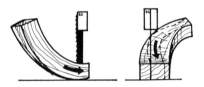

Fig. 304 The final top and bottom cuts are made on the bandsaw to follow the lines drawn on the inside curve. Keep the handrail flat on the table at the saw.

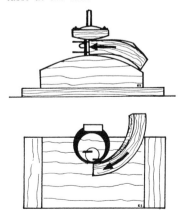

Make the final bandsaw cuts for the top and bottom faces of the handrail by following these drawn lines. Keep the section where the saw actually cuts flat on the bandsaw table by following a curved path in feeding. Finally, clean-up and size the handrail on a disc and bobbin sander using a shaped saddle similar to that shown for moulding. This is very much a hand trial and error operation. Controlling jigs and templates would be so complex as to be impractical, and would, in any event, vary from stair to stair.

The final operation is moulding the rail on a table saddle, held down by a shaped Shaw guard to run against a double ring fence. The saddle should have a single curve only side to side with the top dead-centre section opposite the cutterhead and level front to back. Some use a double-curved saddle or pudding-bowl, but this type is extremely unstable and dangerous to use.

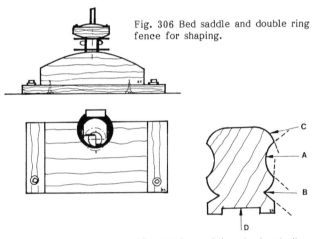

Fig. 306 Bed saddle and double ring fence for shaping.

Fig. 305 In moulding the handrail make cuts in the sequence A, B, C. The groove at 'D' is the baluster seating.

Fig. 307 Top and front views of the shaping operation showing the starting position.

Use only the type of saddle shown, together with a small-diameter cutterhead and the largest diameter rings which will follow the inner curve of the handrail. Set one ring above and the other below the cutterhead to contact the side of the handrail. Guard the cutterhead with a cage guard open only at the front between the ring fences. Form the mould one small section at a time starting from the centre and working out to retain contact with both rings for all except the final top cut.

Feed the handrail underside down. Keep it level at the point of contact and in contact with the marked point of the top ring. For the final top cut, run top surface down, and with both rings set to contact suitable points on the profile. On a fully top-rounded handrail do not attempt to meet on centre when using a saddle. This ensures that the part remains stable during moulding. Leave the overlap for hand finishing. Form the inside curve first and the outside curve as the final cut.

Bear in mind always that this is a dangerous operation, take great care to check and double-check before making any cut. If practicable fasten a rigid holding jig to the ends of the handrail and with fitted handles to give better and safer control. Similar methods can be used to those shown in making curve-on-curve rails.

Jigging for curved handrails

The type of handrail described above is only used with kite treads. The more common types, which are easier to make, are used on stairways with quarter or half-space landings at the turns. The sketch shows a U-turn on a staircase with a halfspace landing laid-out so that only a single curve is used at any point, either a level quarter turn or an up or down sweep. Usually each section is made individually for bolting together with handrail bolts.

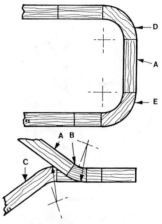

Fig. 308 Sections of a handrail:
A – straight sections.
B – short upsweep.
C – downsweep and straight section.
D & E – level quarter turns.

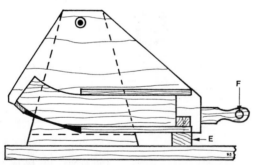

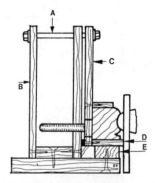

The level quarter turn inside and outside faces can be handled flat with conventional jigged templates of the types previously described. After planing and bandsawing, shape and mould them on jigged templates using a small diameter cutter-head and a ring fence. Use separate wide-based templates to form the inner and outer curves individually for safer hand-ling.

The same machine setting is used, first completing the inside curve, then using the second jig for the outside curve. (The inner curve has more contact with the cutterhead, so the assembly needs to be as stable as possible for this first cut.) Because the jigs are used interchangeably make sure they match perfectly for height and size. Volutes and similar are formed in more or less the same way, but using router cutters and preferably a router.

Fig. 309 Sectional and front views of a sliding base and carriage for moulding up and downsweeps, either as short curves as an extension of a straight section, showing:
A – pivot.
B – support frame.
C – swinging carriage.
D – bearing strip.
E – levelling block.
F – extended control handle for the swinging carriage.

The edge profile on the up and down sweeps cannot be moulded flat on a jigged template. The top and bottom curved faces can by moulded flat, after bandsawing, using two jigged templates, generally as for quarter turns. It is also possible, and very convenient at this stage, to form the centre groove for the balusters and the central section of the top curve on the handrail. Form these at a following operation to square-edge shaping, possibly using the same jigged templates.

For side or edge moulding use fixtures similar to that shown. It consists of a sliding base with two vertical supports carrying a substantial horizontal pivot. Hung from this pivot is the carriage for the handrail, with the distance from pivot to handrail correct for the curvature wanted. This can usually be made a standard dimension.

The carriage supports the handrail in a trough and against an end-stop for precise location. If several rails are being machined, end-trim them precisely to the same length relative to the curve, as they have to be re-fitted several times. Form the underside of the trough and the end support for the curved section as a rubbing strip to bear against the fence. Lock the rail in place by captive brads through the top section of the trough. Fit a block to support the carriage when the handrail is level.

Fit controlling handles both to the carriage and to the sliding jig. Fit and break through a fence for each cut, gauging the height from a section tacked or drawn onto the leading end of the handrail. Fully mould one side before forming the opposite using a separate fixture, but make sure both fixtures correspond. A fixture could be made to mould both curve-leading and curve-trailing sides, but this might be unwieldy if the level sections are long.

Work the mould in the sequences shown, matching to the previously formed central top curve at the final cut. Always work with an upward curve; top 'up' with an upsweep and top 'down' with a downsweep.

When the curve leads, first position the pivot directly opposite the cutterhead and fix a backstop behind the sliding base. Check that the proper movements are possible before making the cut, then mould as follows. Raise the carriage by its handle to clear the cutters when the sliding base is pulled back against the backstop. Holding the sliding base back and with the rubbing strip in contact with the fence, start-up the spindle and gradually lower the carriage making a sweeping cut until level, then hold the carriage handle down and feed forward against the fence until clear of the cutters.

Try to make to make the level cut a continuation of the curved sweep so that no static-cut marks are formed. It is possible to interlock the fixture so that forward movement is impossible until the handrail is level and in contact with the stop. This consists of a curved stop fastened to the infeed fence to follow the path of the extended handle of the carriage in moving. The only gap is at the level position.

When the curve trails fix a front stop for the sliding jig to locate it with the pivot directly opposite the cutterhead. This time hold the carriage handle down, starting the cut clear of the cutterhead to the right.

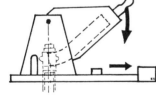

Fig. 310 Starting position for a leading curve.

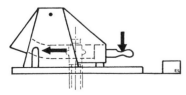

Fig. 311 Level run.

Feed forward until against the front stop, then, holding the sliding jig down, gradually raise the carriage handle until the rail clears the cutters. Again try to make it a continuous cut from level to curve and out. Fit a spring latch to hold the carriage when raised to allow the machine to be stopped in safety. An interlock is possible using a level rail fixed to the fence to contact the extended carriage handle and with a gap only when the sliding jig is against the stopblock.

The up and down sweeps described extend into straight sections when used for spanning short distances. The same part is also made as a curve only. In this case the same jig is used but is fixed in position opposite the cutterblock. With both types the curvature is always extended beyond the point actually needed to allow trimming on site. By doing this the precise angle of the stairway does not need to be known. The stairway angle can vary slightly yet still use a standard curve. Simply trim the handrail at the correct point of curvature to precisely match the stairway rake. Use the pitch plate as a guide to find the proper joint-line point, then draw across square to this to show the joint-line needed.

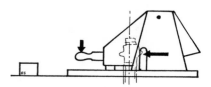

Fig. 313 Starting position for a trailing curve.

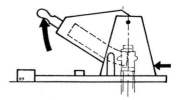

Fig. 314 Finishing position for a trailing curve.

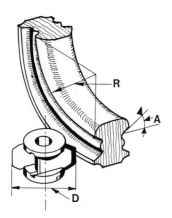

Fig. 312 Check dimensions R and D to find the smallest acceptable mould angle A on the chart.

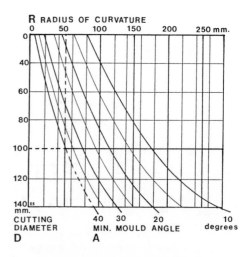

Fig. 315 Chart showing minimum mould angle on upsweeps, downsweeps and similar.
Example shows 100mm cutting diameter which allows a minimum mould angle of 40 degrees when the handrail has a curvature of 50mm at the mould.

When moulding curved handrails of this type and similar there is a chance of the cutter fouling other parts due to the complex geometry. This is governed by the angle formed on the cutterhead, its diameter at the deepest point and the radius of curvature at the point being moulded.

CHAPTER 13

ROUTING

The spindle moulder can be used for some routing, but is no real substitute for an overhead router: the spindle speed is too low for small diameter cutters, there is no convenient fast movement into a blind cut, also the cut is out of sight and is difficult to monitor. Any fault can only be seen when routing is complete which, in most cases, is then too late to correct.

Router cutters are ground in their flutes. They fit in the split collet of a stub arbor replacing the regular arbor.

Fig. 316 Below: Forming open-end grooves. The workpiece is controlled between hardwood guides and butts against an end-stop. A Shaw guard is needed on all routing operations but is ommitted on all drawings for clarity.

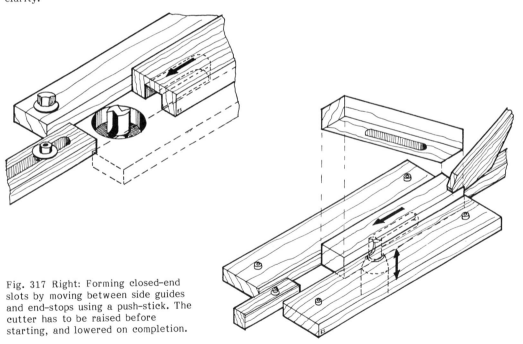

Fig. 317 Right: Forming closed-end slots by moving between side guides and end-stops using a push-stick. The cutter has to be raised before starting, and lowered on completion.

USING GUIDES AND JIGS

Where straight slots are needed parallel to the sides of a narrow workpiece, guide these by hardwood fences at each side, and hold down by a Shaw guard.

When the slot is open to one end, run-in from this end up to an end-stop set to the length needed. For closed-end slots fit stops at both ends. Wind the head up into the cut at the start position, then form the slot, using a push stick to give a smooth and even feed movement. Finally stop and lower the head before removing the finished workpiece and inserting the next. Working this way means removing and replacing the Shaw guard each time. This is tedius, but essential, as running without a top pressure is dangerous.

The spindle moulder should, preferably, have positive vertical setting via an adjustable stop on the slide. It is possible to rely on marks or a scale on the vertical movement or an angular setting of the handwheel, but these can give variation between one cut and the next and it is all too easy to overrun.

If the slot is straight but at an angle to the workpiece edge; for example, sloping shelf grooves in cupboard sides; some form of jig is needed. A simple type is a pair of guides between which a sliding piece operates and having a centre groove through which the cutter projects. The jig fastened to the slide is merely a piece of plywood, having side fences to angle the workpiece so that the required slot is parallel to the guide. Eccentric clamps hold the workpiece in place. For accuracy, first fit the router cutter, then slot through the plywood as a guide when fitting the fence. Add a hardwood block to guard the router cutter when in the rest position.

Stops are needed at front and rear to limit the slide movement, and to regulate the slot length. If open one end, set the cutter at the proper height and run into and out of the slot. Open-end slots can be handled very simply. The jig is drawn back clear of the Shaw guard so that the finished piece can be removed and the next quickly fitted. If closed both ends, the piece must be positioned at the start of the slot and the cutter raised into it as described before. Reverse the angle of the fences for opposite hand sides.

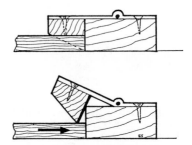

Fig. 319 An end-stop made in this way lifts automatically when the workpiece is pushed against the fence.

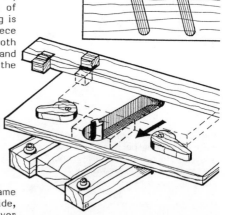

Where a number of parallel slots need cutting in the same piece, again taking the example of shelves in a cupboard side, the jig has a rear fence with front eccentric clamps. Flip-over stops on hinges provide end-wise location.

Alternatively, for easier operation, make the stops taper upwards and away from the fence. By placing the side flat or corner-on the table clear of the stops, all the stops lift automatically when the side is then pushed towards the fence. In operation; shift the workpiece sideways clear of the next stop to be used, so that this drops into place, then back against it for positioning. Repeat for all the remaining cuts.

Fig. 318 Forming stopped or through angled slots or housings on a sliding jig.
Flip-over end-stops allow several housings to be cut.
Eccentric clamps hold the side in place and a block guards the cutter.

Plate 76 A scale close to the rise and fall handwheel on this Delta spindle moulder shows the precise relative height.

Fig. 320 Forming a sill groove using a small-diameter flush-top circular cutterblock.

Plate 77 Height stops on this SCM spindle moulder give precise vertical setting control.

MOULDING

Being a flush-topped cutter, the router bit can be sunk into the cut to reduce projection on deep mouldings. This type is not a heavy-duty tool and is unsuitable for the heavy cuts common with larger cutterheads. There are, however, some uses that it is particularly suited for.

It is suitable, for example, for stop moulding where sweep-in and out needs to be of small radius. Fences and pressures are used in much the same way as with regular cutterheads, and with similar techniques.

Router cutters can reduce projection on what would otherwise need over-long cutters in conventional set-ups. One example is in forming the throating groove in large sills. Normally these need long cutters to reach across the long sill bevel, if worked with regular cutterheads from the side. A suitable router-type cutter for this operation forms only the groove, and can either be a solid router cutter, or a flush-topped circular cutterhead with loose cutters fitted. The sill is worked upside-down, supported on guides fastened to the table. Cutter projection is quite small, with the cutter under-cutting well inside the bevel.

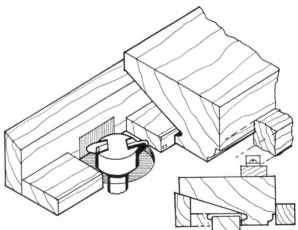

A jig is used when forming a stopped throating on windows where fixed and opening lights alternate, but in this case the jig mounts the sill supports, and has eccentric clamps to lock the jig and sill together. The cutter operates through a slot in the jig base, and the jig and sill assembly runs against a regular through-fence fitted with stops or a cam system. The same arrangement can be used to modify rebates for opening lights.

167

USING A TEMPLATE

Template routing is difficult on the spindle moulder because the cutter is not visible when working, and with inside cuts the cutter has to be wound up before the cut, and down again after. In all cases a Shaw guard is essential to steady the cut. The template can be used below or above the workpiece.

Template below

The template lies on the table and supports the workpiece, which is fastened to it. It needs to be large enough to be both stable itself and support the workpiece. This is not easy with small workpieces, which are better worked two-up on a double-size template making the cut at two passes.

The template can contact the plain shank of the stub arbor as a guide. This not really suitable because it spins with the arbor, tends to burn the template, and gives a rough 'feel' to the work. It is better to use a ball-bearing follower, but templates then have to be made even smaller and less stable. To make operation safe, use a ball-bearing follower only with large templates.

Because the shank or ball-bearing is bigger than the cutter at its planing diameter, the size and shape of the template has to be modified to take this into account, so template-making is complicated. In use, neither the template shape nor the cut can be seen clearly, so the operator works blind with inside shapes and is badly sighted with with outside shapes. In practice, this method is only suitable for the simplest of work, perhaps cutting the drain grooves in drainer boards. (It is possible to taper drain grooves on this, or other similar routing work, simply by tilting the workpiece on the template).

Template above

The template is fastened to the top of the workpiece, which then lies directly-on the table. It is sometimes possible with an over-template to use a router with a small ball-bearing fitted at the end as a follower. This can be used for a light trimming cut, when the workpiece is already virtually the right shape and overall size, or for corner trimming, either by using a template, or by running against the edge of an already trimmed workpiece.

When routing from a blank, the template follower must be separate from, and suspended above, the router cutter, but absolutely concentric to it. Some manufacturers provide a dowelled fixture for this so that alignment is guaranteed. In other cases the support adjusts, and is aligned by lowering the follower near to the chuck and setting concentric to it. This relies on the operator for accuracy of alignment, and can vary each time. The template follower is a ball-bearing on some machines intended to roll with the template and give that essential light touch, but more often is a static pin.

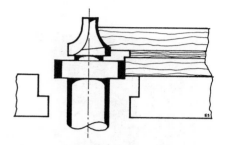

Fig. 321 Routing with the template underneath to contact either the shank or a ball-bearing.

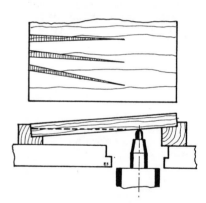

Fig. 322 Forming tapered grooves by tilting the workpiece.

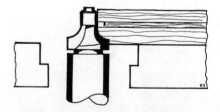

Fig. 323 Routing with the template above to contact either a plain shank, a small diameter ball-bearing or a pin suspended above the cutter.

A starter pin or block should be used where the shape is a full outline, as with regular shaping. This is not normal practice with regular routing, but spindle moulder speeds are lower, so there is a tendency to snatch on initial contact. When cutting inside shapes, the cutter needs raising when in the cut. Use a Shaw guard to hold down and steady the assembly and place the pin firmly against the template in a suitable position before switching-on.

With outside shapes, feed counter-clockwise when spindle rotation is also counter-clockwise, but with inside shapes rotate clockwise. In both case, movement is such that cutter rotation keeps the pin hard against the template. With wrong feed direction the cutter runs uncontrolled away from the template to a much greater extent than on a router because of the lower spindle speed. Preferably, take a heavy cut in two or more stages, raising the cutter between cuts so that no cut is excessive. This takes longer but makes the work easier and gives less chance of kick-back.

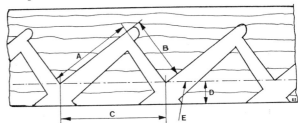

Fig. 324 Basic measurements of a string.
A - going.
B - rise.
C - pitch.
D - margin.
E - pitch line.

STAIR HOUSING

The spindle moulder is quite efficient at housing stair strings. A jig for this is available from some machine makers as a light-weight, clamp-on template, which usually has fixed tread and riser thickness and a standard tread nosing, together with an overhead guide follower.

First make a plywood pitch board to the required going, rise and pitch. The going is the distance from the face of one riser to the face of the next measured horizontally. The rise is the distance from the top of one tread to the top of the next, measured vertically. The pitch is the distance from one tread/riser intersection to the next, and the pitch line is that parallel to the string edge to join the inside corners of the tread/riser. All these dimensions must be within specified ranges or the stairs will be difficult to climb because they are too shallow, too steep or have too long or too short a tread.

There are somewhat involved guide lines to be followed to give the right combinations, and these vary between different countries.

In the UK domestic guides, the rise should be between 160 and 220mm, and the going between 220 and 280mm to give a pitch angle of not more than 42 degrees. The sum of twice the rise plus one going should be between 550 and 700mm.

In the USA, the rise should be between 7 and 7 5/8in, and the going between 10 and 11in to give a pitch angle of between 32 and 37 degrees. The sum of twice the rise and one going should be between 24 and 25in, and the sum of one rise and one going should be between 17 and 18in.

To find the precise dimensions, the overall height of the stairs, floor to floor, must be measured accurately, also the overall going. The calculations needed are quite simple when measured metrically, using a modern calculator with squares and square roots. (The following calculations apply to UK domestic stairs, but similar calculations are used for USA stairs).

Assume an overall height, floor to floor, of 2 340 mm. Divide this by the average rise, say 180mm, to give, in this instance, 13 treads. (If the number is not even, round this up or down to the nearest whole figure, then divide back into the overall height to find the correct rise. This may be hard to measure accurately, but necessary to get the pitch board right.)

Next find the total going which should be 13 x 220 (the average going) in this case 2 860mm. Check if this distance is acceptable and, if so, make this the total going. (Actually the overal distance is less by one going because the top tread is actually where the upper floor starts, but for calculation purposes it is easier to include an imaginary full top tread). If the distance available is a bit short, cheat by shortening the going to fit in with this, but don't overdo things. It can also be stretched, but not by very much.

In all cases, however, the final figures must comply to the guides. In the example, the total of 180 + 180 + 220 is 580mm, well within the UK recommendations, also the pitch angle is 39 degrees, again well within the UK limit of 42 degrees.

Finally, calculate the overall stair pitch, so that the total pitch line, floor to floor measured along the stair slope, can be found. Calculate the square root of the sum of the going and rise after squaring both. The rise is 180mm, squared this is 32 400. The going is 220 mm, squared this is 48 400mm. Add these together to give 80 800mm, then find the square root which in this case is 284.25mm. The pitch board must be made to these dimensions precisely. Multiply the pitch by the number of treads, 13, to give an overall pitch of 3 695mm, to which the string length is made.

The plywood is triangular in shape, with two adjacent sides square to one another. Mark in from the square corner the going on one edge and the rise on the other. Join the two marks with a straight line, the pitch line, and check that this corresponds exactly to the pitch calculated.

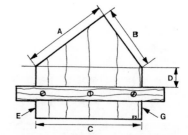

Fig. 325 A typical pitch board. Dimensions as Fig. 324, but with the two gauge lines E & G added.

Assumming that this measurement is correct, draw gauge lines about 100mm long square to the pitch line from these two points, and carefully cut along them. The dimension between the two gauge lines must correspond exactly with the calculated pitch. The two obtuse corners are where the outside faces of the next tread below and the next riser above intersect.

Draw an underedge line parallel to the pitch line and spaced between 25 and 75mm from the pitch line. Fasten fences on both faces, to this line, as a margin gauge. The margin is the distance from the pitch line to the underedge of the stair string - which is not critical unless the string itself is narrow. To maintain the correct distance from the nosing line (a line joining the nosings of the treads), the margin width can be varied, as necessary, to compensate for any width error of the string. This top edge is sometimes moulded to add interest, but then needs extra width in this case.

Preparation

Make the string to the overall pitch calculated, plus extra for trimming on site at the foot and the head of the stairs. A rule of thumb is to allow 125mm from where the bottom riser crosses the floor line to the bottom end of the string, and beyond the upper floor line. This allows enough room for a vertical mitre with a 150mm skirting board. Preferably make the string over-long to trim on site.

To make sure the string is housed correctly for the treads and risers, one string needs marking out in full using the pitch board. Mark the reverse face so that the correct positions for clamping the template are clearly visible. Use the pitch board first to mark the upper floor line on the string. With the margin fences against the under edge, mark along the tread line. Extend this line, using a straight-edge, to the upper edge of the string. With the pitch board still in place, also mark along the lower gauge line and the top rise face line.

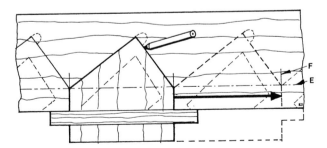

Fig. 326 Marking out a string using the pitch board. The pitch line is E and the gauge line F.

Move the pitch board along, its fence still firmly against the under edge of the string, until the top gauge edge of the pitch board corresponds with the drawn gauge line. Draw around the tread, riser and leading gauge line, then repeat, moving along the string in stages, until the lower floor end is reached. The lower floor line cuts the pitch line where the lowest riser meets the floor. Check that the overall length is what was calculated in the first place.

Another way is to draw in the overall pitch line, floor to floor, and divide equally for the number of treads needed. It can be done with a rule, but is easier using a pair of joiner's dividers. Set these to the calculated pitch and step along the pitch line adjusting, as necessary, until the distance pitches-out exactly for the number of treads needed (including the top floor line). Square across from each point to the pitch line to show the gauge lines. The pitch pitched-out should also correspond with the spacing of the gauge lines on the pitch board. After pitching-out fully, mark the reverse face of the string using the pitch board.

Machine setting

Set the template follower concentric to the router bit and adjust it vertically to barely clear a single string. Set the height of the router cutter to form the full depth of stair-housing needed. (It is tempting to cut the housing in two steps when using a light spindle moulder. Preferable, though, cut the full depth at a single pass, but more slowly. Many stair-housing cutters are slightly tapered, so that the treads and risers bite-in at the string face to give a better fit. Cutting the groove at two bites reduces this effect).

Place the left-hand string inside-face down on the machine table, and set the fences on the template so that the outer edges of the tread and riser slots in the template guide correspond exactly with the lines drawn on the string for the first housing. Clamp the template in place. Position the assembly so that the template slot is directly below the follower, when the router cutter is clear of the string. Lower the follower to engage in the template, check again that the cutter is clear of the timber, then start the machine.

Plate 78 Stair housing attachment on a Dominion spindle moulder.

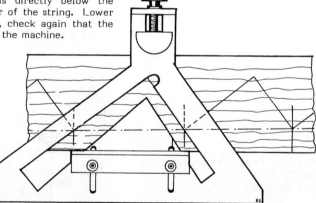

Fig. 327 Typical stair-housing template positioned via guide lines drawn on the reverse of the string.

Move the assembly so that the follower moves around the template as required, so that the router cutter mills an identical housing. Always move the assembly so that the cutter pulls against the template in feeding; otherwise it is difficult to control. If the left-hand string is being housed the tread template is to the right, (assumming the nosing faces the operator - this is the normal direction when stair housing). The sequence is to cut-in and follow-round the outer face of the riser, the nosing, the top face of the tread and out.

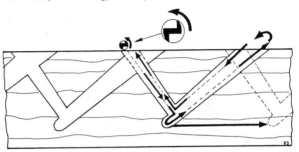

Fig. 328 Follow the sequence shown to keep the follower against the template and to avoid spelching where it shows. Note that the string is shown from above, but the housing is shown as solid lines for clarity on this and the following sketches.

Enter a second time against the under face of the tread, then back along the inside face of the riser and out. Make sure each housing is cut properly by going around a second time. Any lump formed during the first cut is easily removed at this time, but much more difficult to make good later.

Move the string well clear of the cutter and stop the machine. Raise the follower then re-set the template for the next tread and riser and mill as before, and so on until complete. Take care to set the template accurately or tread and riser width will vary.

CAUTION: If the cutter is sharp and the timber mellow little spelching will occur, but it can happen. Break-out at the unseen parts is not so important, for example the underedge, but, if excessive, cure this as follows:

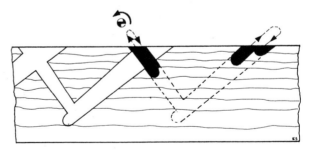

Fig. 329 To avoid under-edge spelching form initial cuts as shown in black prior to the main cut.

Before making the complete housing first notch-in about 50mm deep at the tread under face and the riser outer face, as though to start the housing, but withdraw along the same path before completion. Then cut in the same direction but just short of 50mm deep and, this time, against the opposite faces, the top edge of the tread and the inside face of the riser. The cutter will try to run, so feed slowly and carefully. Doing this forms the full width at the exit points and reduces breaking-out along the back edge.

The only other point that break-out is likely, and which must be avoided, is at the outer internal corner between tread and riser. When cutting the left-hand string, this only occurs when cutting top tread first and working down to the bottom tread, so always start with the bottom tread and work up. The housing for the riser cuts across the previous housing for the next tread below, but in the right direction, so that spelching doesn't occur where seen. It might spelch at the inside face of the next lower tread, but this is acceptable if crossed slowly.

Spelching is always possible if the route described is not followed exactly. See Fig. 328.

Housing the opposite string

The right-hand string can be housed by flipping-over the template and repeating the sequence described above, but with the following changes: Assuming the tread is now to the left, begin to house the outer top of the tread, then around the tread nosing, riser outer face and out. Re-enter against the inner face of the riser, then back against the under face of the tread and out. To avoid spelching make notching cuts intially against the riser inside face and tread top face, then against the opposite faces of both. Start at the top housing and work down to avoid spelching at the external corner between tread and riser.

Using a string as the template

An alternative which is faster, simpler and error-free, is to use the first string as a template for its pair. (The strings will match precisely, but any error in the first string repeats exactly in the second).

Nail the two strings back to back, taking great care where you place the nails of course, and work left-hand string up as a template. The first housing must be absolutely clean-cut, and the router cutter must be precisely the same diameter as the follower. (The cutter is the same when new, but wear reduces its diameter, so check. This is no problem when housing strings individually).

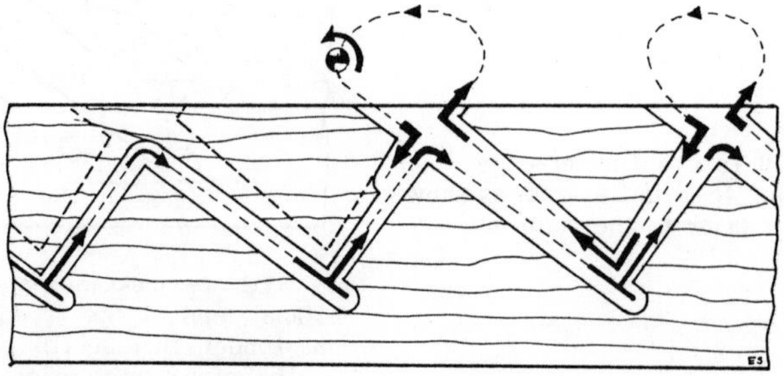

Fig. 330 House the second string as shown here when using the finished string as a template.

The second string can be worked in two stages. Start with the outer face of the top tread, around the nosing and outer face of the top riser, the top face of the second tread, around the nosing and outer face of the second riser, and so on, until the lower end is reached.

The second cut is a series of individual cuts starting this time at the bottom riser inside face, then along the under face of the bottom tread and finally out along the remaining housing for the outer face of the next riser. Re-enter to cut the remaining top face of the next tread, then along the inside face of the next riser, under face of the next tread and exit via the remaining section of the outer face of the third riser, then repeat. Sounds complicated, doesn't it? well, it isn't really, just follow the routes shown.

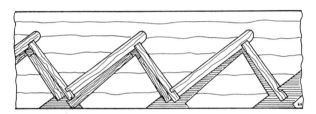

Fig. 331 The string is finally fitted with treads and risers interlocked as shown.

Variations from standard

Templates provided for housing strings on a spindle moulder have a fixed tread and riser thickness, though going, rise and pitch can be varied. Most incorporate wedge room to tighten the treads and risers after assembly. If thinner treads or risers than allowed for are to be fitted, house as before and make-up the difference with thicker wedges.

If thicker treads or risers than the template allows for are to be used, fit a router cutter which is bigger in diameter than the follower by the difference needed. For example, if the regular tread is 30mm but a thickness of 40mm is called for, use a 30mm router cutter (or 20mm follower (or 40mm and 30mm respectively) to cut the correct width. When setting the template on the string it must, of course, be off-set from the gauge marks of the tread and riser by half the difference between cutter and follower.

The most accurate way is to align the upper tread line of the template with the upper tread line drawn from the pitch board. The cut does not then precisely align, but off-sets each time by the same small amount. The riser housing is also housed wider pro-rata, so cut thicker wedges to suit. If subsequently using the first string as a template, replace the router cutter, or the follower, because the diameter of both must correspond exactly for this operation, even though, in housing the first string, using the machine template, the cutter and follower are of different diameter.

Other changes possible are: to fill in the nosing with hardwood shaped to produce an alternative nosing profile, either shorter or of a different shape; and filling in the riser slot to produce tread-only (riser-less) stairs.

After completing the strings, fit treads and risers individually to mark out, on the tread, the housing for the riser and the rebate on the back edge to tongue-into the next riser. Mark on the riser the groove to accept the tread tongue.

Plate 79 Dominion dovetailing attachment being used on the Dominion spindle moulder.

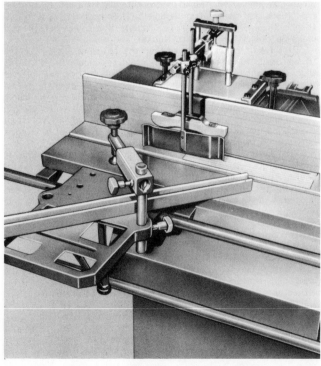

Plate 80 Startrite spindle moulder fitted with a sliding table for tenoning, end moulding and similar operations.

CHAPTER 14

DRAWER AND FRAME JOINTS
Dovetailing

When dovetailing was a primary method of jointing solid cabinets, some spindle moulders had attachments for dovetailing the frames - in addition to drawer dovetailing. They were versatile, but produced a square pin which did not seat properly in the rounded tail formed by the dovetailing cutter. Modern ones produce rounded pins which match the tails precisely.

Most current attachments are designed for drawer dovetailing only and, whilst very good for this, will only dovetail other sorts of frames within this capacity range. The attachment is a casting, with a finger-guide to form pins and tails at the same time, clamps for sides, fronts and backs, also left and right-hand side-stops to locate them.

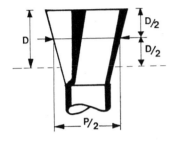

Fig. 332 The dovetail cutter diameter measured as at P/2 is half the pitch for which it is intended.

OPERATION

Clamp the drawer side upright to rest end-on the finger guide with its inside-face 'out'. Clamp the front horizontally inside-face down and butt firmly against the outside face of the drawer side.

The router-type dovetail cutter fits in a collet of a stub arbor and should run at the highest speed available on the machine. Slide the attachment on the spindle moulder table, manually guiding it so that the plain shank of the dovetail cutter follows around the finger plate. By doing this, pins are cut on the drawer side and tails in the drawer front at the same time. Dry-lubricate the spindle moulder table so that movement is easy.

Fig. 333 All these types are used in dovetailing.

Left: without spurs.
Centre: with two spurs.
Right: with multiple spurs.

SETTING

To vary the pitch of the dovetails the attachment often has interchangeable finger plates with dowel-pin location. The normal pitch is 25mm (1in), but others of 20 or 40mm (1/2 or 1.1/2in) can be substituted. Fit the appropriate plate for the drawer size; small pitches for small drawers, large ones for extra large drawers, but the common 25mm (1in) pitch for most regular sizes.

Different dovetail cutters are needed for each pitch. Makers can give details, but if in doubt measure the dovetail cutter diameter about 1/3 down from the top. It should equal half the pitch for which it is intended. A cutter 10mm diameter is for a 20mm pitch finger plate and to produce dovetails pitched at 20mm.

Some dovetail cutters are plain, that is without spurs. Others have spurs, either a single spur per edge, or multiple spurs. Those with spurs are less likely to spelch at lower spindle speeds. Sharpen and fit the appropriate cutter.

Dovetail cutters of different sizes usually interchange on the stub arbor, but have different shank diameters where they contact the finger plate. Set the cutter to the correct height (see notes on adjusting dovetail fit) and add fill-in rings to close the gap around the stub arbor.

Drawer side

Position the drawer side front-end down, with the groove central to one finger of the finger plate. This pin then neatly fills in the drawer groove. Set the side-stop against its under edge.

Check where the top edge of the drawer side then lies on the finger plate. Preferably it should be between fingers so a full pin is formed near the top. If a part pin is formed this looks untidy, so shift the side so that it does not - provided the groove still lies largely on a finger. If this is not possible there are two options:

a) Position the side so that a full pin forms close to the top edge ignoring the under edge, which is normally unseen, and fill the groove gap after assembly.

b) Position the side with the groove central on one finger, but do not form the part-cut at the top edge of the drawer front when dovetailing. Match this by cutting off the part pin on the top of the drawer side. See notes and Fig. 335.

Drawer front

Fit the drawer front firmly up to the drawer side with its under edge off-set inwards from the drawer side under edge by half a pitch. Set the side-stop against the drawer front under edge. Make sure this leaves the under edge of the side projecting beyond the under edge of the front for two reasons:

a) When the drawer side top pin needs cutting off, the corresponding part-cut must not be formed on the drawer front. If off-set as described it can easily be missed-out; if off-set in the wrong direction, it forms automatically when cutting part of the top pin on the side

b) Part of the side is unsupported when dovetailing because of the off-set - which may lead to spelching. This is less conspicuous if close to the under-edge.

A quick, simple and accurate way of off-setting, when positioning the drawer front stop, is to use a setting piece. Notch-out a scrap drawer front to hook onto the underedge of the drawer side and give the correct off-set for the pitch of drawer being dovetailed. Flip for the opposite hand. Keep different setting pieces for different pitches.

Tail depth

On some attachments the pin and tail depth are fixed so that no machine setting is necessary, but the joint strength remains

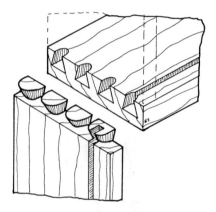

Fig. 334 Drawer fronts are preferably positioned so that the drawer side pins fills in the drawer front groove on assembly.

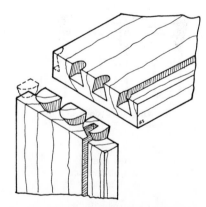

Fig. 335 Leaving part of a pin looks untidy; instead, cut it off and take care not to form the corresponding tail. Both are shown in dotted outline.

exactly the same regardless of drawer side thickness. As the tail depth suits a regular drawer side, there is no gain in joint strength by using thicker sides.

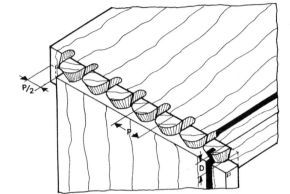

Fig. 336 Right: Off-set for dovetailing by half a pitch (P/2). D is the dovetail pin height.

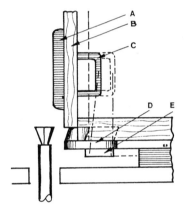

On other attachments the tail depth cut is manually pre-set to correspond with the drawer side thickness - to give the strongest possible joint. Check it by cutting a test dovetail using scrap pieces of the same size.

On the Robinson attachment the tail depth is set automatically to the thickness of the drawer side, to give the strongest possible joint. It also guarantees a flush fit without need of adjustment or trial and error machine setting.

Fig. 337 Above: Section through a Robinson dovetailing attachment with automatic tail depth control:
A - fixed front plate.
B - drawer side.
C - adjustable clamp.
D - finger plate.
E - depth control bar.

Fig. 338 Right: Joints produced on drawer sides of different thicknesses as shown by the corresponding distances between arrows. The right hand sketches show an attachment with fixed depth control; and the centre sketches show an attachment with automatic depth control.

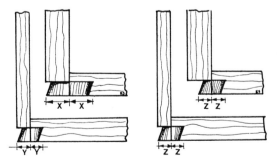

Dovetail fit

Check tightness of the assembled joint on any suitable scrap timber by dovetailing and fitting. Adjusting the dovetail cutter height varies the tightness of the joint; so if tight, lower it, and if slack raise it.

When correctly set, clamp a scrap drawer-front in the attachment to project just beyond the fingers and form a dovetail in it. Use this as a guide when setting height in future - but always check the fit before starting the run. The setting guide must be properly seasoned timber or it can shrink or warp to become useless. As the dovetail cutter is sharpened its diameter reduces and a lower height setting is needed, so replace the setting piece periodically to take account of this.

DOVETAILING OPERATION

Some makers show the dovetail attachment held from the rear, but this is so that the attachment shows clearly - it is not the way to use it. Most users, including the writer, work with the attachment on the far side of the dovetail cutter and span this to grip it either side. The inside of the drawer side faces the operator and the drawer front extends away from him at the rear. This gives better control and allows the cutting action to be seen clearly.

Before starting the dovetailing cut proper, form a scribing cut across the full width of the drawer side, moving the attachment so that the cutter cuts 'in'. Only a shallow scribing cut is needed, perhaps between 1 and 2mm deep. No guide is normally used so careful control of the cut is essential. A depth guide could be fitted temporarily on the finger ends, but most users find scribing in this way easy enough after little practice. If a scribing cut is not made prior to dovetailing there is a chance of spelching when using spur-less dovetail cutters.

Finally, cut the pins and tails simultaneously in the drawer side and front by carefully following round the finger guides. To prevent the cut running out of control move the attachment so that cutter rotation forces it against the guide fingers (as when routing). With normal rotation, start the cut at the right to finish at the left. Take care that contact is maintained throughout the full cut otherwise the joint may not be a flush-fit on assembly.

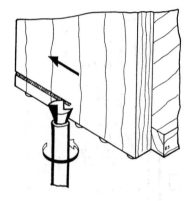

Fig. 339
Above: Scribing movement.
Below: Dovetailing operation.

Notes

1. When cutting the pin at the groove end of the drawer side move slowly so that it does not spelch-out at the back (the outer face when assembled). If this still happens, fit a hardwood backing piece alongside the front arranged to butt against, and lap, the drawer side. If the backing piece is firmly fixed it could, in practice, replace the normal side-stop.

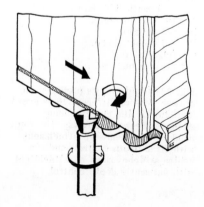

2. When the top part-pin on the drawer side is to be cut off, do not form the corresponding part-tail in the drawer front. Either stop at this point, or start further along - depending on the hand being cut. To cut off the pin, release the drawer side only and move it sideways so that the part pin overhangs

a gap between fingers, and re-clamp. Leave the drawer front in its original position for support, then cut-off the part tail by running-in the dovetail cutter.

3. It is essential that drawer parts are cross-cut square. If not, the drawer alignment will be incorrect on assembly. This is because the side-stops are distanced from the finger plate.

4. When fitting, press the drawer front hard against the drawer-side to prevent break-out on dovetailing.

Opposite hand

Drawer sides are dovetailed in pairs, so, if several drawers are being dovetailed, set the machine for both left and right-hand at the same time. Take care that the methods detailed are followed exactly, including the cutting sequence which is precisely the same for both hands.
    The most convenient way of dovetailing is to complete dovetails at both ends of the front and one end of both sides in a following sequence. In this way the front is handled once only, simply reversing it end for end for following cuts.

Drawer back

Drawer backs are normally flush on their underside with the top of the drawer side groove so the drawer bottom can be fitted after assembly. There are two alternative methods:

a) The drawer side can be dovetailed to a pin, and the back to a tail, as a duplicate of the drawer front fitting. In this case the drawer front and back are the same length. Use the drawer front stop settings, simply inserting a spacer between the side-stop and drawer back for the off-set needed. The spacer should equal the distance from the drawer side under-edge to the groove top. Make just one spacer and use it at both sides. When forming the pins on the drawer side do not form pins below the groove or above the back top edge, merely round them over.

b) Alternatively, form the drawer back as pins, and the drawer side with tails, to make a neater fitting. This may also allow better placing of the pins and tails. Part tails are acceptable on the under-edge, but the top pins must be whole. With this assembly the drawer front and back are different lengths, so carefully calculate this or the finished drawer will taper.
    Clamp the back in position vertically, and butt the side against it. Set the stops to correctly align the drawer back under-edge with the groove top. Use a scrap drawer back which is notched for easier setting, or the spacer previously described (equal in thickness to the under-edge to groove-top distance).

Lapped and open dovetails

Most dovetails are lapped; that is the drawer sides and back

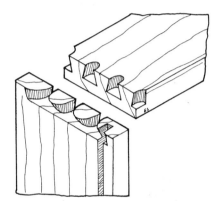

Fig. 340 One side-to-drawer back dovetail joint.

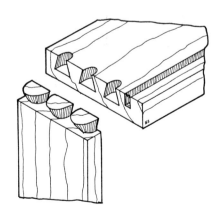

Fig. 341 An alternative side-to-drawer back joint.

are thicker than the pin length so the tail does not break through. This masks the assembled joint to give a neat appearance. If the sides are too thin for lapping, use a worn cutter which has less height, a stubbier cutter for the same pitch, or a smaller pitch-plate with a shorter pin.

Some users like to see the dovetail ends. They can look well in hardwood when varnished, but must be a good fit. They are easy enough to produce simply by making the drawer back thinner than normal so that the cutter breaks through on dovetailing. It is usual to make the parts thinner than the pin length so the pins project for sanding flush after assembly. Take account of this when sizing the drawer parts.

Lipped drawers

Kitchen drawers are often lipped at the top edge and both ends to disguise an otherwise poor fit. Dovetailing gives problems on some attachments, but is practical on those machines having an adjustable depth bar. Cut the drawer front to drawer width plus double the lip needed. Normally the lip is trimmed, so initially allow more than really necessary. After dovetailing and assembly, trim the projecting tails flush and round over the lips as a final operation. (See previous chapter).

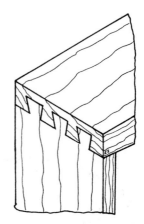

Fig. 343 Lapped dovetail assembled.

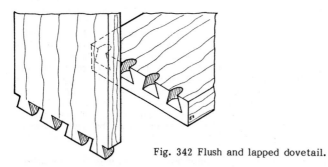

Fig. 342 Flush and lapped dovetail.

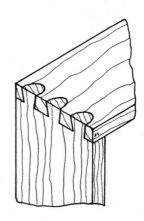

Fig. 344 Open dovetail assembled.

With attachments having a fixed tail depth, first dovetail the sides in the usual way using a scrap drawer front as back-up. Take care always to fit this in the same position, or the cut gradually widens to give inadequate support. If practical, leave the back-up piece in position and only switch the side.

When dovetailing the front, set the end forward of its normal position by the lip depth needed, and dovetail this alone. An easy way to locate the front is to rebate the end of a scrap drawer side by this amount, and clamp it at a higher position so the front butts against the rebate. The finished joint looks a bit odd, but allows the side to set-in by the lip-depth needed on assembly and gives an acceptable appearance when cleaned-up. See Fig. 349.

182

With adjustable depth-stop types, the front and side can be dovetailed at the same time by adjusting the depth bar to suit. On the Robinson attachment, the side and back are also dovetailed at the same time, simply by inserting a spacer between drawer side and clamp to automatically deepen the tails. The spacer should equal half the lip depth needed.

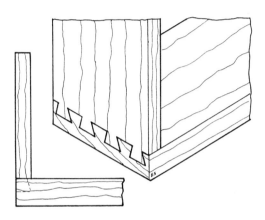

Fig. 345 Flush and lapped dovetail assembled.

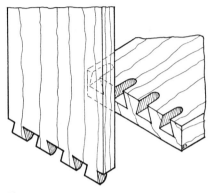

Fig. 346 Lipped and rebated drawer dovetail exploded.

Fig. 347 Lipped and rebated drawer assembled.

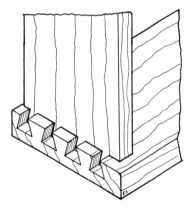

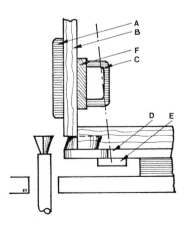

Fig. 348 Section through a Robinson dovetailing attachment set up for lipped drawers and showing the parts as under Fig. 337, plus the spacer F.

Sloping front drawers

It is possible to dovetail drawers with a sloping front by cutting off the sides at an angle and placing them so that the angled end seats properly on the fingers. The slope angle limits the width that can be dovetailed - wide pieces or large angles will not fit. The front is butted squarely against the side, off-set by half a pitch, and the dovetail formed as before. It isn't easy to position the front and side with absolute accuracy, so make the fronts a little wide, and off-set a little more than normal to allow fitting after assembly.

The same method can be used to make other frames with a sloping front and/or back, but the two sides must be upright. Trying to make these slope also simply is not viable.

Hidden dovetails

Most users think a machine cannot form hidden dovetails, but this is possible on some attachments if the side is double the normal thickness, or roughly equal to the pitch. The fixed-depth types cannot do this; fronts and sides need separate settings.

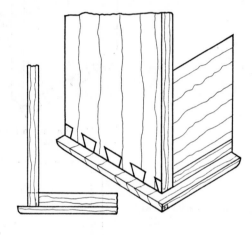

Fig. 349 Assembled drawer after rebating and nosing.

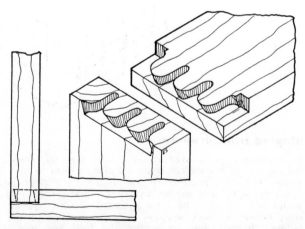

Fig. 350 The machine version of a hidden dovetail needs some hand work.

Clamp the side in position and set the depth bar accordingly to limit the cut depth so that the cutter is just

184

short of breaking through. This gives the appearance of a combination pin and tail. On the Robinson attachment wedge a spacer against the automatic depth bar (equal in thickness to the side) to give the same effect and leave the spacer in position. Raise and reclamp the drawer side to allow the front to barely slide underneath. Use the drawer side as a guide to set the drawer front end in line with the outer face of the side (and off-set as usual). Dovetail as before.

When assembled, the joint looks like a lap dovetail, but which is actually a blind dovetail. To completely baffle the curious, form the two outer edges of the side as part pins, then stop short of the edge to leave this square. Chisel-in the drawer front to form an assembled joint which gives no clue as to the way it was actually formed.

Finger jointing

Both jointing and tenoning operations are possible with make-shift set-ups on the spindle moulder, but for safe operation and dependable results use the proper attachments.

The finger-joint attachment consists of a table with a front fence and side clamp rolling on a guideway fixed to the spindle moulder table, or a sliding section of the main table. The cutters used are two-wing type, stacked between spacers of equal thickness and mounted on a special keyed spindle. Cutters have a keyway so that, when correctly assembled, the cutting edges spiral to stagger the cut. The diameter is around 150mm, and they to run at 5 000 revs/min., or thereabouts.

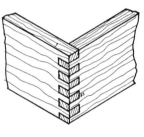

Fig. 351 Finger-jointing, showing the two settings with cutters off-set half a pitch.

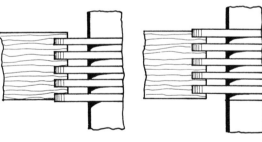

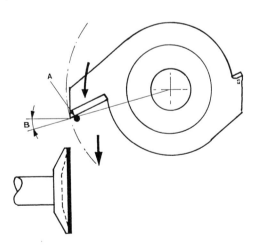

Fig. 352 Grind all finger joint cutters to the same cutting diameter by butting and clamping the cutter front-face against a fixed pin A. This is off-set from the centreline to give the required clearance B.

Set the assembly so that cutters just clear the leading fence. Set the height initially so that the underside of the lowest cutter is barely below the rolling table surface. Check the workpiece depth against the cutters, and adjust the height, if necessary, so that the bottom cutter lap equals the lap of the top cutter, or the lap of the space above it. Fit the guard to protect the cutter assembly.

Use the regular steel fences to gauge the length of the fingers, but make sure they are in line and absolutely parallel to the slideway. Do this by clamping a setting block on the attachment to just touch the cutters. By moving the attachment fully across, with a spacer fitted between block and fence, the fence position can be set accurately at both ends. The spacer should equal the finger length needed.

Parts for finger jointing are cut to neat length and stacked several together all face to back. Carefully butt their ends against the infeed fence and seat them properly before clamping against the front fence. With the cutters running, pass the assembly across the cutterhead, then draw fully back before stopping the machine to unclamp and reload. Finger joint the opposite end after turning end for end, keeping the same under-edge down. Repeat as necessary.

The opposite-hand pieces are clamped the same-edge down, but move the cutterhead up by the thickness of a single cutter so that the joint matches properly when assembled. This is possible by using the vertical adjustment of the machine, but a simpler and more accurate method is to release and remove the cutter assembly complete, then insert a single spacer before replacing and relocking.

GROOVED SIDES

When finger jointing grooved sides, position two cutters in the first set-up one above and the other below the groove, and finger joint as before. For the second set-up use an extra spacer as before and replace the finger now opposite the groove by a cutter smaller in cutting radius by the groove depth. By doing this the groove is filled-in by the finger joint.

Preventing spelching

In finger-jointing as a pack the feed is steadier and the pieces each support one another, so spelching only occurs at the back of the trailing piece. To stop it altogether, sandwich a piece of hardwood between the pack and the clamp as a back-up. Take care that this seats properly, then screw it to the clamp to keep it in the position needed.

Sharpening cutters

As with all cutters, finger joint cutters should be kept sharp. Normally they are a specially-made set to correspond exactly in cutting width both with one another and with the spacers supplied with them. Sharpening is only carried out on their outer faces, and care should be taken to keep them all precisely the same diameter. Don't sharpen them on the face or edge as this reduces their thickness. Use a universal type of grinder. Position the front face firmly against a fixed pin, and clamp in place. The pin positions the cutter to form the correct clearance angle, so adjust it accordingly. Grind all at the same setting using a CBN wheel for accuracy.

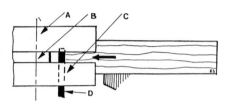

Fig. 353 First cut on square-cut tenons:
A – top tenon head.
B – spacer made-up to tenon thickness required.
C – bottom tenon head.
D – end-stop.

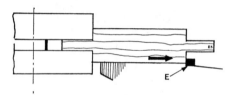

Fig. 354 Second-cut on square-cut tenons. Butt the first shoulder against the spring-loaded shoulder stop E.

Plate 81 Robinson finger-jointing attachment for their spindle moulder.

Tenoning

The attachment for this is similar to the finger-joint attachment, but with a wider table and a back fence, top clamp, an end-stop for the first cut and a spring-loaded shoulder-stop for the second. The cutterhead is a large diameter type, usually about 300mm (12 in) diameter, in two halves which are separated by spacers fitted according to the tenon thickness needed.

Each cutterblock carries two cutters. These form the shoulders with their cutting edges, and the tenon proper with the inside corners. Only a relatively short tenon can be produced - limited by the cutterblock and spacer diameters.

Fit the cutterblocks with the cutters staggered, and with spacers between the two halves. Spacers are provided in 2, 3 4, 5mm (1/16, 1/ 8, 1/4in) thicknesses, etc., so any tenon thickness can be made up using the right combination. Set the spindle speed to 3,000 revs/min for 300mm (12in) diameter heads and 4,200 revs/min., for 230mm (9in) diameter heads, then fit the cover guard. Position the slideway so that the cutters clear the edge of the attachment tenon table, then adjust the spindle arbor vertically to give the proper underface-to-tenon distance.

Place the piece for tenoning on the table and back against the rear fence, then clamp in position. Tenon a scrap piece to check alignment on assembly. To use the attachment, butt the workpiece against the end-stop to gauge the length of the first tenon. The endstop usually fits on a bar projecting from the slideway base, and first needs off-setting from the cutting line to the required tenon length. It is practical to measure this from the shoulder of the backing piece. Tenon the end by slowly feeding the piece clear past the heads, then draw back well clear of the cutters and release.

Keeping the same face down, turn end for end and set the shoulder against the spring-loaded shoulder-stop for tenoning the opposite end. The shoulder-stop is pre-set from the cutting line, again measuring from the shoulder on the backing piece.

STEPPED TENONS

The regular cutterblocks are fitted with square-end cutters to produce square tenons which are also square across. It isn't safe to project cutters more for the stepped tenon needed to match a rebate. For these, first cut tenons square to the longest shoulder length, with the shoulders to be shortened face-down. Remove the top tenon head, then fill-up with spacers and re-lock. Do not alter the height of the spindle arbor. Fit an end-block against the back fence to butt against the top shoulder when the bottom shoulder projects beyond the cutting line by the step needed. Re-tenon all the pieces same-face down locating the top shoulder against the end-block.

Plate 82 Dominion tenoning attachment fitted on their spindle moulder.

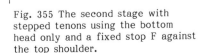

Fig. 355 The second stage with stepped tenons using the bottom head only and a fixed stop F against the top shoulder.

An easy way to set the end-block is to first secure it against the top shoulder of the last piece whilst this remains in position for the initial tenon. Re-clamp the workpiece nearer the cutterhead so that a spacer equal to the rebate depth is sandwiched between shoulder and block (or measure this distance), then simply re-set the end-block against the top shoulder.

SCRIBED TENONS

When the tenon has to fit a mortised part which is moulded it needs reverse-moulding (scribing) to suit. The regular tenon cutters can be replaced by others shaped to the scribe profile, but because very precise setting is needed it isn't worth the trouble for only a few pieces. An alternative is to first tenon pieces with square shoulders, then add the scribe at a following setting. Use either a router cutter fitted in the stub arbor or Whitehill cutters ground to suit in a flush-topped block. In both cases the tenon attachment needs re-setting nearer the spindle arbor so that the tenon projects over the top. Gauge the workpiece position for both ends from the same shoulder-stop, preferably against the top shoulder.

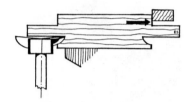

Fig. 356 Adding a scribe to square-cut shoulders using a flush-top Whitehill head or a router cutter.

FINGER JOINTING SASHES

The attachment is also suitable for finger jointing small window frames and similar using two-wing cutters of different thickness, together with matching spacers. Often these are provided in matching sets so they form scribed profiles to suit standard window sections. The most convenient method is to change one complete set for another when setting for the opposite hand. In this way no vertical spindle adjustment is needed, yet face-alignment is ensured. In some cases one or more cutters may be used in both set-ups. Grind cutters only on their outside faces as a complete set, grinding the same off each to retain correct alignment.

NOTE: The tenon attachment can be used for finger jointing thin boards, but only when clamping a single piece at a time. If a pack needs finger-jointing add a horizontal G-clamp to hold them solidly together to prevent individual pieces being pulled violently out. To do otherwise is dangerous. In preferrance, of course, use a finger-jointing attachment which has the proper front-to-back clamping action.

Plate 84 Oppold tenoning cutterheads fitted with disposable cutters and scribers.

Using a backing piece

A small fence only is provided on these attachments, but there is less spelching if a wooden backing piece is also fitted. Make this from hardwood to project beyond the table edge, and always set the slideway so that the cutters just clip this to give a clean leading edge. Feed past the rotating cutters once the machine is set, then use the shoulders formed on the backing fence to accurately set both tenon and shoulder length. If only a few pieces of different length are to be tenoned, mark these individually. There is no need to set the

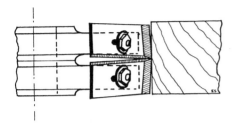

Fig. 357 Showing clearance angles on the cutters when set together and against a square-ended piece.

tenon and shoulder gauges; instead simply set the marked lines against the backing fence shoulders.

Cutter sharpening

Grind cutters slightly out-of-square so that the tenon shoulder fractionally leads the root, and so that the inside edge of the cutter only contacts at the leading corner to taper-away beyond. Set cutters to a precise tenon equal in thickness to spacers fitted between the cutterheads.

To sharpen cutters, place the heads one on the other with cutter faces in line and with a 2mm (1/16in) spacer so the inside corners do not foul. Sharpen, using a hone across both cutters as though they were a single cutter. This keeps them both precisely to the same cutting circle and prevents the hone dubbing-over the root corner.

Plate 83 Using the tenoning table on a Wadkin Bursgreen BEL/T spindle moulder.

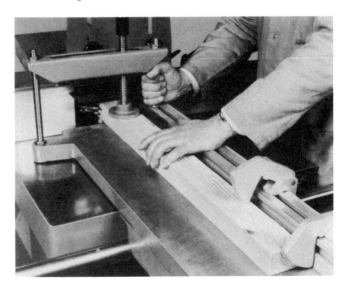

Index

Abrasives, grinding – 81, 83
Aluminium oxide – 81-88
Arbor
  collet – 2, 49
  spindle removable – 2, 11, 52
Arkansas hone – 88
Back stop – 20, 123, 131
Back-up block – 105
Back-up pieces – 114
Ball-bearing follower – 2, 21, 23, 30, 31, 52, 141, 143, 145, 146-47,

149, 157, 168
Balancing cutters – 17, 35, 40, 61, 70
Balancing stand – 62
Bandsawing
  for curved handrails – 160, 161
  for shaping – 155
Bauxite – 81
Bed saddle – 157, 161
Belt drives–
  infinately variable – 5, 11
  flat & vee – 4, 5,

Bevel angle on cutters – 10. 26, 29, 35, 40, 60, 64
Bevel angle chart – 10
Bevelling – 99, 109
Bite of cutters – 33, 38, 48
Bonnet guard – 21
Borazon – 87
Brads for templates & jigs– 119
Brake, electronic – 12
Burr – 81, 89
Burnishing cutters – 26

Cage guard - 21
Cam stops - 124-126
CBN (cubic boron nitride) -
  73, 87, 88
Chair back rails - 145, 149,
  157-159
Chair legs - 150
Chamfering - 109
Chip bruising - 8
Chip limiting - 48, 49
Chip packing - 37
Circle rounding - 136, 137
Clamps - 119, 120
Clearance angle - 7, 9, 10,
  26, 29, 35, 60, 65, 66
Climb cutting - 7
Collet - 2, 49
Compax - 90
Combination moulds -
  17, 46, 111, 114, 115,
Conventional cutting - 6
Coolant (grinding fluid) -
  81, 86, 88
Copy grinding - 63, 64
Corner rounding - 134-135
Creep in cutters - 28
Crown moulds 17, 111, 115
Curly-grained timber - 6, 8
Curved bandsawing -
  155-160
Curve-on-curve work -
  156-164
Cut relieving - 135, 155
  166
Cutter balancing - 17, 35,
  40, 61, 66, 70
Cutter blanking - 61, 67-68,
  77
Cutter bevel angle - 10, 26,
  29, 35, 40, 60, 64
Cutter bevel angle chart -
  10
Cutter bite - 33, 38, 48
Cutter burnishing - 26
Cutterblocks & heads
  chip limiting - 48, 49
  circular - 8, 17, 38, 43, 79
  collet - 2
  diameter - 6
  direction of rotation - 33
  disposable - 47-48
  French - 21, 25-28
  grooving - 107, 109
  hydraulic - 43-44, 46
  mounting - 15-16

panel raising - 90, 112- 114
profiled 8-9, 44-47, 71-74
rebating - 38, 47, 106, 109
safety keyed - 28, 32, 39,
  41, 47, 49, 75
securing 15-16
slotted collars - 3, 21,
  28-31, 75
Cutterblocks & heads
  speed - 3
  square - 17, 33-37
Cutter clearance angle
  main - 7, 9, 10, 26, 29, 35,
    60, 65, 66
  secondary - 10
  side - 9, 30, 45, 60-68,
    69
Cutter creep - 28
Cutter development
  approximate - 19, 53
  geometric - 55-58
  by profile grinding - 63
  rule - 56
  template - 57
Cutter dimensions
  circular block - 41-42
  French head - 28
  slotted collars - 32
  square block - 35, 37
Cutter grinding - 17, 26, 35,
  40, 47, 51, 59-81
Cutter land - 10
Cuttermark depth, pitch - 5
Cutter packing - 36
Cutter projections - 16, 18,
  27-28, 32, 35, 37, 41, 42
Cutter pre-setting - 20, 22,
  76
Cutter selection - 16
Cutter setting
  for disposable-cutter
    heads - 48
  for moulding - 18, 19, 22,
    23, 27, 29-31, 40
  for planing 18, 22
  for routers - 49
  using rollers - 22
  to a sample - 22
  to a straight edge 23
  using a template - 18, 23
    31, 41-42
Cutter setting screws - 28,
  32
Cutter width - 18, 29, 34,
  46, 76

Cutters
  circular block - 38
  Compax - 90
  diamond - 51, 89, 90
  disposable - 47, 47-51
  French head - 26
  grooving - 43, 107, 109
Cutters
  HCHC (high carbon, high
    chrome) - 29, 38, 89
  HSS (high speed steel) -
    10, 19, 33, 45, 89
  PCD (polycrystalline
    diamond) - 51, 89, 90
  profiled - 45, 46, 71-74
  router - 49-51
  segmented - 43
  serrated-back - 39, 42, 43
  slotted - 33, 39
  slotted collar - 28, 75
  square block - 33
  stair housing - 169, 173
  Stellite 20, 33, 89
  Syndite - 90
  Tantung - 20, 33, 89
  tungsten carbide - 45, 51,
    66, 88. 90
Cuttermark depth, pitch - 5
Cutting action - 5
  climb - 7
  conventional - 6
  resistance - 6-7
Cutting
  against the grain - 8, 151
  angles - 7-9, 25, 33, 38,
    45, 47, 53, 54, 71
  angle chart - 9
Development (of profiles)
  approximate - 19, 53
  by profile grinding - 63
  geometric - 55-58
  rule - 56
  template - 57
Diamond
  cutters - 51, 89, 90
  grinding wheels - 87-89
Disposable-cutter heads - 47,
Dividing head - 51, 72-74, 85
Double spindle - 58, 138, 154
Dovetailing
  cutters - 177
  drawers - 178-184
Drawer
  dovetailing - 178-184
  moulding - 117, 128

Dropping-on - 122-126
Drunken saw - 108
Electronic brake - 12
Edge moulding 30, 91, 99,
    112, 116, 137
End-grain moulding -
    127-131
False fence - 93-101
False table - 101
Feed
    direction - 120, 124, 125,
        127-129, 131, 133,
        135-137, 139, 173
    manual - 6, 13, 49
    mechanical - 6, 13, 21, 91,
        116, 117
    speed - 5, 6
    speed chart - 6
Fence
    breaking-through - 95-101
    gap width - 93, 98, 99
    gap chart - 98
    off-setting - 99
    ring - 3, 21, 23, 30,
        140-144, 155, 156, 161,
    saddle - 145, 158, 159
    setting methods - 92, 95,
        97-99, 101
    spacer-guide - 20, 114
    straight - 91-101
    strip - 128-135, 144
Finger jointing - 185-186,
    188
Followers for shaping
    ball-bearing - 2, 21, 23,
        30, 31, 52, 141, 143,
        145, 146-149, 157, 1682,
    pin - 172
    plain - 21, 172
    starting block - 141
    table ring - 140
French head - 21, 25-28
Front bevel on cutters - 9
Front stop - 122, 165
Grecian moulds - 111
Grinding cutters
    copy - 63-64
    manual - 39, 59-62
    profile - 39, 63, 65-70, 85
    profiled - 70-74
Grinding wheel
    burr - 81, 89
Grinding wheel
    coolant (grinding fluid) -
        81, 86, 88

defects 87
dressing - 66, 86,
fluid (coolant) 81, 86, 88
mounting - 84, 85, 87, 88
profiles - 59, 66-67, 89
shed - 81
speed - 85
specifications - 82-83, 87
Grinding wheel types
    ABN - 87
    aluminium oxide - 81-88
    Borazon - 88
    CBN (cubic boron nitride)
        - 73, 87, 88
    cup - 83, 88
    diamond - 87-89
    dish - 83, 88
    grit - 67, 81-88
    plain - 59-69, 76-79,
        83-84, 88
    saucer 51, 71, 73, 83, 88
    silicon carbide - 81, 88
Grooving tools
    cutters - 43, 107, 109
    drunken saw - 108
Grooving
    across the grain - 166
    slots - 165, 166
Guard
    bonnet - 21
    cage - 21
    Shaw - 14, 16, 58,
        102-104, 113, 117, 146
Guide, outer - 117
Hand feed - 6, 13, 49
Handrails for stairs -
    159-164
HCHC (high carbon, high
    chrome) - 29, 38, 89
Hones - 88
Housing
    cutters - 169, 173
    stair strings - 169-175
HSS (high speed steel) - 10,
    29, 33, 45, 89
Hydraulic
    cutterblock - 43, 44
    sleeve - 44, 73
Indexing profiled cutters -
    72
Inside shaping - 141-144
Jigs - 118-128, 139-172
Kick-back - 16, 48, 49, 122
Locknuts, double - 16
Manual feed - 6, 13, ⌐

Mechanical feed - 6, 13, 21,
    91, 116, 117
Mould angle chart - 164
Mould blending - 112
Moulding operations
    corner rounding - 134-136
    dividing the cut - 17, 111,
        115, 161
    edge moulding - 30, 91,
        99, 112, 116, 137
    end-grain moulding -
        127-131
    sinking a cutterhead - 17,
        20, 101, 105-107, 114,
        115
    stopped moulding - 20,
        120-126
    straight moulding - 20, 26,
        30, 91-134
Moulding - 110
    drawer fronts - 128
    drawer pulls - 118
    drawer sides - 117
    newels - 129
    to size - 129
    to thickness - 118
    to width - 117
Moulds
    beads - 116
    combination - 17, 46, 111,
        114, 115
    crown - 17, 111, 115
    Grecian - 111
    newel caps - 129
    newel posts - 127, 129
    raised panel - 90, 112-114,
        127
    Roman - 110
    rounds - 116
Outer guide - 117
Outside shaping - 140-146
Over-cutting - 94, 113-114,
Panel raising - 90, 112-114,
    127
PCD (polycrystalline
    diamond) - 51, 89, 90
Pitch
    board - 170
    of cuttermarks - 5
    of stairs - 170
Planing circle (diameter) -
    34, 38-39, 53
Planing line - 18
Planing to thickness
Pressures - 102-104

191

Profiled cutters - 45, 46, 71-74
Profile grinding - 39, 63, 65-70, 85
Q3S - 28, 75-79
Quality of surface finish - 5
Radial relief - 9, 45, 50
Raised panels - 90, 112-114, 127
Rebating
    cutterblock - 47, 105-107, 109
Ring fence - 3, 21, 23, 30, 140-144, 155-166, 161
Rings, table - 20, 100, 140
Risers, stair - 169
Riving ahead - 5-8
Rocking jig - 157, 182-165
Roman moulds - 110
Router - 1
Router cutters
    for shaping - 49-51, 167, 168
    housing - 165-175
    routing - 165, 166
    slotting - 165, 166-175
    stair housing - 169-175
    tapered grooves - 168
    throating - 167
Saddles - 145, 157-159, 161
Safe operation - 12-13, 27, 31, 36-37, 42-43, 47-49, 51, 84-85, 104, 114, 117, 122, 126, 139, 141, 146
Safety aids - 10, 104, 105, 114,123
    cam stop - 124-126
    clamps - 119, 128-131
    end stops - 20, 123, 131
    jigs 118-128, 139-172
    push block - 20, 105, 114, 127
    push stick - 20, 105,
    spacer guide - 20, 114
    spike - 20, 105
Safety cutter heads - 27-28, 32, 39, 43, 44, 47-49, 75-79
Saws
    drunken - 108
    grooving - 107-109
Secondary clearance angle - 10
Setting stand - 20
Shaper heads (U.S.- slotted collars) - 3, 21, 28-31

Shaping
    and bandsawing - 155, 160, 161
    chair back rails - 145, 149, 157-159
    chair legs - 150
    curved stair handrails - 159-164
    curve-on-curve - 156-164
    cut relieving - 135, 155
    double spindle - 58, 138
    feed direction - 139-146
    inside - 141-144
    nosing start - 142
    outside - 140-146
    rocking jig - 157
    saddle - 145, 157-162
    starting block 141
    start strip 142
    straight-fence - 144
    template 21, 140-146
    with the grain - 151
Shaw guard - 14, 16, 58, 102-104, 113, 117, 146
Side clearance angle - 9, 30, 45, 60, 66, 68, 69
Silicon carbide - 81, 88
Sills, throating - 167
Sinking a cutterhead - 17, 20, 101, 105-107, 114, 115
Sizing
    to a frame 128-130. 132-134
    to a template - 130
Sliding table - 44, 52, 80, 127, 176, 187, 189
Slotted collars - 3, 21, 28-31, 75
Snipe - 20
Spacer guide
Spacing washers - 15
Spindle
    brake - 12, 13
    drives - 4, 5, 11
    speed - 3, 4, 6, 12
    speed chart - 3
    tilting - 2, 17, 24, 107,
Spelching - 106, 131, 173
Splitting ahead 6, 7
Stair
    going - 169
    handrails - 159-164
    housing - 169-175
    housing cutters - 169, 173
    pitch board - 170

    tread - 169
Stellite - 29, 33, 89
Starting block - 141
Straight fence - 1, 13, 29
Stubb arbor - 2, 165
Support for long pieces - 20, 91
Surface finish - 5
Superabrasives - 87
Syndite - 90
Table line - 19
Table rings - 20, 100. 140
Tantung - 20, 33, 89
Tear-out - 5
Template
    double - 150
    for cutter grinding - 63-68
    for cutter setting - 14, 18-19, 22, 23, 31
    for routing - 168
    for shaping - 22, 140-164
    for sizing - 130, 131
    for stair housing - 172
    for stop moulding - 124-126
    full outline - 22, 145-147
    lead-in - 22, 149
    multiple - 22, 149
    part-outline - 22, 148-150
    position - 147
    sandwich - 152
    size - 146
    stacked - 151-153
Tenoning - 187-189
Tenoning table - 14, 52, 80, 176, 187, 189
Throating sills - 167
Tool speed chart - 3
Tool steels - 89
Tread (going) - 169
Trimming
    boxes - 132
    corners - 134-136
    circles - 136-137
    horns - 133
    panel skins - 132
    tenons - 133
Tungsten carbide - 10, 29, 33, 45, 47, 51, 87, 89-90
Undercutting - 112
Washers
    keyed - 16
    spacing - 15
Washita hone - 88
Wooden bed or table - 101, 114, 115